FROM BARBARISM
TO UNIVERSALITY

From

BARBARISM
TO
UNIVERSALITY

⚜

*Language and Identity
in Early Modern France*

CHRISTOPHER COSKI

The University of South Carolina Press

© 2011 University of South Carolina

Published by the University of South Carolina Press
Columbia, South Carolina 29208

www.sc.edu/uscpress

Manufactured in the United States of America

20 19 18 17 16 15 14 13 12 11   10 9 8 7 6 5 4 3 2 1

Library of Congress Cataloging-in-Publication Data

Coski, Christopher.
 From barbarism to universality : language and identity in early modern France / Christopher Coski.
   p. cm.
 Includes bibliographical references and index.
 ISBN 978-1-61117-036-8 (cloth : alk. paper)
 1. French language—History. 2. French language—Middle French, 1300–1600—Rhetoric. 3. French literature—16th century—History and criticism. 4. French literature—17th century—History and criticism. 5. Rhetoric—History. I. Title.
 PC2075.C67 2011
 440.9'031—dc23

2011017788

This book was printed on a recycled paper with 30 percent postconsumer waste content.

CONTENTS

Acknowledgments vii

Introduction
Themes, History, and Ideas 1

One
Du Bellay's *Deffence et Illustration*
The Vernacular Inferiority Complex 9

Two
Montaigne's *Essais*
The Baroque Mind, Language, and Being 32

Three
Descartes' *Discours*
The Mind/Identity Complex and Human Language 54

Four
Vaugelas' *Remarques*
Language, Quality, and Communal Identity 77

Five
Condillac's *Essai*
Language, Analytical Method, and Identity 103

Six
Rivarol's *De l'Universalité*
French Superiority 128

Conclusion
Binary Relationships and the Making of Myth 149

Appendix
Historical Overview of French's Rise in Status 153

Notes 157
Bibliography 187
Index 199

ACKNOWLEDGMENTS

There are a number of people to whom I must express my gratitude for their assistance in producing this work. First, I would like to thank the Provost's Office at Ohio University for granting me a sabbatical leave in fall 2007, during which the heaviest portions of research and analysis were completed. Second, I wish to thank several colleagues at Ohio University. Tom Franz and the members of the Modern Languages Faculty Fellowship Leave committee helped me to make a successful application for my sabbatical leave. Lois Vines gave me invaluable advice on book proposal writing and took the time to help with proofreading and offer feedback. Brigitte Moretti-Coski, Herta Rodina, and Mary Jane Kelley also devoted time to proofreading and giving feedback, while Neil Bernstein assisted me in deciphering citations in Latin. In conclusion I wish to thank all the teachers, colleagues, and students with whom I have had the opportunity to discuss literature, culture, and ideas over the years.

Introduction
Themes, History, and Ideas

*I*n the early modern period the cultures and vernacular languages of Europe struggled to pull themselves out of an inferiority complex they derived from self-comparison with Latin language and a culture inherited from classical Rome. In the desire to leave this complex behind, the French were not different from anyone else in Europe. However, France ultimately did distinguish itself; by the end of the era the French language was spoken, written, and read across Europe more than any other vernacular. France's language and culture alone, among those of all the nations of Europe, could legitimately claim to have risen from the depths of "barbarism" to the heights of "universality," with French supplanting Latin on the continent and with French culture having a disproportionately large influence across national borders.[1] This journey from barbarism to universality is not just a journey of language but also one of identity. The present work examines the themes of language and identity in the history of ideas in early modern France as this linguistic and cultural transition took place. These three concepts—themes, history, and ideas—are crucial to the dialogues that unfold in this book.

First, the emphasis on the *themes* of language and identity, rather than the actual origins, development, or evolution of language and identity, defines this work as a literary study and thus as the study of a fiction. Lipiansky has asserted that identity belongs less to reality than to social representations, myth, and ideology (3). This is a fundamental notion underpinning my analyses, and it positions this book as a study of the myth of a language and an identity, as perceived by early modern French writers. The perceptions and ideas of these thinkers sometimes do not correspond to today's views of historical, linguistic, or cultural truths.

At the same time the notion of *history* evokes a certain basis in fact, despite the fictions outlined above. While deviations may exist between the views of the authors analyzed and the reality in which they were writing, there is never a complete divorce between perception and reality. The fiction studied here is a historical fiction. The language and identity myths are to some degree rooted in fact. If there is a shift in how early modern French intellectuals viewed their language and identity—moving from barbaric to universal, advancing from an inferiority complex toward a superiority complex—it is because in the world around them the use and prestige of the French language and culture truly increased during this period.

Next, in terms of *ideas* this book is about philosophy and ideology, even though many of the writers were not actually philosophers and ideologues. While Descartes and Condillac were philosophers and Rivarol was a political pamphleteer and ideologue, others were quite different. Du Bellay was a poet, Montaigne a personal essayist, and Vaugelas a grammarian. Nevertheless, when examined in retrospect with the tools of literary explication, the concepts expressed by these writers converge to form a coherent tableau of an evolving and emerging view of language and identity (in general philosophical terms) that ultimately justifies the ideology (in specific nationalistic terms) of France as an entity whose language and culture have progressed from a state of barbarism to a state of universality.

This text, then, is not a study of history, linguistics, sociology, or psychology, though it brushes elbows with all of these disciplines. Instead it is a literary analysis of nonfiction works narrating a language and identity fiction inscribed in a specific historical period.

French treatments of language in the early modern era focus on three main components—expression, thought, and reality—and the relations between them. Preoccupation with these three elements of signification are not unique to France or to the early modern period. They can be found at least as far back as the thought of the Greek Stoics. Formigari, for example, has described how Sextus Empiricus summarized the semantic paradigm of the Stoics, who distinguished between "the thing signified . . . , the thing signifying . . . and the thing existing" (*History*, 28). This view of language prevailed throughout the early modern era and even beyond—Saussurian semiotics, for example, reflect this conception. The examination of these three elements in early modern French thinking on language is a primary concern of this study. The elements can be considered as an ideological triangle, as a coherent figure in which they are inseparably connected and in which the connections between them delimit and define identity, thus:

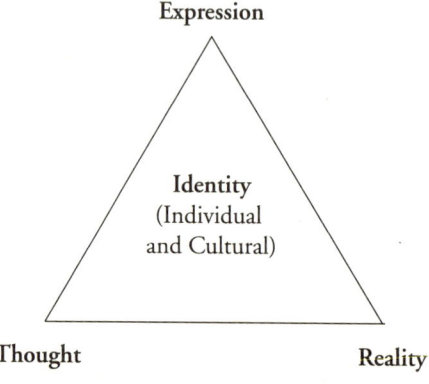

Representations of the interplay between these three language elements vary considerably from author to author and from century to century within the early modern era. However, it is always in the framework of language that the question of identity appears. John Joseph has asserted and convincingly argued in his exploration of language and identity that "the entire phenomenon of identity can be understood as a linguistic one" (*Language*, 12). His assertion is another fundamental assumption of this book.

Identity can mean many different things. Joseph's study, for example, lists up to six potential separate analytical categories of identity.[2] For the purposes of this study I limit the number to two—individual and cultural—as these are the categories highlighted by the authors analyzed in the following chapters and, in and of themselves, they represent a substantial degree of complexity even in their most basic forms. From one perspective, identity is what makes the individual unique, that which identi*fies* a person and distinguishes that person from all other individuals. It is the state of being oneself and not someone else. At the same time, however, identity is the condition of resemblance between several individuals, or of the qualities of those individuals, such that the individuals can be considered in some way identi*cal* and therefore as forming a group. So identity, even in just these two fundamental senses, simultaneously separates and connects, excludes and includes. This complexity is deepened by the fact that the individual is part of the group, the fact that groups are often part of larger groups, and the fact that individuals and groups continually interact and intermix with each other, so that relationships of sameness and difference, and the sense of what identity truly means, become increasingly difficult to define. The authors of the early modern era frequently slide from one of these meanings of identity to the other, and they often conflate the two in their discussions.

The play of individual and communal levels of identity is crucial to this study. The broadest of the communal identities treated by the authors considered in this book, that of a French national identity, is the primary focus of only two of the early modern works examined here—namely the earliest, du Bellay's *Deffence et illustration de la langue françoyse* (Defense and Illustration of the French Language, 1549), and the last, Rivarol's *De l'Universalité de la langue française* (On the Universality of the French Language, 1784). If one were asked to name early modern texts dealing with language and French identity, these two works would be the first to come to mind for practically anyone with a knowledge of early modern French culture and literature. Across the 235 years separating these two works, it is more difficult to name other significant texts that focus specifically on the same primary theme. So this is a key question: just what lies between these two books?

Most works written in the interval between the publication of the *Deffence* and *De l'Universalité* do not focus on the question of language as it relates to a specific

French national identity. However, numerous authors do address more generic concepts of language and either individual or communal identity (and indeed sometimes both). These middle works played a pivotal role in laying out the basic ideological, philosophical, and mythological concepts that would define the paradigm shift evident in the two bookend texts of the *Deffence* and *De l'Universalité*. This study is organized accordingly.

First, I explore du Bellay's *Deffence* and the expression, thought, and reality issues related to the reputation of French as "barbaric" when compared to the ancient languages (in particular Latin). For du Bellay, the value of a language is not inherent. All languages in their essence have the capacity to express all ideas, and reality, equally well. French is not therefore by nature barbaric. As du Bellay views it, the French of his time is inferior but only for acquired, not inborn, reasons. Consequently French can change and improve, if people opt to employ it as a medium for literary expression. Translation is not adequate for promoting improvement since all languages have an acquired character, and translation would not further the development of a truly French character; it would only transfer another language's character to the French language. Creative literary imitation, however, is a proper tool for developing the character of the French language since the writer can thus imitate not the character of another language and literature but the method by which another language and culture developed their character. Underlying du Bellay's text is the idea that the writer brings his own character into his writing through the manner in which he expresses thought and reality, and he ultimately is responsible for creating a national cultural identity through his development of the language and the language's ability to express thought and reality.

Next is an examination of Montaigne's *Essais* (Essays, 1580–95) and the concept of baroque language expressing baroque identities. For Montaigne, thought is an internal discourse, and writing is a means of painting individual identity by converting this internal discourse into the external discourse of language. However, this process is problematic. Montaigne holds that identity, reality, and thought are continually in flux. So the question becomes one of determining how language can express, in any meaningful way, things and ideas that are constantly changing. If our ideas and opinions change with time, how can what we write (since writing is static once it lands on the page) express the truth of who we are and what we think?

The universe too is continually in motion, which again begs the question of whether language can express the reality of the world. Additionally, as a philosophical skeptic, Montaigne believes that we cannot ever truly know the world around us, such that even if thought and reality did not fluctuate ceaselessly, there can never be true concordance between the two. The one characteristic that all languages have in common is an expression rooted in affirmation, which makes language a problematic medium for expressing a thought and a reality in which nothing can be affirmed. The only solution for Montaigne lies in accepting that we cannot know the truth of reality or thought or who a person actually is and in accepting that we cannot use language to define these things. However, Montaigne's text is informed by the belief that we can know *how* a person attempts to articulate language with thought and world and self. It is this *how* of expression that constitutes the only linguistic truth and the only means of knowing the identity of an individual and, by extension, of a community.

Descartes' *Discours de la méthode* (Discourse on Method, 1637) is parallel and an antidote to Montaigne's *Essais* in that the text presents the idea of a classical language expressing a classical identity—simple, direct, knowable, and true. Descartes, in contrast to Montaigne, is the quintessential antiskeptic. Descartes begins from the fundamental assumption that the world, thoughts, and identities can be known and that language can be used to reflect and transmit this knowledge. Men reason differently from each other, some better and some worse, but Descartes' view of human reason is similar to du Bellay's view of different languages. All human beings share reason, and their reason is not inherently superior or inferior to that of others. Instead what differs is how individuals use and apply their reason. The self is, in its essence, a thinking substance, and the manner in which a person reasons defines him. Language is reflective of a person's manner of thinking; it is the means by which thinking individuals come together to constitute a thinking community. These points implicate language as the marker by which superiority and inferiority of thought processes can be recognized in Descartes' philosophy and also imply that as such a marker, language establishes a hierarchy of intellects and by extension a hierarchy of both individual and communal identities.

Vaugelas' *Remarques sur la langue française* (Remarks on the French Language, 1647) addresses language as the means for defining communal identities. In essence Vaugelas takes the hierarchical principle suggested by Descartes' text, that some means of expression are superior to others, and then divorces expression from reason, instead using expression as a means of distinguishing between social subgroups within a culture. In place of Cartesian truth, Vaugelas' goal is linguistic correctness, and in place of rational method as a means of attaining his goal, Vaugelas has recourse to the concept of usage. Good usage is defined by the finest part of the court and by the best authors, and in cases where these two groups are at odds in their usage, the grammarians decide. Ultimately what is good is decided by the authority of the highest classes in the social, artistic, and intellectual domains, thereby establishing a hierarchy of social and cultural groups in which language is a marker of individual and group identity. The perfection of the language spoken by the elite has, for Vaugelas, developed over time through the innovative efforts of writers and grammarians. Linguistic perfection, however, is problematic, in that artistic and grammatical innovation become the mechanism for both change and stability. This paradox leads later thinkers, such as Condillac, to reexamine the notions of linguistic evolution and perfection.

Condillac's *Essai sur l'origine des connaissances humaines* (Essay on the Origin of Human Knowledge, 1746) posits a chain of cause-effect relationships between reality and language, language and reason, reason and individual and group identities, and finally reason and specifically national identities. Condillac approaches language and identity from the perspective of Lockean sensualism. Starting with Locke's idea that all thought originates in the senses, Condillac expands upon this notion and proposes that all human reason is rooted in language, in a vein similar to Montaigne's thought as internal discourse. Language in turn, as the source of human reason, has its origins in sensation and our environment. Like Descartes, Condillac holds that reality is knowable and that human thought constitutes identity. However, since language and therefore human thought and identity are environment-based, they evolve and change in a continual process of improvement. This process of evolution is driven by both reason and feeling, as individuals perceive the world in their own particular ways and then effectively "rewrite" the languages of their cultural groups, which then, in turn, affect the ways in which those same individuals perceive the world. Condillac fleshes out du Bellay's conception of the individual contributing to the language and identity through his or her own particular means of expression, reworking that conception as a cycle in which individual and communal identities contribute mutually to each other. Additionally Condillac redefines linguistic perfection, breaking from the problematic Vaugelasian tension between change and stability, and positing instead the vision of a perfect language as one that evolves and progresses continuously in a cycle of never-ending improvement. At the same time Condillac recreates a Vaugelasian hierarchy of languages based on this new definition of perfection. While French is, for Condillac, one of the better languages in the world, it is not the best for him because, leaning more toward reason than toward feeling, it does not evolve as efficiently as a language more balanced between reason and feeling.

Then there is Rivarol's *De l'Universalité* and the linguistic justifications for the universal quality of French its title announces, along with Rivarol's declaration of the superiority of French over other modern languages. Rivarol adopts concepts from all of the other thinkers mentioned earlier in order to establish the idea that

French at the end of the eighteenth century has finally reached a state of universality in which its native speakers can claim that their language has replaced Latin as the world's lingua franca. Rivarol explains the universal nature of French in part through the concept of language and culture marketing. Yet such marketing is not in itself, even for Rivarol, an adequate explanation of the status of French language and culture. There is a quality to French that other languages do not possess. Rivarol takes the idea from Montaigne and Condillac that language creates reason and crosses it with the Cartesian notion that reason is the most commonly shared characteristic of all human beings. Further, Rivarol argues that French is fundamentally more rational in its syntax and structure than other languages and that this is the feature that makes French the universal language it has become. French appeals to the most common denominator of humanity: reason. Consequently members of other cultures seek to speak French and thus define their own identity as being in some manner connected to the French. In this way language becomes not just the marker of a social superiority as Vaugelas had presented it but rather a marker of the national superiority that du Bellay had once anticipated and hoped for.

The myth of French superiority was not simply born from Rivarol's pen 235 years after du Bellay's *Deffence;* rather the myth evolves through the successive mutations of the philosophical concept of the language triangle throughout the early modern period. By building the myth of an identity on the philosophical foundation of the language triangle, the thinkers of the early modern era divorce their individual and cultural self-views from the historical factors that truly were responsible for the rise of French linguistic and cultural prestige in that period. Unwilling to attach their sense of self-worth to the vicissitudes of political and economic forces external to the language in which their identity is subsumed, the period's authors seek to justify step by step the validity, prestige, and increasing universality of French. They do this not through elements exterior to the language and its speakers' identity but rather through factors that reflect what they perceive as the fundamental qualities of language—and often specifically of *their* language—thereby giving an inherent and inalienable substance to their sense of who they are.

While this study does not deal with language and identity issues in contemporary France, it is worthwhile to highlight that the myth of a French linguistic identity, rooted in the distant depths of the early modern era, does have relevance even in our own time. Françoise Gadet sums up the current state of French language and identity studies with her interrogative section heading "Une identité linguistique française?" (208). The question mark is telling. Works on contemporary French linguistic identity explore a continuing complex of myth and reality—most notably in the relationships and tensions between French and Francophone identities, between French and regional languages and cultures within the hexagon, and of course in the long-standing resistance in some quarters to the incursions of English, as the postwar lingua franca, and Anglo-American culture into French linguistic and cultural space.[3] Though the main goal of the present work is to serve scholars and students of language and identity in the early modern era, it is also my hope that this study will simultaneously help to shed some light on the early modern origins of issues still being discussed today.

One

Du Bellay's *Deffence et Illustration*
The Vernacular Inferiority Complex

Joachim du Bellay (1522–60) was a poet, a friend of Pierre de Ronsard, and one of the most celebrated members of the group of poets that Ronsard was to name the Pléiade. This group of young writers, originally calling themselves the Brigade, had come together around 1547 as students of the humanist Jean Dorat at the Collège de Coqueret. At Dorat's school the young men were educated under the principles of the new humanistic academia and were submerged in the study of Greek, Roman, and modern Italian literature. Studies and reading ran daily from daybreak to midnight. There was little time for anything else, and even during their limited leisure hours the students continued to discuss literature (Keating, 7–8). It is not surprising that young men thus educated became the foremost poets of their time.

Du Bellay wrote the *Deffence et illustration de la langue françoyse* in 1549 as the first part of a text including the *Olive* and *Vers Lyriques* while still at Coqueret. The text was to a large extent a response to Thomas Sébillet's *Art poétique françoys*, published a year previously. Sébillet's work gave an overview of poetry from biblical times through the reign of Henri II; discussed aspects of poetic composition, including rhyme, invention, rhythm, and meter; explored problems particular to French, such as the pronunciation of certain letters; and cataloged and examined poetic forms. In addition to recommending imitation of the ancients as models, as du Bellay and the Pléiade poets would do, Sébillet strongly promoted the imitation of medieval and recent French poets—notably Marot and his disciples—and recommended the continued development of medieval genres as the means to perfecting French poetry.[1] These ideas prompted the composition of du Bellay's manifesto on behalf of his classmates. The scholars and poets of the Brigade had been for some time distressed at the poverty of French verse and were not happy with the poetry written by preceding generations. So this point of disagreement with Sébillet was certainly one of the driving forces behind the *Deffence et illustration*. Du Bellay's critique of the Marotic poets would draw no small amount of fire from Des Autelz, Aneau, and Sébillet (Chamard, 145–58). However, there was another motivating element as well.[2] Alongside what Dorat's students perceived to be a weak French-language poetry was the production of neo-Latin poetry. Among the many texts studied at Coqueret was Jacques Peletier's translation of Horace's *Art Poétique,* in which Peletier had advocated the use of French as a literary language (Keating, 9; Chamard, 35).

Latin had been the main language of the church, the universities, diplomacy, and the courts throughout the Middle Ages and was considered more prestigious than the vernaculars. Theological works, histories, science, philosophy, treaties, and many laws were written in Latin.[3] Vernaculars were typically relegated to more common (both in the sense of "everyday" and in the sense of "base") uses. Latin, thanks to the church, whose influence continued to transcend national borders, also had the advantage of serving as a universal language that enabled foreign travelers to communicate with their hosts—even if the Latin was somewhat corrupted and sufficient only for ordering meals and lodgings at inns or asking directions (Burke, *Languages,* 47). These uses of Latin continued to a greater or lesser extent throughout Europe from the Middle Ages into the early modern period.

What was of prime concern to the members of the Brigade, however, was not simply that people were writing in Latin but rather that many French neo-Latin poets believed that Latin, having produced so many literary masterpieces, was inherently better suited than French to the creation of great literature. A glance at Céard and Tin's relatively recent *Anthologie de la Poésie française du XVIe siècle* shows many French poets writing in Latin rather than their native tongue, including Macrin, Bourbon, de Bèze, Muret, Dorat, and even du Bellay.[4] In the epistle to the reader of his *Poematum Libri Quatuor* (1558), however, du Bellay refers to the French muse as his wife, while the Latin muse is merely his mistress (Céard and Tin, 258). This suggests that his own relationship to Latin is an on-again, off-again fancy, a flight of passion, while his relationship to French is long lasting, heartfelt, and durable—as evidenced by the fact that the vast majority of his work was in the vernacular.

So du Bellay's Latin poems should not be viewed as a counter to his own argument in favor of French as a literary language. Other scholars and writers of the era, such as Dolet, were able to maintain a love for Latin even though they argued forcefully for the promotion of the French language.[5] It is possible to attribute their stance to du Bellay as well—though he loves Latin, he loves French still more. Such a stance enables du Bellay to avoid contradiction and permits him, while writing occasionally in Latin, to reject the idea of neo-Latin poetry as a genre that must surpass, or should be considered to surpass, French poetry. It is not neo-Latin poetry that du Bellay condemns but rather the attitude of those poets who choose a dead language as a preferred literary medium while looking down on their own native tongue.

These two contextual elements—the old-school literary conservatism of some of Sebillet's ideas and the denigrating attitude of the neo-Latin poets—give the reader a starting point for examining the text of *Deffence et illustration de la langue françoyse*. The very title contains two key words that reflect this double preoccupation. First, there is the "defense," denoting the intent on du Bellay's part to intervene in favor of French, against Latin (or Greek and modern Italian as well), and to uphold his mother tongue against attacks and accusations of inadequacy and inferiority. The book also addresses the question of "illustration," the problem of rendering French—and its highest manifestation, its literature—"illustrious" and worthy of an admiration and esteem that it had not acquired up to that point. In this sense du Bellay's text represents an intellectual and artistic identity crisis, manifesting itself in the recognition that French language and literature *have* been inferior up to this point in history, coupled with the desire to transform that linguistic and literary status. Du Bellay's is an inferiority complex revolving around both his language and his muse, and it represents the beginning of an attempt to transform that perceived inferiority into greatness.

Du Bellay logically begins by treating the origin of languages in his first chapter, stating that "les Langues ne sont nées d'elles mesmes en façon d'herbes, racines & arbres: les unes infirmes & debiles en leurs espéces: les autres saines & robustes, & plus aptes à porter le faiz des conceptions humaines: mais toute leur vertu est née au monde du vouloir & arbitre des mortelz" (languages are not born in and of themselves like grasses, roots and trees: some infirm and weak in their species: others healthy and robust, and more able to carry the weight of human conceptions: rather all their virtue is born of mortal desire and will, 12). The core of du Bellay's first argument is the comparison of languages to plants—a comparison taken almost word for word from Sperone Speroni's *Dialogo delle lingue* (1542).[6] Du Bellay's borrowing from Speroni's text suggests above all that a language is a living thing. All languages are born, grow, develop, and even die. Additionally the adopted image from Speroni's text allows du Bellay to acknowledge the existence of a taxonomy of languages, reflecting different characteristics of languages just as with living organisms. This taxonomy is centered on the opposition of characteristics such as weakness and strength, flaw and advantage, imperfection and perfection, effectiveness and ineffectiveness, health and sickliness, resistance and susceptibility. Each of these characteristics is derived from the constitution of any given language's forms, the morphological structure of the language-as-organism, its "anatomy" or "physiology," and provides the basis for underscoring differences between tongues.

However, du Bellay's intent, paralleling that of Speroni, in adopting this organic metaphor is to stress that the quality of a language is actually *not* congenital. He insists on this point from the outset by indicating this one prime difference between languages and plant life in his comparison. While languages can be classed taxonomically like living organisms, they are not born in the same manner, which is to say that languages are not created with the characteristics that ultimately place them in one class or another. Such traits are not innate.

It may be true that some languages are superior to the extent that, at present, they better execute their primary task, which is the conveyance of ideas, but this conveyance occurs on two levels. First, it takes place in the transmission of the substance of ideas individually, in the relationship of signifier to signified, of expression to reality. Second, it occurs as a corpus, in the relationship of language as a system to the sum total of ideas, or ideology, of a community of speakers. In each case a language's ability to engage in each type of connection is an acquired capacity. The relationships of expression to reality and of expression to thought are man-made.

Du Bellay's considerations on the origin of language therefore set in opposition the principles of nature and art. Within the natural/artificial opposition, du Bellay emphasizes that linguistic differences, in their entirety and without exception, originate in acts of human choice and free will. Signification for du Bellay is entirely arbitrary—human beings invent language and make it what they want it to be. This is an important point since if language were of divine origin, as church and biblical tradition suggested, du Bellay's goal of changing language would be impossible. Presumably one could not improve upon divine creation. However, because language is man-made, it can be elevated and perfected. Through the natural/artificial opposition, the idea emerges that it is in the *art* of language that linguistic progress is made—in other words, in poetry. This principle also has two important implications. The first is that language, in a larger, cultural sense, evolves through the efforts of poets. The second is that this evolution can take place only if poets leave behind Sebillet's proposed reliance on natural talent and natural composition.

The idea that language can evolve, that nothing linguistic is carved in stone, leads du Bellay to the conclusion that "on ne doit ainsi louer une Langue & blamer l'autre: veu qu'elles viennent toutes d'une mesme source & origine: c'est la fantasie des hommes: & ont eté formees d'un mesme jugement à une mesme fin: c'est pour signifier entre nous les conceptions & intelligences de l'esprit" (one must not thus praise one language and blame another: given that they all come from the same source and origin: which is the fantasy of man: and were formed of the same judgment and for the same ends: which is to signify between us the conceptions and intelligences of the mind, 12–13). The expression of favorable or unfavorable judgments relative to the *essence* of a given language *as a whole* is unjustifiable. However, the negation of this manner of judgment by du Bellay contrarily legitimizes the praise or condemnation of accidental language-related *factors*.

Du Bellay identifies two such factors in this passage by way of association. First there is the element of language's starting point. The beginnings of a language are associated with the concept of human "fantaisie." This association not only links language to its aforementioned characteristics of free will and arbitrariness but also semiotically connects it to the productions of human imagination and the writer's power of invention. The fact that du Bellay employs the term "source" designating not only a commencement but also a spring or fountain evokes the mythological Hippocrene, the legendary spring on Mount Helicon, home of the muses and the font from which all poetic inspiration flows. This mythical association reinforces the previously suggested role of the poet in the formation of a broader poetico-cultural facet to linguistic development.

Additionally du Bellay identifies a second element upon which legitimate evaluations can be made. Following the creation of language, its development into a particular form is based on human judgment. Here language is linked not with imagination but with reason. If imagination creates changes, then intellectual discernment and good sense regulate the changes provoked by imagination. In this way a parallel is established between the dual associations of linguistic creations to imagination, and linguistic formation to the intellect, that bring together both personal inspiration and humanistic erudition and intellectualism. A language must have writers of both imagination and intellect driving it in order to make progress toward the ends for which language exists in the first place—the signification of concepts. Further, the language must not simply signify and manifest thought; it must also create community. What it expresses it must express "between us" (excluding "them"), and it must express both concepts and "intelligences." This latter term not only indicates the general notion of ideas but also suggests relations between members of a group, of a closed circle or society, to which access is difficult, indeed impossible, to those not initiated and granted admission by way of speaking the language.

This notion of initiation to the community through the speaking of the language provides du Bellay with a segue into his second chapter: "Que la Langue Francoyse ne doit estre nommée barbare" (That the French Language Should Not Be Called Barbarous). Many writers of du Bellay's time were frustrated by the all too common perception of the French tongue as barbarous. Dolet, for example, viewed his work on the art of translation as a starting point for arriving at a moment in time when foreigners would no longer consider the French to be barbaric (4–5).[7] The concern over a French language perceived as barbarous is echoed by Pasquier's *Recherches de la France* (1566), which railed against the Italian tendency to qualify French this way, and eventually Estienne, in his *Deux dialogues* (1578), played a reversal and tagged as barbarisms only the Italianisms becoming increasing popular in court French.[8]

Indeed the question of the barbarity and inferiority of all vernaculars relative to the classical languages was not limited to France or its language and may even have had its beginnings in Italy. Speroni's entire *Dialogo* centered on this very question. Most of Speroni's text consists of a debate between Pietro Bembo, supporter of the Tuscan vernacular, and Lazaro Bonamico, arguing for the superiority of the classical languages (the choice of the latter historical personage as a character being most appropriate, as even the famous philologist's name suggests the raising of the dead tongue). Lazaro maintains the barbarity of Tuscan, while Bembo insists that the vernacular has greater harmony and measure than Lazaro is willing to admit and proposes that it can and should be used for higher things (Speroni, 11).[9]

Given the sheer quantity of ink spilled on the topic of Latin versus the vernacular in France, one must question the opinion of Aneau, who in the *Quintil Horatien* (1550) criticizes du Bellay for employing the term "deffence" in his title. Aneau argues that the term is inappropriate because "il n'est point defense sans accusation precedent" (there is no defense without a preceding accusation, ix–xiv).[10] Despite Aneau's protestations to the contrary, the barbaric reputations of vernaculars in general and of French in particular were very real.[11]

The concept of barbarism is significant in establishing a link between language and identity because, as suggested by du Bellay's text, it carries the concept of inclusion and exclusion from the community within it: "quand à la signification de ce mot *barbare:* barbares anciennement etoint nommez ceux qui ineptement parloient Grec" (as for the signification of this word *barbarous:* antiquity named barbarians those who ineptly spoke Greek, 15). Though the term is applied to the French by the Italians, whose pride is rooted in the achievements of their Roman ancestors, the etymological origins of the term force du Bellay to shift his attention from the narrow focus of the Latin tradition to concentrate on the other great tradition of European antiquity, that of ancient Greece. The term "barbarian" is historically, as du Bellay emphasizes, used by the ancient Greeks to identify those who did not speak their language or who spoke it poorly. However, the term "barbarian" is highly charged with connotations that extend beyond simple linguistic matters. In addition to the linguistic element, the barbarian is someone who by race or by nationality is primitive, uncivilized, and uncultured; ignorant of manners and taste; and lacking in reason. Such characteristics render him and his people inferior in the eyes of the people using the term. These two strains of ideas are fused together by the ancient Greeks in du Bellay's mind. The Greeks, as he sees them, view their society and culture as superior in equal measure to their language. The logical extension of this is that anyone who does not speak the language cannot possess the same qualities of mind, culture, and community that they do.

However, du Bellay, while acknowledging the connection between language, culture, and community, obviously rejects the idea that there is something inherently special about the Greeks, stating that the Greek perception of the other "ne doit en rien diminuer l'excellence de notre Langue: veu que cest arrogance Greque, admiratrice seulement de ses inventions, n'avoit loi ny privilege de legitimer ainsi sa nation & abatardir les autres" (should not diminish at all the excellence of our language: given that this Greek arrogance, admiring only its own inventions, had neither law nor privilege to thus legitimize its nation and bastardize others, 16–17). Reiterating the communal nature of "our" language, du Bellay insists that there is absolutely nothing to render French, by nature, less important or of less value when compared to Greek. Indeed, French is capable of achieving the ideals of representation and might even acquire superiority in certain domains. The idea that languages other than Greek would be considered unworthy of esteem or even of interest is the result of an insulting and scornful conceit. The exclusive and exalted pleasure felt by the ancient Greeks while gazing into a mirror at their own intellectual, creative, aesthetic, and moral achievements is, for du Bellay, simply narcissistic.

On the one hand, there is in du Bellay's text an acknowledgment that the nation of Greece did many things first in western civilization and that the country is, in a sense, the father of all subsequent European cultures. On the other hand, while the Greek culture was the first born of all cultures tracing their origins to that land, there is no general imperative, no authority human or divine, no necessary and constant natural relation that would provide this firstborn with any claim to privilege over other European languages and societies. Greek language and culture do not have nor did they ever have any natural, divine, or legal right to claim advantage or to claim to be the only rightful cultural and linguistic heir to those father islands. Nor does Greek culture have the right to claim only itself as being of pure blood. All European cultures, for du Bellay, are of the same original blood, are derived from the same parental land, from the same original cultural and historic traditions, from the same ethnic, social, and religious conditions, giving them a coherence such that all have the legitimate potential to aspire to claims of the same greatness of heritage. Thus, contrarily, no one group or set of groups can be singled out by its inborn characteristics as bastardized, either in terms of not possessing the requisite qualities and vigor to achieve greatness equal to that of Greek culture or in the sense of not having the right to lay claim to a cultural inheritance from the Greek islands.

So it may well be that Greek culture was the first child, but French culture is nonetheless a legitimate heir. However, du Bellay argues, even if in some respects French culture could be truthfully regarded as barbarous, the fact that these facets of French culture are not natural but acquired allows for the possibility of change:

> quand la barbarie des meurs de nos ancéstres eust deu les mouvoir à nous apeller barbares, si est ce que je ne voy point pourquoy on nous doive maintenant estimer telz, veu qu'en civilité de meurs, equité de loix, magnanimité

de couraiges, bref en toutes formes & manieres de vivre non moins louables que profitables, nous ne somme rien moins qu'eux: mais bien plus: veu qu'ils sont telz maintenant, que nous les pouvons justement apeller par le nom qu'ilz ont donné aux autres. (17–18)

(while the barbarity of our ancestors' mores might have moved them to call us barbarians, nonetheless I do not see at all why one should now esteem us so, given that in civility of mores, equity of laws, magnanimity of courage, in sum, in all the modes and means of living no less laudable than profitable, we are no less worthy than they: indeed, even more: given that they are such now, that we can justly call them by the name they gave to others.)

Temporarily distilling the question of culture from that of language, du Bellay focuses on the issue of superiority from the standpoint of the customs, tastes, and collective behaviors of the two respective nations, France and Greece. This distillation is focused on the temporal opposition of past and present. If the Greek islands were the father of all European culture, the lands within the boundaries of France were the mother of French culture, and hence, in contrast to the "connecting" bloodline from Greece common to all European nations, the territory of France constitutes a differentiating bloodline unique to du Bellay's civilization. The opposition of past and present is crucial because the imperfections of comportment and social interaction derived from the mother's side are not inherent to the bloodline but rather are inherent to a point in time. As these imperfections were acquired aspects of "Frenchness," it was indeed in the past legitimate for the Greeks to apply the word "barbarian" to the French (along with all other non-Greeks).

However, du Bellay's use of the term *appeler* framing the past French barbarism as a signifier employed to denote the French people brings the notion of French barbarity back to the fundamental conception of language expressed in his discussion of the origin of languages—the idea that signifiers are arbitrary and man-made, and therefore subject to change. By contrast, du Bellay's present view of his own nation's civil and social value is expressed through the term *estimer,* which, unlike the semiotic act of appellation, implies rather a view of the signified, the substance of a thing, and the mind's determination and judgment of its value. The value that du Bellay presents is, of course, positive, as the term suggests. Furthermore the arbitrary, changeable signifier associated with the past is articulated by du Bellay with the more substantial, signified, real value of French culture associated with the present. This articulation evokes the concept of progress and movement, the idea of an increase in substance and in worth, that is as real and concrete as any cause for past denigration was unsubstantial and indefensible.

Du Bellay's view of his own nation's present degree of civil and social development is, ironically, as self-satisfied as anything he attributes to the ancient Greeks. With respect to the observation of social rules and obligations, the respect for the citizen and for justice, and the "male" virtues of selfless sacrifice that he considers so necessary for the maintenance of these values, du Bellay shamelessly announces that France has reached the absolute fullness of any nation's potential for societal (though not necessarily cultural) achievement.[12] There is no trait or aspect of civil life that France fails to possess, from which France's people benefit and for which France is worthy of admiration.

At this stage we see a reversal of roles in du Bellay's mind for ancient society and French society. Not content to argue that France has equaled the ancient Greeks, he posits French superiority. Again the temporal element of flux comes into play, as he identifies the Greeks, *such as they are now*, as being inferior to the French in the realms of civil life. The reprise of the opposition of name versus being is also crucial. The reality of things as they *are* justifies for du Bellay the act of attributing the *name* of "barbarian" to the Greeks. Of course, this ironic denigration of the Greeks applies only to civility, as opposed to civilization. The missing element is that of the language, distilled out of the equation from the start, and with it the question of poetry as linguistic culture and as an indicator of a broader civilization beyond simple civility. The language and literature element is fundamental to the overall cultural community identity of a nation for du Bellay.

The temporary elimination of the language and literature portion of the question is made by du Bellay for the strategic purpose of demonstrating that if the role reversal could be made in the realm of civil life, there is no reason whatsoever that it cannot be made in the linguistic and poetic domain, thereby announcing the argument for an overall progress of French civilization beyond civility. In fact, it is not long before du Bellay returns to the question of language. If French is not as abundant, complex, and varied as Greek or Latin, this is due to the failings of "our ancestors," who restricted the language's development to mere necessity, preferring "deeds to words" and leaving examples of virtue rather than precepts—an explanation for the lack of a Gallic national literature that was a commonplace at the time.[13] While some later authors—Rivarol, for example—will consider the simplicity of French a positive trait, this is not so for du Bellay. This failure on the part of his ancestors represents more than a nostalgic regret. The hole in the Gallic linguistic and literary past is an identity issue. It led to a lack of models for posterity to imitate, such that "nostre Langue si pauvre & nue, . . . a besoing des ornements et (s'il faut ainsi parler) des plumes d'autruy" (our language so poor and naked, . . . needs the ornaments and [if one must speak thus] of the plumes of others, 22–23). Armed with a language of insufficient resource and barely able to meet the needs of expression, composing in a language lexically, structurally, and stylistically stripped, the French poet has no choice but to seek embellishment and decoration in non-French literary models—a point driven home by the double meaning of "plume" as both an aesthetic ornamentation and a writing instrument.

However, du Bellay's view of the current state of the French language is mixed, fusing a pessimistic consideration of the past with an optimistic vision for the future:

> Ainsi puys-je dire de nostre Langue, qui commence encores à fleurir sans fructifier, ou plus tost, comme une plante & vergette, n'a point encores fleury, tant se fault qu'elle ait apporté tout le fruict qu'elle pouroit bien produyre. Cela, certainement, non pour le défault de la nature d'elle, aussi apte à engendrer que les autres: mais pour la coulpe de ceux qui l'ont euë en garde, & ne l'ont cultivé à suffisance, ains comme une plante sauvaige, en celuy mesmes desert ou elle avoit commencé à naitre, sans jamais l'arrouser, la tailler, ny defendre des ronces & epines qui lui faisoint umbre, l'ont laissée enveillir & quasi mourir. (24–25)

> (Thus can I say that our language, which is still beginning to flower without giving fruit, or rather, like a sapling, has not yet flowered such that it has not yet brought forth the fruit it is capable of producing. This, certainly not through any fault of its nature, since it is just as capable of engendering as others: but through the fault of those whose charge it was to care for it, and who did not cultivate it sufficiently, thus like a wild plant, in that very wilderness where it had been born, without ever watering it, or pruning it, or defending it from the brambles and thorns which overshadowed it, allowed it to shrivel and nearly die.)

Returning to the metaphor of the language as a tree, du Bellay employs it to paint a picture of the present state of French superposed upon its past.[14] The present state is one of beginning. French is now, however late it may be, accomplishing the first phase of its true development. It is starting to blossom in the plenitude of its youthful springtime color and vigor, beginning to develop the lexical, structural, and stylistic reproductive organs that will allow linguistic and poetic (pro)creation. The "fruits" of this flowering have not yet made themselves felt, and no genuine increase in the quality of the language or its literature has yet been seen. Du Bellay acknowledges that we still may not even quite be at the "flowering" stage, though his "encore" implies that this phase, if it is not here now, is at the very least on the horizon and represents a positive affirmation of change. Regardless of whether French has reached the flowering period or not and regardless of how its development toward adolescence and adulthood has been retarded and its growth stunted, that growth and development will happen nonetheless. The retardation of the language's development is the reason that French has produced, literarily, so little of value to this point. French has reached the maximum potential it can reach given the conditions in which it has existed. However, du Bellay reiterates the idea that this is not due to some flaw of linguistic genetics, underlining again that this tree has the capacity to generate the fruits of a great national literature as much as any other does.

If the flower of French is sickly, this is not the fault of the tree but rather the fault of the gardener. In an abstract metaphor of writers and intellectuals as caretakers of the garden, du Bellay inserts into his painting a harsh attack on those writers who preceded his generation. He accuses them of having committed a sin against their language, at the very least a sin of omission, by not properly tending the tree in its garden. Proper cultivation produces exploitable utilitarian and aesthetic benefits; it brings about the fruitful development of the plant's qualities beyond their initial and natural condition—the artificial perfecting of the natural state of things. The term *cultiver* is of crucial significance. "Culture" relates not only to the agricultural endeavors inherent in the metaphor but also to the more human (or humanistic) sense of the term: the means of augmenting our knowledge, the development of the mind, the improvement of our faculties of judgment and of taste, the concept of intellectual and moral progress—all derived from education and the diffusion of the arts.[15] The sin of du Bellay's forbears consists of having failed in this charge, and instead of a beautiful tree growing in a garden of plenty, his generation inherited a shrunken shrub.

Du Bellay even acknowledges that in its present state the French language actually *is* barbarous. His qualification of the plant as "sauvage" denotes a conformity to the state of nature and a lack of human intervention. At the same time, however, the term highlights specific characteristics of the plant (its roughness, lack of grace, lack of delicateness) that make the word a synonym for "barbarous." Again this barbarism is the result of neglect and abandonment. Du Bellay's ancestors failed to nourish the language, failed to prune it (in agricultural terms, necessary for improving production in fruit trees), failed to give it proper light such that it shriveled and nearly died.

Du Bellay's view of the language that he and his contemporaries inherited manifests itself as a humanistically altered Garden of Eden motif. The picture painted by du Bellay centers on the image of a tree in a garden. It presents du Bellay and his fellows as the victims of the crimes of their forefathers, being punished for a humanistic original sin. The punishment of this sin is to carve out a literary life amid thorns and thistles in an arid cultural wilderness. Yet at the same time du Bellay's *Deffence et illustration* acts as a literary New Testament, carrying in its optimism the potential for cultural redemption and the promise of a poetic immortality: "Le tens viendra . . . que nostre langue . . . qui commence encor' à jeter ses racines, sortira de la terre, & s'elevera en telle hauteur & grosseur, qu'elle se pourra egaler aux mesmes Grecz & Romains" (The time will come . . . when our language . . . which is only beginning to sprout roots, will rise up from the ground, and grow to such height and girth, that it will be able to equal even those of the Greeks and the Romans, 27–28). Just as Speroni had argued the future greatness of Italian language and literature, du Bellay holds that the tree that is the French language will grow in glory, and French culture will be no longer a desert but a new Eden. France's poets, like those of antiquity, will have everlasting life.[16]

The idea of the *Deffence et illustration* as a testament or covenant is reprised in the concept of a contract as the fundamental link between the two elements of defending the French language and rendering it illustrious:

> Et qui voudra de bien pres y regarder, trouvera que nostre Langue Francoyse n'est si pauvre, qu'elle ne puysse rendre fidelement ce qu'elle emprunte des autres, si infertile, qu'elle ne puysse produyre de soy quelque fruict de bonne invention au moyen de l'industrie & diligence des cultivateurs d'icelle, si quelques uns se treuvent tant amys de leur païz et d'eux mesmes, qu'ils s'y veillent employer. (29)

> (And he who is willing to look closely, will find that our French language is not so poor that it cannot render faithfully that which it borrows from others, so infertile that it cannot produce some fruit of good invention by means of the industry and diligence of those who cultivate it, if there are but some who have enough love for their country and themselves, that they are willing to use it.)

This passage both defends the language and lays down the beginnings of a prescription on how to make the language better. In terms of defense, du Bellay argues that French's supposed insufficiency of resource for expression is countered by the quality of French translations. Thinkers such as Louis Meigret in his *Tretté de la grammère françoèse* (1550), Beaune in his *Discours* (1548), and Pasquier in his *Recherches* upheld the idea that French could express any idea under the sun and was up to any task.[17] For du Bellay, the ability to translate anything into French proves this beyond doubt. Additionally du Bellay plays with the double meaning of "rendre fidèlement" to drive the point home and to make the link with the notion of illustration. To render faithfully, in one sense, denotes the precise reproduction and exact expression of ideas and texts borrowed from other nations. At the same time the idea of borrowing texts from others leads into the second part of the play on "rendre fidèlement" in that French is giving back what it borrowed from the other culture, or notably, French "borrows" glory through the translation and extends equally (if not more so) the glory of the original text. This part of the contract is being fulfilled in du Bellay's time through the translations undertaken by his humanist contemporaries.

The problem with translation, though, is that the little glory France gets from these endeavors is not really its own.[18] As Peletier would later underline in his *Art poétique* (1555), translation is unforgiving—if you do it well, then people say you have done nothing but walk in the original's footsteps, and all the glory goes to the original author; if you translate badly, then all the blame gets laid on you as a translator; and even if people recognize that the original itself was bad, you get blamed for having chosen to translate something unworthy in the first place (30–31).[19] So translation can never be a means of truly improving the status of one's own culture and language, or of one's sense of identity.[20]

One step beyond translation is where the real illustration portion of the new covenant begins. Illustration starts with du Bellay's assumption that the so-called infertility of the French language is not inborn. He proposes that poets of his own generation should simultaneously abandon translation and break with the tendency to write in Latin.[21] French can deliver not only simple reproductions of other cultures' work but also original works of its own if writers adhere to four basic principles. The first two are industry and diligence. If French writers bring enough intellectual genius and artistic inventiveness to the table, and if to that they attach sufficient determination, then the French language will have a chance of standing with the best of the ancient and modern languages. The hard work required to bring about linguistic prestige was a frequently encountered concept at the time.[22] Du Bellay adds to these basic principles two qualities he sees as necessary to pave the way to such industry and diligence: love of country and of self—two essential ingredients insofar as these qualities fuse together the identity of the poet with that of the nation. By identifying himself with the nation and the language, the poet will transform the French civility previously praised by du Bellay into a genuine culture. This French culture will stand alone and by developing its own identity will distinguish itself from other cultures, ceasing to be the bastard child of the ancients. This, in a phrase, is the new covenant: devote your love of country, your industry, your discipline, your creative energy, your individual identity to writing in French, and a new French linguistic and cultural identity will be given to you.

The formation of an independent French identity is the main point behind du Bellay's continued and reiterated rejection of translation in subsequent chapters. In addition to the problem of sacrificing all glory to the originals, du Bellay further stresses that translation does not develop the language. It may serve as a sort of "standardized test" to determine what the language has previously acquired, but it does not drive the language forward.

Furthermore, from the standpoint of identity issues, translation has other flaws for du Bellay. He holds that translators can never really render orations or poems with the same grace as the original author since "chacune Langue a je ne scay quoy propre seulement à elle" (each language has a certain je ne sais quoi unique to it alone, 36).[23] Each nation's language has, for du Bellay, an indescribable and indefinable spirit or character. Translation may be fine for philosophical or scientific texts that depend "only" on the reproduction of ideas. However, the poetic or oratorical text contains meaning not only in the words as such but also in the fusion of sonorous and stylistic harmonies among those words that alter, augment, and add subtleties to the text's signification. No translation can ever reconstruct the simultaneous concurrence of those elements in the same way that they were constructed in the original language. For this reason du Bellay points out that translation is incompatible with the poetic spirit that "les Latins appeleroient *genius*" (the Romans would call *genius*, 40). Poetry is ultimately the form of linguistic production that best expresses *genius,* both in its creative sense of superiority in invention and talent and in its linguistic sense referring to the distinctive characteristics that define the individuality of a particular language.

Therefore, du Bellay admonishes the aspiring poet patriot: "Se compose donq' celuy qui voudra enrichir sa Langue, à l'immitation des meilleurs aucteurs Grecz & Latins: & à toutes leurs plus grandes vertuz, comme à un certain but, dirrige la pointe de son style" (Let he himself compose therefore who wishes to enrich his language, by imitating the best Greek and Latin authors: and toward all their greatest virtues, as toward a target, direct the point of his style, 45). Imitation of the authors of antiquity is well known as a central point of du Bellay's *Deffence et illustration,* and indeed he would be echoed in the work of thinkers such as Pasquier.[24] However, a number of points make the formulation of this counsel particularly interesting in terms of identity. To begin with, du Bellay opens this exhortation with a play on the meaning of *se composer*. On the surface he is, of course, arguing for a poetic composition based on the reproduction of classical poetic tendencies. At the same time, however, the use of the reflexive form, while literally indicating mere literary creation, is also suggestive of the poet's individual identity in the sense of composing or making oneself. Poetic creation and self creation are blended into a single act. The poet's sense of self becomes indistinguishable from the poet's artistic sense.

In addition, if the reproduction of the literary qualities of classical authors becomes an objective toward which the poet should aim the "pointe de son style," this too can be read in two ways. The "style" evokes the stylus, the writing instrument, the tool with which the poet performs his labor and craft, reiterating the emphasis on the link between invention and diligence and providing an objective toward which invention and diligence should work. At the same time the term implores the budding author to focus on an aesthetics reflected through the association of all elements of expression, an aesthetics that will distinguish him from all other writers, that will express his individual personality, and that by association with the character of his country and language will again serve to produce a communal cultural identity.

The objection could be made that this is paradoxical, in that the imitation of other writers should, like translation, only lead a writer to reproduce someone else's identity in the new poet's language. However, du Bellay suggests that one should imitate only the best of the authors of antiquity rather than all of them. Additionally he intends that the poet imitate only the best qualities rather than every characteristic of a given author, and not, certainly, the overall spirit or genius, since this would comprise the author's poetic and cultural identity. As Peletier du Mans puts it in his *Art poétique,* imitation is necessary but must not become a form of slavery. Peletier du Mans states that the author who imitates must always "ajouter du sien" (add something of his own, 23–24).[25] Indeed in du Bellay's own text the possessive "son" modifying the French poet's style is a small but significant detail emphasizing that the French poet's style is never to cease to be his, that he is to focus not on reproducing the other's genius but rather on creating his own.

Conscious of the difficulty inherent in this task, du Bellay highlights the subtlety of what he means by imitation:

> Mais entende celuy qui voudra immiter, que ce n'est chose facile de bien suyvre les vertuz d'un bon aucteur, & quasi comme se transformer en luy, veu que la Nature mesmes aux choses qui paroissent tressemblables, n'a sceu tant faire, que par quelque notte & difference elles ne puissent estre discernées. Je dy cecy, pour ce qu'il y en a beaucoup en toutes Langues, qui sans penetrer aux plus cachées & interieures parties de l'aucteur qu'ilz se sont proposé, s'adaptent seulement au premier regard, & s'amusant à la beauté des motz, perdent la force des choses. (46)

> (But let he who would imitate understand, that it is not an easy thing to follow the virtues of a good author, and to almost transform oneself into him, given that Nature, even with respect to things which appear very similar, was not so successful that they cannot be distinguished by some note or difference. I say this because there are many in all languages who, without penetrating to the most hidden and internal parts of the authors they have undertaken, satisfy themselves with only a first glance, and amusing themselves with the beauty of words, lose the force of things.)

The author of the *Deffence* reiterates the idea of adopting the best qualities of the best authors. This task involves nearly giving up one's own being in order to adopt that of the author being emulated. It is important to emphasize the qualification "nearly" in this identity swap, as du Bellay doubly qualifies the metamorphosis with the terms "quasi" and "comme." The transformation is selective. In defining the *partial* adoption of the other's identity, du Bellay employs two lexical associations that exist in opposition with each other. The first lexical group consists of the virtues of a good author, evoked by expressions such as the "plus cachées et intérieures parties de l'auteur" and "la force des choses." What is of value is that which is invisible, intimate, situated beneath the surface of the text. It is here that the aspiring French poet can locate the energy of poetic effect, the power of subject matter, the moral and intellectual resources informing both the signified and the *manner* in which signifier is attached to signified. What is not important is the signifier, as evidenced by the opposition of this first semantic connection to the second semantic network of "the first glance" and the idea of the poet "s'amusant à la beauté des mots," the imitation of which, by means of the opposition, is presented as a vice. Imitation of the external appearances of things is superficial, frivolous, vain, and trivial. It is the occupation of the mind in a futile endeavor unworthy of merit. The external appearances of signifiers may have an aesthetic beauty, but they have no substance of use to the poet in another language.

In other words, the French poet, for du Bellay, must look to the ancients for types of subject matter and general poetic techniques, as opposed to the specific *linguistic expression* of such subjects and poetic techniques, since these fall into the category of the genius, the je ne sais quoi, the poetic spirit. Not only can this external linguistic expression of the genius not be translated, but it also cannot be reproduced by an author in imitative works. Should a writer attempt its reproduction, he would simply lose his own identity.[26] In addition the possibility of contributing to a wider French cultural identity would be diminished in the process.

The difficulty of the poet's work lies in separating the one form of imitation from the other. Du Bellay acknowledges that the separation is made only with great effort, and this is because in the nature of things signifiers, signifieds, and the means of attaching one to the other are intricately interwoven. Distilling one from the other is a task accomplished only through pinpointing subtle and nearly imperceptible distinctions between them. It is not enough to stop at the visible beauty on the surface of the object of emulation. The aspiring poet needs to get underneath to the delicate shades of musicality informing subject and technique.

However, attempting to dig to the underlying musicality of past French poets is not a sufficient means of accomplishing the dual task of developing the language and building a literary culture: "Je t'amoneste donques (ò toy, qui desires l'accroissement de ta Langue, & veux exceller en icelle) de non immiter . . . les plus fameux aucteurs d'icelle . . . chose certes autant vicieuse, comme de nul profict à nostre vulgaire: veu que ce n'est autre chose (ò grande liberalité!) si non luy donner ce qui estoit à luy" (I admonish you therefore [oh you, who desire the growth of your language, and wish to excel in it] to not imitate . . . its own most famous authors . . . a practice certainly as vice-ridden as it is unprofitable to our vernacular: given that to do so is nothing more [oh great generosity!] than to give it what already belonged to it, 47). The paradox, for du Bellay, of French linguistic evolution and cultural development lies in the fact that it is not from the French past that the French future will develop.[27] Indeed he launches a two-pronged attack against the imitation of France's own past poets, qualifying the endeavor as both an unprofitable act and a vice. Imitation of French poets is unprofitable to the extent that the poet gives to the language only what he has taken from it, which du Bellay emphasizes by his sarcastically underscored exclamation of "admiration" for such "generosity."

What is worse is the expression of vice in this act. In essence, imitating one's own poetic family is an incestuous activity since poetic creation, as du Bellay previously evoked through his images of fruit and flower, is an act of reproduction. By borrowing from his own poetic traditions, the author engages in literary, linguistic, and cultural inbreeding. Inevitably this inbreeding leads to literary, linguistic, and cultural deformity and retardation. From a perverse seed results a perverse offspring. Again we come back to a scathing attack on Sebillet's views. The latter's poetic conservatism does not, in fact, maintain the status quo for du Bellay but, on the contrary, results in the crippling debilitation and devolution of French literature and cultural identity.

Du Bellay also explains why, although he recommends imitation of the ancients, he is against the writing of poetry in their languages. Many humanists tried to copy the ancients, having what Chamard calls "un désir violent de les imiter" (a violent desire to imitate them, 61). The drawback of this "violent desire" is that many poets undertook to copy the classical models in the ancients' own languages, which led to the explosion of neo-Latin literature. More often than not this form of imitation was unsuccessful. Du Bellay recognizes this, arguing that it is, in fact, impossible to equal the ancients in their own tongues. Referring to contemporaries who write in Latin or in Greek, du Bellay inquires:

> Pensent ilz donques, je ne dy egaler, mais approcher seulement de ces aucteurs en leurs Langues? Recueillant de cet orateur & de ce poëte ores un nom, ores un verbe, ores un vers, & ores une sentence: comme si en la façon qu'on rebatist un vieil edifice, ilz s'attendoint rendre par ces pierres ramassées à la ruynée fabrique de ces Langues sa premiere grandeur & excellence. Mais vous ne serez ja si bons massons (vous qui estes si grands zelateurs des Langues

Greque & Latine) que leur puissiez rendre celle forme que leur donnerent premierement ces bons & excellens architectes: & si vous esperez . . . que par ces fragmentz recuilliz elles puyssent estre resuscitées, vous vous abusez, ne pensant point qu'à la cheute de si superbes edifices conjointe à la ruyine fatale de ces deux puissantes monarchies, une partie devint poudre & l'autre doit estre en beaucoup de pieces, les queles vouloir reduir en un seroit chose impossible: outre que beaucoup d'autres parties sont demeurées aux fondementz des vieilles murailles, ou egarées par le long cours des siecles ne se peuvent trouver aucun. . . . Parquoi venant à redifier cete fabrique, vous serez bien loing de luy restituer sa premiere grandeur, quand, ou souloit estre la sale, vous ferez paravanture les chambres, les etables ou la cuysine, confundant les portes & les fenestres, bref changeant toute la forme de l'edifice. (78–80)

(Do they really think then, I do not suggest to equal, but even to approach these authors in their own tongue? Picking up from this orator and that poet here a noun, there a verb, and there a sentence: as if in the way one rebuilds an old edifice, they were expecting with these gathered stones to render to the ruined structure of these languages their original grandeur and excellence. But you will never be such good masons [you who are so zealous toward the Greek and Latin languages] that you can give back the form that was originally given to them by their own great and excellent architects: and if you hope . . . that from these gathered fragments they can be resurrected, you are sadly mistaken, not realizing that in the collapse of such superb edifices joined to the fatal ruin of these two powerful monarchies, one part became dust and the other must be in innumerable pieces, to want to put them back together again would be impossible: apart from the fact that many other stones having remained in the foundations of old walls, or having been carried off by the long passage of the centuries, none of them can be found. . . . Which is why, coming to rebuild that structure, you will be far from restoring its original grandeur, when, where a hall was to be, you will randomly place the bedrooms, and stables where the kitchen was, confusing doors and windows, and in a word changing the form of the whole edifice.)

The problem with writing in the languages of the ancients, as du Bellay exposes it, is one of comparative quality, and he posits that in terms of quality, the modern author cannot arrive at anything even close to equality. In this sense du Bellay breaks with Speroni, whose character Bembo, despite his own defense of the Tuscan vernacular, advises Lazaro to continue writing and speaking in Latin, as befits a man who speaks and writes much better in Latin than in the vulgar tongue (13–14). For du Bellay, as it would later be for Peletier du Mans, what Bembo advises Lazaro to do is simply beyond the realm of possibility. To drive home his point, du Bellay's discussion of the problem centers on a semantic network of architectural terms. The ancient cultures, like the remains of their buildings in contemporary times, are nothing more than remnants—foundations and old walls and loose stones, representing the basics of grammar and vocabulary, complete works of some few authors and literary fragments of the rest. The modern poet writing in the ancient tongues, most notably in Latin, seeks to reconstruct a literary body and culture that re-creates the original structure out of these elements.[28]

However, the rudimentariness and overall incompleteness of the materials with which the neo-Latin writer has to work are problematic. Du Bellay insists on the fragmentary nature of these materials through a semantic subnetwork of terms suggestive of broken bits.[29] Along with these he uses terms representing the scattered and disordered nature of those bits (*égarés*) and even explicitly reconnects the elements of language and poetic creation to these scattered pieces (beginning with the smallest of linguistic elements or individual words and progressing upward in size and significance through the rhythmic and musical elements of poetic lines, along with the ancient wisdom or moral lessons informing such lines), all of which lack order and unity and come haphazardly from one ancient writer or another without distinction or discretion.

This very lack of distinction or discretion constitutes an inevitable lack of cohesion in the literary constructions built by neo-Latin authors. Du Bellay reflects this missing cohesion in his extension of the metaphor by contrasting the modern French author writing in Latin as "mason" with the writers of antiquity as "excellent architects." The contemporary writer of Latin may well be able to do some "stonework" putting together words, phrases, and ideas in some rough manner of structure, but such a rudimentary structure is far from a grand palace, with all its complexity and sweeping unity of design. The mason can pragmatically connect blocks, foundations, walls, and joints. However, he lacks the art, science, and technique of the architect to create and conceive. The contemporary neo-Latinist is but an artisan, while the ancient poets were artists of the highest caliber.

Worse still, the neo-Latinist is not even a good artisan. The neo-Latin poet's attempts at construction are not simply rudimentary; they are convoluted monstrosities jumbled together with every element out of place. The neo-Latinist builds his poetry in the same manner in which he found its elements—broken and scattered. The French writer of verse in ancient tongues is reduced in du Bellay's eyes to the ignoble status of the scavenger collecting, scooping up, and picking through the linguistic and cultural junk heap of others. For the author of the *Deffence*, from junk comes junk. All pieces of verse the neo-Latinists write are corrupted, twisted versions of the sublime originals. Neo-Latin verse lacks both rhyme and reason, and those who think otherwise, for du Bellay, are fooling themselves.[30] There is no question of rebuilding the lost civilization of Rome. One must rather treat the cultural space where Rome once stood as an already cleared, empty plain where a *new* civilization can be erected.[31]

The mechanism that has rendered the re-creation of the ancients in their own languages impossible—the passage of time—is the same element that gives to the French language so much potential for progress in du Bellay's eyes. Whatever one may think of his views on translation, neo-Latinism, and imitation, du Bellay suggests that we cannot argue that the ancients are better than we are and will always be better just because they came first.[32] On the contrary, in the sciences and in technology we far outstrip them, so why should language and language's art be any different (53)? Such progress and the ultimate reversal of roles are, in fact, for du Bellay part of the natural order of things. If the Frenchmen of du Bellay's time have surpassed the ancients in so many fields, it is because God "a donné pour loy inviolable à toute chose créée de ne durer perpetuellement, mais passer sans fin d'un etat en l'autre, etant la fin & corruption de l'un, le commencement & generation de l'autre" (set down as an inviolable law that no thing created can endure perpetually, but must pass ceaselessly from one state to another, with the end and corruption of one being the commencement and generation of another, 57). The notion of progress is part of a necessary and constant sequence of temporal and cultural phenomena that are regulated by a divine imperative and cannot be altered by the acts of men or nations. The very form of imperative that du Bellay denies for granting privilege to any particular language and culture is contrarily at the root of the guarantee that no language or culture having reached a privileged state will ever be able to remain there. In essence that divine and natural law is one of finiteness. All glory is fleeting, and the superiority of any people is a priori forbidden indefinite continuity.

At the same time, however, the lack of permanence in and of itself is paradoxically a form of continuity. Rather than true and absolute beginnings and endings, what one sees in du Bellay's discourse of language life span is a metamorphosis that extends the original plant metaphor borrowed from Speroni and used to express the origin and progress of language. While nothing can last forever, any given thing will "passer sans fin d'un etat en l'autre"—the process of movement from one form to another being itself an infinite one. Indeed du Bellay even presents beginnings and endings as equivalent, such that identities intermingle and such that it is difficult to determine where one linguistic community's identity ends and another commences. If each language and culture is a plant, when it dies, it decomposes ("corruption" of the living organism), thereby nourishing the soil and preparing the terrain, as it were, for the next seed to spring into germination, in an endless cycle of life. From this perspective both translation and neo-Latin poetry can be regarded as necessary steps in the cycle but steps that have now served their purpose and prepared the way for French to be used first in imitation of the ancients and ultimately on its own at some future point without recourse to imitation at all. The further logic of this is that eventually French will, as du Bellay suggests, reach the same degree of eminence that the ancient languages did and will then finally decline and die out in its own turn, preparing the ground for other languages to translate, employ, and then imitate.

Since, like the ancient languages, French too must eventually decline and fade, transforming into something else, the only question is, how long will the glory period last? Du Bellay states that the French language can be certain of maintaining its eventual perfection for quite a long time, "l'ayant acquise avecques si longue peine, suyvant la loy de Nature, qui a voulu que tout arbre qui naist, florist et fructifie bien tost, bien tost aussi envieillisse et meure: & au contraire, celuy durer par longues années, qui a longuement travaillé à jeter ses racines" (having acquired it with such long effort, following the law of Nature, that any tree which is born, flowers and yields fruit early, must also quickly shrivel and die: and contrarily, that tree will last long years, which worked long to take root, 57). What French will have going for it, allowing it in its future phase of prominence to survive longer than did the languages of the Greeks or Romans, is a natural law of inverse proportions. The ancients were meteoric and fast burning. They wrote fast, died young, and left beautiful literary corpses. The developmental curve of French, in contrast, has up until du Bellay's era been a gentler one, so the downslide of the arc will also be longer and gentler, giving French more time to accumulate and retain literary glory. French's more slowly budding flowers will be more colorful and long-lived. French's more slowly developing fruit will be sweeter and more succulent. It will take longer for the leaves (the laurels of poetic glory) to fall from French's branches.

The remainder of du Bellay's *Deffence et illustration,* the whole "second livre," explores the question of how to achieve and maintain this lengthy period of glory. Nearly the entirety of it is devoted to the topics of precisely whom and what to imitate and how to do so. A survey of the chapter titles reveals an unbreakable link between the poetic act and a national/linguistic identity. Of twelve chapter titles eight make explicit reference to expressions such as "le poëte francoys," "le poëme francoys," or writing in "nostre langue" (the French poet, the French poem, our language). The link between poetics and the national linguistic identity reaches its climax in the final chapter, which consists of an "exhortation aux Francoys d'ecrire en leur Langue" (exhortation to the French to write in their language), the fundamental root of the compact by which French authors will create their new, true identity.[33]

In the end there is much that derives from the national identity crisis and inferiority complex at the root of du Bellay's *Deffence et illustration.* Language's purpose is to convey ideas. This conveyance consists of substance, form, and the fusion of form to substance—or in more modern terms, of signifieds, signifiers, and the processes of signification. Signifiers and the process of signification are arbitrary. As such they are artificial and therefore exist in opposition to the very signifieds they represent, which are completely natural. For du Bellay, signifiers and signification produce culture. A culture is not inferior by nature but only by a deficiency of human processes. Thus the art(ificial) holds a privileged position in the opposition of nature and the natural with art and the artificial for du Bellay. Language is the artificial material of the poetic art, and this art creates a sense of identity and community. Only because they are artificial can language and culture evolve. The mutual evolution of language, poetic art, and cultural identity hinges on intellectual erudition; natural inspiration is too rooted in immutable nature to aid change and progress. Progress is the key to defining the quality of a nation. Laws and virtues may provide for civility, but it takes a (literary) culture to make a true *civilization*. It is this criterion that divides the civilized from the barbarous; hence the necessity of du Bellay's efforts at "defense."

The evolution of a national identity (and in particular a French identity) is riddled with paradoxical fusions and distinctions: us and them, I and us, past and future. As far as the us-and-them relationship goes, French language and literary culture must be derived from those of the ancients while simultaneously distinguishing themselves from it. In terms of the I-and-us relationship, the poet must carve out his own identity while simultaneously being infused by and infusing his national identity. Where the past-and-future connection is concerned, it is by engaging on individual and communal levels in a relationship with both the past and the future that poets participate in a larger cycle of linguistic and literary cultural life. They commit themselves to an endless spiral of progress, privileging the descendant over the ancestor. This spiral is at the heart of the "illustration" of the French language. By borrowing from the past and from the other, by adding to the mix the individuality of the self, the poet will write great works, thereby contributing to his nation's sense of communal identity, creating his nation's glory, and further laying the groundwork not only for the next generation of his own nation but also for the benefit of future generations of *other* nations.

Hartley has underlined the fluidity of the notion of *patrie* or *pays* in the sixteenth century in the sense that it could have a range of meanings, from "the locality in which the individual was born" to his nation (1). We see this in a number of du Bellay's poems, which express love sometimes for France, sometimes for the Loire valley. I would add to this that for du Bellay, the fluctuation extends even further in that he envisions France's place in a larger cultural milieu, such that the potential *patrie* of the artist can be viewed even as the world, anticipating the general intellectual and artistic cosmopolitanism of the seventeenth and eighteenth centuries as well as anticipating the possibility of a universal French culture (if not its language) that will appear in the work of Rivarol at the end of the early modern period.

In this way du Bellay's *Deffence et illustration* is fed by and feeds the humanist ideal—individual poetic glory contributes to national glory, and national glory contributes to the long-term glory of the human race: *humanitas* as letters, *humanitas* as culture, *humanitas* as the fundamentally human. The duty of the individual is to the tribe; the duty of the tribe is to the race. The greatest individual crime is to fail in duty to the community; the greatest communal crime is to fail in duty to humanity. We remember the Greeks and the Romans for what they contributed to the world. France can be glorious, after its eventual decline and death, only if it too has contributed to the overall culture of the human race, and this task lies in the hands of the individual poets. This is barbarous indeed, and an enemy not only of *humanitas* but also of his *patrie* and *himself,* is he who fails in these tasks.

Two

Montaigne's *Essais*
The Baroque Mind, Language, and Being

Michel de Montaigne (1533–92), country gentleman, parliamentarian magistrate, mayor of Bordeaux, traveler, and thinker, is best known for his *Essais*. The first edition of the *Essais,* comprised of the first and second books, was published in 1580; the third book was published in the second edition of 1588; and the author's final edition, containing various corrections, was published posthumously in 1595. An essay by one possible definition is a work that treats a subject in an analytic, interpretive, or speculative fashion. Montaigne's *Essais* treat a wide variety of topics, from cannibalism to idleness, from anger to the greatness of Rome, on which the author writes in a meandering conversational style—sometimes analytical, sometimes speculative, sometimes interpretive. In them he infuses quotations from classical authors, exhibiting the continued influence of the humanist movement on French letters. Like du Bellay, Montaigne forms part of a larger wave of humanistic learning and thinking.

Additionally the concept of the essay connects Montaigne with du Bellay's vision of the French literature of the time. An essay can also be defined as a first production of someone commencing in the field of artistic production. Du Bellay and the Pléiade had seen themselves as literary pioneers, breaking new ground and creating the first productions of a truly French literature through their poetry. Montaigne does the same thing in prose, breaking new ground, establishing a new genre—the personal essay—and giving new direction to French writing.[1]

From a linguistic standpoint, we also see in Montaigne's personal life, as presented in the *Essais,* a parallel image to what du Bellay defines as the natural life cycle of a language. Montaigne tells us that his first language was Latin. To raise Michel when he was still an infant, his father hired a German tutor who spoke no French but was an expert in Latin. The entire household was forbidden to speak any language other than Latin when in the presence of young Michel. At the age of six he still knew neither French nor Perigordin (209).[2] At that point in Michel's life his father sent him away to the Collège de Guienne for a wider education. Montaigne tells us that at school his Latin "s'abastardit incontinent" (immediately became bastardized) and that since then he had lost all use of that language (211).

Montaigne still read Latin into adulthood, however. His first work was a translation from Latin to French of Raimond Sebond's *Theologia naturalis* (1434–36), which he produced for his father. Talking of this book in the *Essais,* Montaigne highlights the general danger of translating into "un idiome plus foible" (a weaker idiom, 482), referring to French. Nevertheless when he was an adult, active Latin use belonged only to his past, and he wrote in French alone. For the *Essais,* his original literary creation, he uses the language of his nation—though not without frequent quotations in Latin rendering homage to antiquity. However, his own thoughts he composes entirely in French.[3]

This brief sketch of Montaigne's "linguistic biography" reflects the general progress of French traced out by du Bellay in his *Deffence et illustration*. In the first stage there is only Latin. This is followed by a period of translation and denigration of the vulgar. Finally there is acceptance of the French language and its use as a legitimate medium of literary production, albeit with awareness and recognition of the contribution of the classic authors.

For these reasons alone it would make sense to study the *Essais* following an examination of the *Deffence et illustration*. At the same time there are, amid the wide variety of topics covered by Montaigne in his work, recurring themes that transcend the textual boundaries of individual essays, and two of these themes will be treated in this chapter. The first is the question of identity. In the case of Montaigne's *Essais,* concern here is with the individual identity of the writer expressed in his text. The second theme is the question of language, in particular its nature and potential for expressing the reality of the world. Essentially this chapter contains an examination of a metaphysics of identity and semiotics across various parts of Montaigne's works. In a way these two themes are two sides of the same literary coin, since the ability of a text to express the linguistic genius of an author, to use du Bellay's term, is entirely dictated by the fundamental capacity of language to signify reality. In the overlapping of these two thematic fields, there will be many echoes of questions raised by du Bellay and foreshadowings of questions to be raised by others, such as the relationship between the natural and the artificial, issues of certainty and doubt, truth and falsehood, language and mind.

The theme of identity appears at the very start of Montaigne's *Essais*. Montaigne explicitly announces this theme as the primary subject of his book in his prefatory note to the reader. He claims to have devoted the writing of this book to "la commodité particuliere de mes parens et amis: à ce que m'ayant perdu (ce qu'ils ont à faire bien tost) ils y puissent retrouver aucuns traits de mes conditions et humeurs, et que par ce moyen ils nourrissent plus entière et plus vifve, la connoissance qu'ils ont eu de moy" (the particular benefit of my family and friends: who having lost me [which they soon must do] will be able to recover certain traits of my conditions and moods, and by this means nourish in a more complete and lively fashion, the knowledge they had of me, 25). In making this announcement Montaigne introduces the reader to four key elements: intimacy, temporality, portraiture, and knowledge. The first phrase of the passage presents the concept of intimacy. The declaration of intentionality, that this work was produced for two explicitly named groups—members of family along with those not in the family but who have a privileged emotional attachment to the author—creates concentric circles of intimacy that act as boundaries of communal identities. One is in a particular circle, a member of a community centered on the individual of the author, or not. The text of the *Essais,* if the phrase is taken at face value, is the property of members of those two circles, suggesting a degree of exclusivity. In other words, anyone not a member of these circles seems, at first glance, to be excluded from the text as an other, as an outsider.

The use of text as the center of these circles is brought on by temporal necessity. The problem of temporality is reflected in the concept of Montaigne's assumed impending death, along with the play of tenses in the passage: "m'ayant perdu" participating at one and the same time in a past and a present, piled on top of "ont à faire bientôt" participating at once in a present and a future, and reinforcing the immanence of that future, along with the use of a *passé composé* "qu'ils ont eu" for the past of a future event that has not yet occurred. The play of time in the juxtaposed use of these seemingly incompatible tenses highlights the text as a unifying element that stretches across time and connects past, present, and future. The text becomes a means of creating a past before it is past and a means of solidifying that past such that in the future it can be consulted as if the subject and the objects of representation were still present. It is as if the definitive loss of center for these circles of community, the loss of the author, will not be so definitive after all, through the eternal presence of the text. The text through its intemporality is a preserver of the individual and of the community.

This facet of representation is the very essence of the act of self-portraiture that Montaigne proposes to undertake. Like lines traced on an artist's sketch paper, Montaigne's lines of text—replacing "traits de crayon" with "traits de plume"—double as "traits de personnalité." With words Montaigne will paint himself through salient facts and anecdotes, through expression of essential elements of his character, his dispositions and temperament—in short, all the particular qualities reflecting his identity. The presentation of select pieces attaches the intention of the author once again to yet another definition of the essay: a small portion of a thing by which one assesses the entirety of it. In other words, each essay becomes a small portion of Montaigne's personality from which we can come to know the overall man.

So the text of Montaigne's *Essais* defines itself as a vehicle for knowing its author. At the same time it becomes more than that. It "nourishes" the intimate knowledge held already by those belonging to the designated circles of community. In other words, it does not simply reproduce what members of the community already know. Nourishing is an act that encourages growth and expansion; it is the provision of life. Knowledge of the author, paradoxically, even after the author is dead is still a living thing in that it continues to grow, expand, evolve, just as if the author were still alive. This idea suggested by the term *nourir* is reinforced by the comparative *plus* modifying both the development and extension of the intimate knowledge possessed by the author's inner circles of family and friends, and modifying also the intensity and level of intimacy of that knowledge. In addition the adjective *vif*, so suggestive of this intensity and intimacy, evokes equally the living nature of the intimate knowledge provided by the text. The text becomes a living and breathing source of the author's self.

The inclusive/exclusive nature of the text is also underlined by Montaigne's announcement in the prefatory note to the reader of the style he will employ. If the purpose of his text "eust esté pour rechercher la faveur du monde, je me fusse mieux paré, et me présanterois en une marche estudiée. Je veus qu'on m'y voie en ma façon simple, naturelle et ordinaire, sans contention et artifice: car c'est moy que je peins" (had been to seek the favor of the public, I would have better adorned myself, and would present myself with a more measured step. I want to be seen in my simple, natural and ordinary fashion, with no effort or artifice: because it is myself that I am painting, 25).

Montaigne expresses the existence of two forms of literary motivations existing in opposition to each other. On the one hand, there is the private, intimate (even confessional) literature, written for the exclusive readership designated above and intended for after the author's death. On the other hand, there is a completely inclusive public literature, aimed at the broadest possible community, whose purpose is the acquisition of social recognition and acclaim, and the resultant benefit to its author during his lifetime. This opposition of intent is reinforced by the opposition of two competing semantic networks, centered on the traditional tension between *l'être et le paraître*, between reality and appearance. Private literature is positively associated by Montaigne with a lexical network of terms relating to reality.[4] This network highlights honesty, lack of cultivation and finesse, lack of subtlety and complexity, and ease in the flow of ideas directly from the inherent qualities of the author and from the order of things. Public writing, in contrast, is negatively associated with a network of appearance.[5] This emphasizes ornamentation, outward facades, self-glorification and aggrandizement, manipulation of the gaze of the other, calculation, ruse, fabrication, and imposture.

The manner of expression announced by Montaigne, his overt choice of a private style, is indicated as a logical extension of his intended purposes and readership.

Montaigne finally reinforces both the nature of his text as personal portrait and its exclusive nature: "Ainsi, lecteur, je suis moy-mesmes la matiere de mon livre: ce n'est pas raison que tu employes ton loisir en un subject si frivole et si vain" (Thus, reader, I am myself the matter of my book: there is no reason for you to employ your leisure on a subject so frivolous and so vain, 25). Preceding the colon separating the sentence into two phrases, we have eleven words, of which five are either in the first person, marked as first-person agreements, or used as first-person stresses.[6] Further, the terms *matière* and *livre* are equated with the first-person persona of the author such that the book is nothing more than an extension of the author's being. Claiming to be the matter of his book, Montaigne becomes both grammatical subject and object. He is the subject of his book, the topic. Every author exposes a topic, making the topic of any book a grammatical object. At the same time Montaigne the author is the grammatical subject, since Montaigne writes the book. This play with the notion of the subject of his book, with the author as both grammatical subject and object, gives a double meaning to the concept of creative work.

The *Essais* are creative in the obvious sense that they can be considered a work of what would be termed today creative nonfiction, while at the same time they are creative of the author himself, for they are a vehicle of self-creation allowing Montaigne to present us with a portrait of the self as *ouvrage*. This concept of the identity or the being of the author as the grammatical subject and object of a work links Montaigne to the preoccupation of du Bellay in the *Deffence* that the author "se compose" as a means of creating an identity through literary composition (45). At the same time the idea of the author as grammatical subject and object is also important in its connection with writers of Montaigne's time, such as Sánchez, for whom the question of "being" is the alpha and omega of the larger concept of understanding.[7] This perspective on the book carries the question of language and identity more clearly into the realm of the semiotic triangle of expression, thought, and reality, which ultimately will be the main thrust of Montaigne's ideas on language. Montaigne's manner of situating language and the self of the author will ultimately lead him to associate, as Speroni did, the means of expression with the writing self.[8]

In the context of the opening to Montaigne's *Essais,* this particular angle on the subject of the book links self-portraiture again to the dichotomy of inclusion/exclusion and connects the identity of the individual with a larger community identity. Montaigne tells his reader (who, as the structure of the phrasing indicates clearly to us, is not inside the circle of family and friends) that there is no justification for him to read the book and to consume his free time in the examination of a subject so "frivolous" and "vain." Ostensibly self-deprecating, Montaigne presents the act of coming to know him through the book as an unimportant, futile, even illusory pursuit. It appears on the surface that the author is trying to drive the reader into a self-exclusion from the inner circles—put the book down now; it is not worth your effort; stop while you are ahead.

However, at the same time this very phrase plays into the domain of inclusivity. If Montaigne seems to drive away the reader, it is only because he is attempting to pull in a certain type of reader, one who believes in the value of getting to know the author for his own sake. It will be shown in later discussion that Montaigne relishes this activity in his own reading. Here he is seeking out kindred spirits to enter the inner circle of friends—he even says as much explicitly near the end of the *Essais* in "De la Vanité" (On Vanity, book 3, chapter 9, 1057–1123), expressing his hopes that "s'il advient que mes humeurs plaisent et accordent à quelque honneste homme avant que je meure, il recerchera de nous joindre" (if it should come to pass that my humors please and agree with some cultivated gentleman before I die, he will seek to join us, 1098). So despite its efforts to scare off some readers, the text is nevertheless also intended for future members of the inner circles. By releasing his book not just to family and friends but also to the general public, Montaigne casts the widest net possible. However, his bait will appeal only to a chosen minority. For the rest, the reading will indeed be vain, but for that happy few, there will be membership and inclusion and the pleasure of a shared communal identity built around the individual identity of the author.[9]

The essay entitled "De l'Institution des enfants" (On the Education of Children, book 1, chapter 26, 176–213), is one of the first pieces in Montaigne's work to make reference to issues of both identity and language and to their overlap. Early in this text Montaigne reflects on one of the principal difficulties of writing the self: "ce sont ici mes humeurs et opinions; je les donne pour ce qui est en ma creance, non pour ce qui est à croire. Je ne vise icy qu'à découvrir moy mesmes, qui seray par adventure autre demain, si nouveau apprentissage me change" (here are my humors and opinions; I present them as what I believe, not as what should be believed. I aim only to discover myself, who will perchance be different tomorrow, if new experience changes me, 180). The primary axis on which this passage turns is the opposition of the descriptive and prescriptive in the writer's work. Negating for the reader the possibility of accepting what he writes as truth, Montaigne instead indicates to the reader that what is on the paper are those ideas currently in the author's mind. The reader is engaged not to believe but only to observe. Judgment of truth value is left to the reader, as Montaigne's first opposition feeds into a second one of description versus definition.

Indeed Montaigne claims not to define, to the extent that nothing he says is defin*ite* or defin*itive*. This lack of the definite and the definitive unveils a semantic network of uncertainty inseparably linked to the self.[10] On this point Montaigne takes the broad abstract claim from Sánchez's *Nothing Is Known* (1581) that being is indefinable, and he applies it to the very specific being of the individual in the person of the author.[11] What the reader will find in Montaigne's book are merely momentary dispositions and temperaments, fleeting character tendencies, points of view devoid of any implication of the absolute or the correct, particular orientations of the author's thought processes, the paradox of being other than what one is, and the temporal forces that drive alterations in being.

The use of the term *humeurs* in particular suggests the completeness of this fluctuation, linking the emotional and the intellectual (good humor, ill humor, ideas, and inclinations) with the physiological (Galen's humors, the fluids flowing through our veins that determine our short-term and long-term conditions of being).[12] In addition the fluctuations of being occur not only from within but also from without, through "education," through experience and external input. Such forms of alteration are basic laws of human physical, psychological, and social existence, and these alterations happen with enormous rapidity from one day to the next.

If such changes are unpredictable, as Montaigne's text suggests, the role of authorial intent becomes problematic as well. If Montaigne has a goal, it cannot be to make the changes occur—they happen to him with or without his consent. All he can do is reproduce them on paper from day to day as they take place. Intent is limited to taking the here-and-now snapshots that in the long term will reflect the changes and fluctuations as they manifest themselves. Indeed, Montaigne is merely coming to know himself through the process, discovering himself, therefore, in both senses of the term—in the most common sense, he is learning things about himself that he did not know (because prior to fluctuation those parts of him did not exist) and also discovering himself, in the sense of *un*covering, before the reading public, stripping bare the self so that it can be seen by all. Suddenly the text as a vehicle for creating the self suggested in the preface to the reader takes on a double character, and along with its capacity for self-creation, it carries with it the function of self-discovery. Language, true to Montaigne's notion of fluctuation, vacillates between creation and *re-*creation.

This dual concept of creation and re-creation through language is presented in the image of the mirror further on in the "Institution." Montaigne writes that "le vrai miroir de nos discours est le cours de nos vies" (the true mirror of our discourses is the course of our lives, 203). Focusing on the concept of reflection, Montaigne establishes a parallel between life and language. Just as the mirror's image and the individual resemble each other, so too do language and life. Language walks hand in hand with existence, the course and *dis*course of human lives.[13] As individuals run and race through life, so language runs about, to and fro, keeping up with it. Or does it? This image of language suggests that language follows life, but the phrasing Montaigne uses, that the true mirror of our discourse is the course of our lives, juxtaposes the relationship—discourse does not reflect life, but rather life reflects discourse. Reality, it is suggested, conforms itself to language, and language is returned to its role of creating rather than re-creating.[14]

Furthermore, in the context of an essay on education, the terms "discourse" and "course" have important pedagogic associations. "Discourse," apart from simply referring to language or its use, denotes also a didactic writing, while a "course" is an education in a particular discipline or field. So when Montaigne speaks of "le cours de nos vies," his phrasing evokes not only the flow of time and events from birth to death but also the sum total of our experiences, what we learn, the "apprentissage qui nous change," to return to a line he employed previously. From this perspective Montaigne's use of *discours* would give a didactic flavor to his essays. This is not, as he mentions in the "Institution," for others to learn from him.[15] It is rather for him to learn from himself, in this way coming about in circular fashion, providing the very education that will change him, such that language, or discourse, simultaneously fulfills its functions of creating and re-creating the self.

A final example shows how Montaigne tries to keep language suspended equivocally in this dual function of creation and re-creation of reality by swinging the pendulum back the other way. In talking about the role he believes language should play in the education of children, Montaigne emphasizes the function of re-creating reality, insisting that the purpose of education is not to make the child into a grammarian or a logician but rather:

> que nostre disciple soit bien pourveu de choses, les parolles ne suivront que trop: il les trainera si elles ne veulent suivre. J'en oy qui s'excusent de ne se pouvoir exprimer, et font contenance d'avoir la teste pleine de plusieurs belles choses, mais, à faute d'eloquence, ne les pouvoir mettre en evidence: c'est une baye. Sçavez vous, à mon advis, que c'est que cela? Ce sont des ombrages qui leur viennent de quelques conceptions informes, qu'ils ne peuvent desmeler et eclaircir au dedans, ny par consequant produire au dehors: ils ne s'entendent pas encore eux mesmes. (204)

(let our disciple be well furnished with things, words will follow on their own: he will drag them along if they do not wish to follow. I hear those who complain that they cannot express themselves, and pretend to have their heads full of many beautiful things, but, for lack of eloquence, are unable to bring them to light: this is a deception. Do you know, in my opinion, what is really the case? There are shadows that come to them of some few unformed conceptions, that they are unable to unravel and clarify within, nor consequently, express without: they still don't even understand themselves.)

Montaigne enunciates a distinction between signifier and signified, between word and substance. Here, however, the substance of the signified is privileged over the signifier, as it is the latter that must conform to the former. If words are not capable of doing so naturally, the speaker will by intellectual force cause them to do so, restructuring them, inventing, creating, bending the word to fit the idea.[16] The emphasis on the primacy of thought over speech is exemplified by Montaigne's views on unclear discourse. One's incapacity to render ideas manifest through signification is never a linguistic difficulty. It is rather, for Montaigne, an intellectual shortcoming. The supposed lack of expressive or persuasive ability made by those whose discourse appears unclear is exactly the opposite of what it seems to be. These individuals are associated with facade and appearance (*font contenance*), the very things they claim to be short of, so it is not artifice, neither the aesthetics nor the persuasiveness of speech, that they have in short supply.

Their deception, as Montaigne calls it, paradoxically unravels the truth of their situation. If they cannot *exprimer* (etymologically "to bring something out") ideas from the mind, if they cannot make visible for others their ideas (etymologically, "visible forms"), it is because they, in fact, have none to bring out or to make visible. The very notion of the *baye,* of dissimulation and ruse, of intentional falsehood, reconfigures how we see such individuals. Everything they pretend is the opposite of what they claim—the mind defined by emptiness rather than fullness, paucity rather than plurality, beautiful words rather than beautiful ideas, a tendency toward eloquent artifice rather than rational substance, and above all confusion rather than clarity. On this last point Montaigne employs a network of terms evoking the lack of light, of enlightenment, and therefore of reason, suggesting the hidden, the forgotten, the misleading and ephemeral, the unstructured and uncontrolled, the convoluted and tangled.[17] If we cannot understand them, it is because they do not understand themselves. These speakers utter words that have no meaning, either because their signifiers are devoid of signifieds or because their signifiers cannot be linked to any one signified in particular. With signifiers not following specific signifieds in a rational sequence dictated by the nature of things, such discourse becomes inconsequent, both in the literal sense of "not following" and in the sense of being of no importance and not worth notice.

Having critiqued those whose language use is poor, Montaigne then turns to issues of language per se, explaining, on the assumption that a speaker or writer actually has clear thoughts, the kind of linguistic style he prefers:

Le parler que j'ayme, c'est un parler simple et naïf, tel sur le papier qu'à la bouche; un parler succulent et nerveux, court et serré, non tant delicat et peigné comme vehement et brusque . . . plustost difficile qu'ennuieux, esloigné d'affectation, desreglé, descousu et hardy . . . non pedantesque, non pleideresque, mais plustost soldatesque. (207)

(The expression I like is a simple and naive expression, on paper as in the mouth; a succulent and nervous expression, short and tight, not so much delicate and groomed as vehement and brusque . . . difficult rather than tiring, distanced from affectation, unruly, casual and saucy . . . not pedantic, not lawyerly, but soldierly.)

He defines his preferred style through two competing semiotic networks. In the first place there is the lexical grouping referring to the simple, virile, soldierly manner of discourse for which he has a particular affinity.[18] Next to this he lays out another referring to the affected, pedantic, lawyerly discourse for which he has no tolerance.[19] The former style is reflective of honesty, substance, compression, and ease of expression coupled paradoxically with complexity of interpretation—few words expressing vast quantities of ideas. It is a language of action, straightforward and economical, saying what is true and what needs to be said without wasting, or mincing, of words. Like other writers of his time, such as Sánchez and Agrippa of Nettesheim, Montaigne equates economy with truth.[20] However, for Montaigne, these characteristics of language constitute not just truth but good "taste" in discourse—this language is, after all, for Montaigne, "succulent." Contrarily, indigestible discourse is linked to affected grace, preening, ostentation, insincerity, confusion, and obfuscation. It is an unnecessarily amplified discourse expressing few ideas with vast quantities of words. It is a *rhetorical* discourse in the worst sense of the term.

There is an underlying problem with such a rhetorical discourse, on a semiotic level, that goes beyond simple personal preference for Montaigne. In his essay "De la vanité des paroles" (On the Vanity of Words, book 1, chapter 51, 342–45), Montaigne elaborates on this shortcoming. Addressing the topic of rhetoric, he writes that "un Rhetoricien du temps passé disoit que son mestier estoit de choses petites les faire paroistre et trouver grandes" (a Rhetorician of times past used to say that his trade was to take small things and make them appear and seem great, 342). Montaigne astutely employs the words of an expert in the art of discursive techniques to define that art. By so doing, the art criticizes and thereby undermines itself. The definition of this employment of language is reduced to two basic concepts. First, there is dishonesty. If we accept this orator's definition, then all rhetorical discourse is inherently, consciously, and intentionally false, operating in the realm of appearance rather than that of truth and reality. The phrasing of this particular definition excludes the possibility of an alternate conception of rhetoric as truth expressed in an aesthetically pleasing manner. Like others of his time, such as Agrippa of Nettesheim, Montaigne designates rhetoric and eloquence here as the polar opposites of truth.[21] Going a step further, Montaigne underlines a second basic concept as being inherent to this definition of rhetoric, and that is the principle of disproportion—the mechanism by which the essential dishonesty of eloquence takes place. In perfect parallel to Montaigne's qualification of poor discourse, rhetoric, as a discipline or a profession, seeks explicitly to overexpress. It gives more emphasis to signifiers than to signifieds and engages in the profusion of words linked to ideas of little substance. Rhetoric makes things appear what they are not and makes the insignificant appear significant.

Montaigne drives home the importance of falsification through disproportion by arguing that "ceux qui masquent et fardent les femmes, font moins de mal; car c'est chose de peu de perte de ne les voir pas en leur naturel; là où ceux-cy font estat de tromper, non pas nos yeux, mais nostre jugement, et d'abastardir et corrompre l'essence des choses" (those who mask and make over women do less harm; since it is of little loss to not see their natural look; but these others [rhetoricians] make a point of deceiving not our eyes, but our judgment, and bastardize and corrupt the essence of things, 342). Montaigne's metaphor of a woman in makeup lays the foundation for two connected binary contrasts. We see mask and makeup arrayed against the natural, the act of covering, hiding, and misleading in counterpoint to reality and honesty. At the same time this contrast is established in parallel with that of the senses and the mind. The woman's makeup is deceptive, yes, but it is deceptive only to the eyes, only in an aesthetic sense. It is a deception rooted in and limited to external appearance. By comparison the orator, the lawyer, and the rhetorician engage in a more treacherous trickery in that their deceit runs deeper, involving not simply a cover-up of reality but instead a fundamental alteration of it in the intellect. They play not only with signifiers but also with the relations of signifiers to signifieds, transforming black into white and night into day. They change the state of reality, denaturing it at its very conceptual level in the human mind. Their discursive composition involves a *de*composition of ideas, a rotting away of the intelligence we have of the essence of things, altering opinion, which is a most basic part of the self for Montaigne.

Indeed, in a vein similar to that of Sánchez, one sees here the faintest suggestion of the impossibility of language to express identity—though while this is clearly expressed in Sánchez's work, Montaigne will ultimately try to work around the problem.[22] For the moment the key point is that the altering of opinion by orators causes their profession to fall into the category of *le mal* both in a practical sense—a *mal* that is damaging or harmful to the truth of our conceptions of reality—and in an ethical sense—*le mal* as evil or a vice that morally corrupts the individual through the disintegration of the connections between idea and reality. The human mind is, in effect, short-changed by rhetoric, which provides the intellect with words that are either unconnected or else poorly connected to concepts. In the end rhetoric fills the mind with language while sapping the mind of substance. In this way it walks hand in hand with the critique uttered by Montaigne previously in the "Institution" of those whose heads were either empty or else filled with unclear ideas. If an individual is not stupid or muddled to begin with, rhetoric will drive him into that state.

These two problems addressed by Montaigne—that of inadequate ideas informing language and the intentional use of language as a weapon to enfeeble others' ideas—are at their core tied to the fundamental relationship between expression and thought, along with the connection of both to reality. Montaigne examines these relationships in his "Apologie de Raimond Sebond" (Apology of Raimond Sebond, book 2, chapter 12, 481–683). Montaigne was one of the key figures of the period who revived the classical tradition of philosophical skepticism and in particular Pyrrhonism. Popkin even claims that Montaigne is the single most significant thinker behind this revival, which would color the critical tradition of French philosophy into the seventeenth century, the Enlightenment, and beyond (44). The "Apologie" is the best-known presentation of Montaigne's philosophical skepticism, which in terms of this study is crucial for its epistemological impact.[23]

This essay takes as its starting point the translation Montaigne had written, earlier in his life, of Raimond Sebond's *Théologie naturelle ou le livre des créatures* (Natural Theology, or the Book of Creatures). In the "Apologie," Montaigne deals with, among other things, the issue of animal faculties for language and reason. The classical skeptic Sextus Empiricus had a substantial influence on Montaigne, and so it is no surprise that Montaigne, like Empiricus, insists that animals do indeed communicate with each other by sounds, by gesture, and by movement (Montaigne, 499–500; Sextus Empiricus, 21). Furthermore, Montaigne claims that animals think rationally, and as evidence he cites various animal actions and constructions—a spider's web, for example—that could not possibly, in his view, be accomplished without "deliberation, et pensement, et conclusion" (deliberation, thought, and conclusion, 500–506).

However, of particular interest is that the two elements of expression and intelligence, both of which are possessed by animals, are not really separate entities for Montaigne. Again following the lead of Sextus Empiricus, Montaigne describes, for example, how some cultures in certain parts of the world observe foxes in winter to determine if it is safe or not to traverse frozen rivers. The fox, according to

Montaigne, stops at the edge of the river and listens for the sound of moving water, near or far, to judge the thickness of the ice:

> n'aurions-nous pas raison de juger qu'il luy passe par la teste ce mesme discours qu'il feroit en la nostre, et que c'est une ratiocination et consequence tiré du sens naturel: Ce qui fait bruit, se remue; ce qui se remue n'est pas gelé; ce qui est liquide, plie soubs le faix? Car d'attribuer cela seulement à une vivacité du sens de l'ouye, sans discours et sans consequence, c'est une chimere, et ne peut entrer en nostre imagination. (507)[24]

> (would we not be right in judging that the same discourse passes through his mind as would pass through ours, and that it is a ratiocination and consequence drawn from natural sense: That which makes noise, moves; that which moves is not frozen; that which is liquid gives under pressure? For to attribute this only to a sensitive capacity for hearing, without discourse and without consequence, this is an illusion, and cannot be imagined.)

What the fox thinks is, according to Montaigne, a discourse comprised of "ratiocination" and "consequence"—not a simple action of the senses but reasoning in the same way that human beings reason. However, going beyond Sextus Empiricus, Montaigne uses this idea in turn to define both human and animal reason as an *internal discourse,* a form of speech within the mind. This conception of thought as internal discourse is directly tied to two other important questions that Montaigne tackles in the "Apologie."

The first of these questions is the fundamental Pyrrhonian one of unknowability: "Le plus sage homme qui fut onques, quand on luy demanda ce qu'il sçavoit, respondit qu'il sçavoit cela, qu'il ne sçavoit rien" (The wisest man who ever lived, when he was asked what he knew, replied that he knew this, that he knew nothing, 556–57). This reference to Socrates is shortly followed by a quotation from Cicero: "*Dicendum est, sed ita ut nihil affirmem, quoeram omnia, dubitans plerumque et mihi diffidens*" (I will speak, but affirming nothing, I will inquire into everything, doubting for the most part, and distrusting myself, 557).[25] Beginning with Socrates, Montaigne dissociates the capacity to correctly judge reality from the possession of a knowledge of things. He divorces judgment from both completeness of knowledge and the linguistic power to affirm truths about such knowledge. The only knowable truth is the truth of unknowability, which in turn is the only absolutely true judgment that any individual can make. Montaigne's citation of Cicero reinforces this view of the unknowability of the world. If Cicero speaks, it is with a conscious separation between thought and reality. Words may be used to express opinions, ideas, conceptions, but the absolute negation of the phrasing prohibits any absolute connection between idea and world.

The distinction of opinion or judgment from reality as well as the disjunction between language and reality are ideas typical of ancient and Renaissance skepticism.[26] For Montaigne, as for other skeptics, affirmation is a linguistic task by which we express the truth of our opinions and beliefs. However, all that we can affirm is that we hold certain beliefs about the world, in essence asserting only that we are expressing beliefs, as opposed to asserting anything about reality. We cannot guarantee that anything we think about the world actually is true. In terms of the truth of actual things, we can only search, examine, question, and judge our perceptions of things, and we cannot judge the things themselves. Above all, to avoid the pitfall of thinking that we know things in themselves and not merely our ideas of those things, it is as important to withhold trust from our own minds as it is to withhold trust from rhetoricians and orators. The self is the least trustworthy person of all. The untrustworthiness of the self is derived from the very nature of language—all thought and judgment consists of interior discourse. So any erroneous (pretentious) judgment we make about the truth of things is rooted in a rhetorical flaw of interior discourse, the language in which the self speaks to the self and which, like the rhetorician, voluntarily deceives when speaking.[27]

The untrustworthiness of both interior and exterior discourse constitutes the second important language-thought question examined by Montaigne in the "Apologie." The unreliability of these discourses is drawn from the inherent weaknesses and flaws of any given language:

> Nostre parler a ses foiblesses et ses defauts, comme tout le reste. La plus part des occasions des troubles du monde sont Grammairiennes. Nos procez ne naissent que du debat de l'interpretation des loix; et la plus part des guerres, de cette impuissance de n'avoir sçeu clairement exprimer les conventions et traictez d'accord des princes. Combien de querelles et combien importantes a produit au monde le doubte du sens de cette syllabe, HOC! Prenons la clause que la logique mesmes nous presentera pour la plus claire. Si vous dictes: Il faict beau temps, et que vous dissiez vérité, il fait donc beau temps. Voilà pas une forme de parler certaine? Encore nous trompera elle. Qu'il soit ainsi, suyvons l'exemple. Si vous dictes: Je ments, et que vous dissiez vray, vous mentez donc. L'art, la raison, la force de la conclusion de cette cy sont pareilles à l'autre; toutes fois nous voylà embourbez. Je voy les philosophes Pyrrhoniens qui ne peuvent exprimer leur generale conception en aucune maniere de parler: car il leur faudroit un nouveau langage. Le nostre est tout formé de propositions affirmatives, qui leur sont de tout ennemies: de façon que, quand ils disent: Je doubte, on les tient incontinent à la gorge pour leur faire avoüer qu'aumoins asseurent et sçavent ils cela, qu'ils doubtent....
>
> Cette fantaisie est plus seurement conceuë par interrogation: Que sçay-je? comme je la porte à la devise d'une balance. (589)

(Our expression has its weaknesses and flaws, like all the rest. The majority of the troubles of the world are Grammatical. Our court cases are born only from the debate over the interpretation of the laws; and the majority of wars, from our incapacity to clearly express conventions and peace treaties between princes. How many quarrels, and how great, has the world seen over the uncertainty of the meaning of this syllable, HOC! Take the clause that logic itself presents to us the most clearly. If you say: The weather is nice, and you speak the truth, then the weather is nice. Isn't this a very sure way of speaking? Still, we will be deceived. To show this, let us follow with an example. If you say: I am lying, and you are telling the truth, then you are lying. The art, the reason, the force of the conclusion of this example are the same as in the first; nevertheless we are stuck in a quagmire. I see Pyrrhonian philosophers who cannot express their general conception with any manner of speaking: for they would need a new language. Our own is formed entirely of affirmative propositions, which are their greatest enemy: such that, when they say: I doubt, one grabs them immediately by the throat to force them to admit that at least they assure and know that, that they doubt. . . .

This fantasy is more surely conceived by the interrogative: What do I know? as I have it on a medallion inscribed with a scale.)

Montaigne looks at the question of linguistic weaknesses from three specific angles in this excerpt—from the standpoint of historical evidence, from that of logical foundations of language, and from the perspective of epistemological and linguistic genius. Like certain other skeptics, Montaigne questions the very ability of language to express anything truly.[28]

The historical picture painted by Montaigne is one of tragic irony. Focusing on the concept of historical upheavals of various sorts, Montaigne associates them all with language. From the smallest, such as individual conflicts in the courts of law, through the largest, such as political and religious conflicts, Montaigne links unrest with the incapacity of language to fulfill its most basic function of expressing ideas. The term "trouble" is associated directly with *grammairien,* making explicit the link between language structure and disturbance. Further, the polysemia of the word "trouble" evokes not only the disruption of order, and the equilibrium of the social group, but also agitation and confusion of the mind and thought.

The irony of these two types of "trouble" associated with language lies in the fact that for Montaigne, language does precisely the opposite of what it is intended to do. The wording of laws is designed to clarify the rules of living in society. Yet the words end up being the source of debate. Treaties and accords designed to establish peace eventually serve as pretext for engaging in violent armed conflict between nations. Even the supposed divine word, rooted in principles of kindness and love, has provoked bloody fratricide.[29] Apart from the historical horror suggested by Montaigne's examples, we are confronted, from a semiotic point of view, with the necessity of taking it upon ourselves to make comprehensible the inherent density, complexity, and ambiguity of language. More than just a question of human ineffectiveness in employing language as a tool to think or communicate accurately, what Montaigne drives at here is an innate quality of language whose meaning exists in a constant state of incertitude. While some thinkers, such as du Bellay, denounce the idea of the innate qualities of particular languages, this does not prevent Montaigne from underlining the innate defect of all language in the broadest sense of language as the mechanism for human communication.

The inherent flaw in language is clearly suggested by Montaigne's examination of the logical underpinnings of signification. Logic, as the science of rational thought and the discursive formulation of truths, would seem to be a remedy for language's ills. However, Montaigne turns this science upside down by again using it to prove that it is, in fact, its own opposite. To do so he compares two statements. The first statement is simple, ordinary, easily verifiable: "the weather is nice." Having empirically verified this statement, one can apparently conclude that the statement is in complete conformity with the current state of reality and therefore is true.[30] However, in contrast to this, Montaigne presents the example of a slightly different sort of sentence: "I am lying." Again the sentence is simple, ordinary, and easily verifiable; we need not even engage in empirical observations of any sort to do so. The phrase is a speech act, which makes it self-verifying. However, this is the slight difference. The very form of the speech act, while self-verifying and, in fact, because it is self-verifying, is necessarily divorced from any reality it might represent. The speech act consists of language referring to language, rather than to something outside itself. To this extent it constitutes a "forme de parler certaine" just as the preceding sentence does. However, since structure both of speech and of the reality represented are the same, language has in this case allowed for a logical impossibility since the phrase is simultaneously true and false and therefore neither. Because the sentence is detached from any exterior substance, it need not conform to reality in order to be true. It can formally conform to itself and in that sense is true, while at the same time it is clearly false in that the constituent parts—individually referring to the realities of the act of lying and the truth of the statement—are incompatible. The technical correctness of the linguistic enunciation is at irreconcilable odds with both observation and reason.[31]

Lest the reader see this as an isolated anomaly, Montaigne tackles the problem from the third perspective of epistemological and linguistic genius. This final tactic allows him to expand the isolated anomaly presented in his second point as a larger disease infecting language and thought as a whole. To do this he offers the reader a similarly performative act, "I doubt," to sum up the entire epistemological position of the Pyrrhonists. Here again the sample sentence offered by Montaigne is a speech act. Once more we are confronted with a logical impossibility. The lexical contents and the grammatical structure of the sentence are at odds with each other. Lexically to doubt is to eschew the enunciation of an affirmation. Grammatically "I doubt" is an affirmation. However, unlike the statement "I am lying," the statement "I doubt" coming from a Pyrrhonist is a global expression of life, the universe, and everything—the summation of an epistemological framework. Nearly all of human language is composed of this type of affirmative structure: even negations are affirmations of opposites. Montaigne's preoccupation with the level of uncertainty and doubt in our perceptions of reality, the entire underlying spirit and structure of just about any language, its genius, therefore implies that any specific language is inherently and necessarily skewed toward falsehood, if only to the extent that it affirms in a universe where nothing can be affirmed.[32]

Even Montaigne's proposed dodge around the particular problem of the Pyrrhonists is not entirely satisfactory, in that it emphasizes only the far-reaching nature of the more general issue. The use of Montaigne's own motto "Que sçay-je?" as an interrogative may seem on the surface to express the uncertainty of our perception of the universe accurately in that it affirms nothing.[33] However, what language could ever possibly be composed only of interrogatives? Such a language, whatever the particular question asked may be, would express only one single idea. However specific the question, the signification would always be the broad concept of a general doubt. Only by limiting epistemology to the sole thought of doubt could language ever be accurate, though then, of course, there would be no point to language or thought at all. This is certainly why Montaigne qualifies the Pyrrhonist position as a fantasy: one cannot avoid affirmation despite the impossibility of knowing the world in any absolute and indisputable way. Paradoxically, even though we can never be certain of anything in reality, we *must* affirm. Only then can language have any degree of meaning. In a nutshell, Montaigne suggests that we have two options: doubtful meaning or nonexistent meaning. The trick is not to refrain either from opinion or from affirmation but rather to maintain awareness that both our perceptions and our affirmations are fuzzy and that they do not necessarily conform to the nature of things.

These considerations on the nature of thought and language come into play if we return to the principle of Montaigne, the author, as the subject of his own book. Montaigne highlights various inconstant aspects of himself and then stresses the resultant fluidity of the interior discourse he seeks to set down on the page:

> En mes escris mesmes je ne retrouve pas tousjours l'air de ma premiere imagination: je ne sçay ce que j'ay voulu dire, et m'eschaude souvent à corriger et

y mettre un nouveau sens, pour avoir perdu le premier, qui valloit mieux. Je ne fay qu'aller et venir: mon jugement ne tire pas tousjours en avant; il flotte, il vague. . . . Maintes-fois (comme il m'advient de faire volontiers) ayant pris pour exercice et pour esbat à maintenir une contraire opinion à la mienne, mon esprit, s'applicant et tournant de ce costé la, m'y attache si bien que je ne trouve plus la raison de mon premier advis, et m'en despars. (636–37)

(In my own writings I do not always recover the thread of my first imaginings: I do not know what I wanted to write, and I often boil to correct and to invent a new meaning, having lost the first one, which was better. All I do is come and go: my judgment does not always move forward; it floats, it wanders. . . . Many times [as I often enjoy doing] having taken as an exercise or as a game to argue for an opinion contrary to my own, my mind, applying itself and turning to that side, attaches me so well to it that I no longer find the reasoning of my initial opinion and I break from it.)

Montaigne's description is built upon three semantic layers: one relating to expression; one attached to mind; and one connected to inconsistency.[34] The three semantic networks overlap one another to such an extent that they form one coherent triple-faceted complex. Beginning with his literary text, Montaigne remarks on the fluctuations of representations and images, the opposition of losing and finding ideas, the notion of erroneous meanings, inferior and superior expressions, and the problem of a temporal transposition between old ideas and new of a text that refuses to progress unilinearly, instead moving away from its original meaning and then back again. His is a text that moves obliquely, tangentially, and indeterminately, a text that is imprecise, disoriented, disorganized, even contradictory.

The author's mind works in the same manner, modified by the same qualifying network of inconsistency.[35] Montaigne's intellectual activity is one of play and voluntary folly, hopping contrarily from one view to another, unfixed, nonlinear, a mind applying itself with equal devotion to a plurality of concepts, turning from one thing to the next, pursuing each in turn and all at once, and then renouncing one, some, or all ideas for yet some different thought. In this way, paradoxically, his language does express the reality of his mind, in that the fluctuation of the one reproduces the fluidity of the other. Thus he can argue that his expression of himself is true, a baroque mind expressed in baroque language.[36] Montaigne does not, furthermore, see himself as exceptional in this respect but rather as a universal model for the human mind and human expression: "Chacun à peu pres en diroit autant de soy, s'il se regardoit comme moy" (Anyone would say more or less the same about himself, if he looked at himself as I do, 637). The basis for these ideas again lies, on the one hand, in purely linguistic inquiries concerned with the transformation of language over time.[37] On the other hand, it also lies in the coupling of this linguistic notion, in the mainstream skeptical thought of Montaigne's day, with the temporal fluctuations of both reality and mind that lead to unknowing.[38] What Montaigne adds to the mix is a sense of identity that attempts to situate itself, through the art of the writer, in the midst of the fluidic chaos that is time and space.

This notion of a baroque mind represented through baroque modes of expression begins to suggest how Montaigne envisions a language that accurately expresses the self in spite of the imperfections of both our knowledge and our language: "cette belle raison humaine s'ingerant par tout de maistriser et commander; brouillant et confondant le visage des choses selon sa vanité et inconstance. *Nihil itaque amplius nostrum est: quod nostrum dico, artis est*" (this beautiful human reason, taking the liberty everywhere of mastering and commanding; clouding and confusing the face of things by its vanity and inconstancy. *Nothing remains that is our own: that which I call our own is the effect of art*, 654).[39] Montaigne again emphasizes the corruption and confusion of the mind's perception of reality and of the irregularity and vanity (in terms of an inherent futility and a voluntary disproportion) in our expression of it. However, it is the clarifying and buttressing citation from Cicero added by Montaigne to the end of the thought that pique's the reader's interest. Here we see an absolute negation of any possibility of a reflection of the self or of identity through ideas or through language as such. Whatever glimpse we can have of the true self comes in the effects of the writer's art, in the means and processes by which the author attaches fluctuating signifier to fluctuating signified. Our knowledge of the author comes from the author's *articulation,* from his articulation not just as expression but as the manner in which the author hinges language and reality together. Truth lies not in what the author says but in how he says it.[40]

Montaigne's essay "De l'art de conférer" (On the Art of Conferring, book 3, chapter 8, 1031–1057) drives home this point. There Montaigne writes that "tous les jours m'amuse à lire en des autheurs, sans soin de leur science, y cherchant leur façon, non leur subject. Tout ainsi je poursuy la communication de quelque esprit fameux, non pour qu'il m'enseigne, mais pour que je le cognoisse" (every day I enjoy reading authors, without a care for their science, seeking their manner, not their subject. Thus I pursue communication with some famous mind, not for him to teach me, but so that I can know him, 1039). Montaigne erects an opposition between the "science" or "subject" of an author and his *façon*. He is not especially interested in the substance or content of the author's writing, which is for him at best doubtful, as are reality and all representations of reality. On the contrary, instead of striving to assimilate the content of the written text, Montaigne aims to soak in the manner in which the text is constructed, the form the author has given it, the articulation of the author, or the genius of the author, to return to du Bellay's term. If, as Zalloua has indicated, "Montaignian subjectivity . . . emerges or begins to take shape in a dynamic space situated *in between* referentiality and textuality" (53), I would claim that we can select articulation as the name of that dynamic space.

Furthermore, this first opposition of "science" and "subject" stands in parallel with a second suggested by this same passage from the "Art de Conférer," which is the contrasting of the two conceptions of knowledge in French, of *savoir* versus *connaître*. It is not the author's knowledge that Montaigne seeks but rather knowledge of the author.[41] This latter form of knowledge flows to the reader through the double meaning of the verb "communicate." To communicate denotes, obviously, the transmission of information by means of language, but it also suggests a different but analogous concept of connection: the way two communicating vessels are connected. Reader and author are the vessels, while the text is the pipe that joins them. In this way Montaigne's phrasing "lire en des autheurs" takes on a special signification. He is not merely using the term *autheur* rhetorically as a reference to the book, but rather his intent is actually to read into the man, using the text as a means to transfer not the author's knowledge but the author's self to his own mind. The writer's manner is the true representation of his self; his articulation of expression to reality tells us truthfully who he is and allows us to appreciate the nature and personality of the author as person, and it allows us to absorb some measure of the author's identity into our own.

This view that the style makes the man is the rationale behind Montaigne's conclusion that the subject of a book, "selon qu'il est, peut faire trouver un homme sçavant et memorieux, mais pour juger en luy les parties plus siennes et plus dignes, la force et la beauté de son ame, il faut sçavoir ce qui est sien et ce qui ne l'est point, et en ce qui n'est pas sien combien on luy doibt en consideration du chois, disposition, ornement et langage qu'il a fourny" (depending on its nature, can make a man appear learned and knowledgeable, but to judge in him what is most his own and most dignified, the force and beauty of his soul, one needs to know what is his own and what is not, and in that which is not his own, how much is owed to him for the choice, disposition, ornament and language which he furnished, 1053). The content treated by the author tells us little about a man beyond how many facts he has stored in his mind, how full his head is, and this material is not "his." To get to a true judgment or appreciation of the man, we need to dig to what is "his," much as du Bellay had suggested in his treatment of imitation. This true essence of the man, as Montaigne has shown through his citation of Cicero, is his manner or style, which here is qualified as the most worthy and elemental constitutive part of the author's work, as well as being the part of the work that is most in conformity with the author's true being. The style of writing gives us a sense of the moral and intellectual power of the man, what drives and animates him, the intensity and grandeur of his being, and the transcendental beauty of his essence. These are what make him, far beneath the surface, what he truly is, the very foundation of his individual identity. Writing style and aesthetic adornments along with choice of subject matter, choice of citations (of particular importance in the case of Montaigne), and methods of order and organization—these are the facets of an author's work that lead us to know him, that allow his identity to come through his work, despite the apparent unknowability of the reality around us and the inherent shortcomings of language as a medium for expressing reality. Regardless of these difficulties, we can always know, in the truest way, those facets of an author's being expressed by these particular aspects of his writing.

In this context the fact that Montaigne writes in French rather than Latin takes on additional significance. In "De la Vanité" (book 3, chapter 9, 1057–1123), Montaigne tells us that he does not intend for his work to endure. Had he wished it to do so, he would have selected Latin: "Si ç'eust esté une matiere de durée, il l'eust fallu commettre à un langage plus ferme" (If it had been an enduring subject, it would have been necessary to commit it to a firmer language, 1100). Unlike the more stable Latin, French is a language in flux. Furthermore, "selon la variation continuelle qui a suivy [notre langage] jusques à cette heure, qui peut esperer que sa forme presente soit en usage d'icy à cinquante ans? Il escoule tous les jours de nos mains et depuis que je vis, s'est alteré de moitié" (given the continual variation that [our language] has undergone up until this time, who can hope that its present form will still be in use fifty years from now? It slips every day between our fingers, and in my lifetime, it has half changed, 1100–1101). Linking the variations in the French language to the course of his lifetime, Montaigne highlights the language's variability, establishing a parallel with the variability of his own being. If Montaigne chooses French over Latin, it is because the former better conforms to the baroque changeability of self that Montaigne seeks to paint in his *Essais*.

What Montaigne ultimately contributes to the evolution of thinking on language, mind, and identity is a play on the concepts of fluidity and solidity. The text, in light of Montaigne's ideas, defines a specific community through inclusive/exclusive boundaries of identity centered on the author—not just self-identity but an identity of readership. The text itself is a fluid principle, oscillating between fixity and motion. For example, the text has a consolidating effect on culture across boundaries of time, thereby stabilizing identity while moving temporally. The written word is a tool for knowing the author, despite the fact that the authorial self changes through time as well. Additionally the text becomes a conduit for community flux—the community changes through time as future members enter its inner circle.

As the foundation of any written text, language has a dual role, vacillating between creation and re-creation of elements of identity; man makes discourse, which in turn makes the man, and the individual with other individuals make up the group. This is part of the underlying reality of our understanding, both of discourse and of things. Expression and perception of reality are both inherently ambiguous, making knowing of any sort, through experience or discussion, doubtful at best. Thought and expression exist together as an internal discourse that is equally doubtful.

Like the general notion of text, however, discourse, whether internal or external, also oscillates between stability and motion, for despite the inherent instability of its constituent elements, perception and enunciation, the manner of expression can nevertheless be true and immutable. Even if we can never be sure of language and things, the author's articulation of expression and thought, how he puts word and idea together, is knowable in an absolute sense and is a true reflection of his being. The text, then, paradoxically acts as a connector between author and reader through which the author's self is in some degree infused into the reader's self across space and time, modifying the reader's identity and impacting the collective identity of a literary community. In this way the community of letters identifies with the author, establishing a broader identity—identity not as that which makes one different but as that which creates a sameness within the group, a cultural identity. This cultural identity then will fluctuate over time as new members of a reading community read the author—read the man—differently. Where du Bellay sees the author as primarily responsible for making a communal identity through the endless polishing of the language of his text, Montaigne presents the notion of a communal identity as evolving from the author's endless polishing of his self through the composition of his text.

Three

Descartes' *Discours*
The Mind/Identity Complex and Human Language

René Descartes (1596–1650) is often called the father of modern philosophy. The prime reason for this is that Descartes' philosophy breaks away from the traditional school of Scholasticism. This was the dominant strain of philosophy in the education that Descartes received at Jesuit Collège de La Flèche in Anjou. Scholasticism at the time was essentially a fusion of philosophy and theology. It centered on the application of human reason to justify the mystical content of religious doctrine, by reconciling that content with classical philosophy and science. Rather than seeking new knowledge, the Scholastics attempted to integrate classical knowledge with Christian dogma, operating on the assumption that both systems contained absolute truth.

After finishing his education Descartes served in various armies during the period of the Thirty Years' War.[1] His interest in mathematics and philosophy led him to pursue further intellectual inquiries in both those domains. He would ultimately apply the inductive method of mathematics to philosophy in his *Essais philosophiques* (1637), of which the *Discours de la méthode* was a significant part.[2] In the *Discours,* and later in his *Méditations métaphysiques* (1641), Descartes' Scholastic education would show through in that he too would attempt to use reason to prove the truth of metaphysical and theological questions such as the existence of God, though he would, of course, do so with a twist.[3] Rather than relying on the authority of the church or the ancients and rather than using so-called natural reason alone, he would employ a more methodical, mathematics-inspired approach; hence the title of the *Discours de la méthode.*

A second reason why Descartes can be considered a writer of modern philosophy is that he was one of the first philosophers, along with a small minority of others such as Pierre de la Ramée and Scipion Dupleix, to write a major philosophical work in French rather than in Latin. It is worthwhile to make the distinction here between this small group and the bulk of other writers of nonfiction in French prior to them, such as the two authors considered in previous chapters. For example, we see in du Bellay not a philosopher but a poet, whose *Deffence et illustration* is primarily an "art poétique," while Montaigne's *Essais* are actually personal essays or pieces of creative nonfiction. The difference between writers such as these two and the smaller, truly philosophical minority is that while the poet and the essayist have philosophical elements in their writing, they are not creating coherent all-encompassing philosophical systems. In this way they are not philosophers as such but rather creative writers of nonfiction. Du Bellay as a poet writes in French in a genre that already had a long-standing vernacular tradition, and Montaigne effectively creates a brand new genre.

The case of the philosophical minority of which Descartes is a part is different in that members of that minority write in French in a genre whose long-standing tradition is in Latin. There was, of course, as Derrida points out in "S'il y a lieu de traduire," an official invitation made by French monarchs of the sixteenth century to French thinkers pushing them to write philosophy in French (295). However, comparatively few writers answered this call, and even into the seventeenth century, while French literature had long left behind the use of Latin as a medium of creative expression, the classical language from Rome had maintained a hold on academia. Latin, in 1637, was still the prevailing language of the universities and the church, and it was still the nearly exclusive language of science, theology, and philosophy.[4] So while it may be possible to inscribe Descartes' language choice into the context of a political project of the French monarchy, as Derrida argues (306), it is nevertheless just as important to highlight the philosophical revolution that this choice represents.[5]

By opting to write his *Discours de la méthode* in French, Descartes linguistically demonstrates his break, as Ramée had similarly done, with a philosophical tradition governed by Latin texts.[6] Rather than utilize the established language of the existing academy, he employs a modern language, to express a modern philosophical approach. He supplants both church and classical authority by replacing the primary vehicle of their expression. He thus engages in an intellectual rebellion whose first representational act is to affirm a linguistic identity other than that of the existing intellectual power of the churches and the universities.[7]

In addition the widespread success and intellectual impact of Descartes' French philosophical text gives increased status to the French language—a point that distinguishes him even from predecessors such as Ramée and Dupleix. Just as du Bellay and company sought to wrench the place of privilege and glory away from the classical languages in poetry, Descartes' *Discours* ends up doing the same for philosophy. While the poets of the Renaissance give glory to the French language in the aesthetic domain, the *Discours* gives glory to the language in the intellectual and academic milieu. French is shown by Descartes' text to equal the languages of the ancients in any endeavor, not just in the artistic ones.

Apart from these points relating to Descartes' position as the father of modern philosophy and choice of language, there is yet another reason why his *Discours de la méthode* occupies an important place in this present study: Descartes' treatment of metaphysics, ontology, and epistemology centers on the very questions of language, mind, and identity that have been introduced in the two preceding chapters.[8] Descartes' approach to these questions is, as the title of the *Discours* suggests, more methodical than that of du Bellay or Montaigne, and it is also more abstract, more general, and more global. As such, it will be the starting point for future writers such as Condillac, whose primary objective will be a refutation of Descartes' broad, sweeping metaphysical ideas.

The full title of the *Discours* is the *Discours de la méthode pour bien conduire sa raison et chercher la vérité dans les sciences* (Discourse on Method for Conducting One's Reason and Seeking Truth in the Sciences). It is a didactic text, aimed at establishing a path for the mind to follow.[9] This path is defined by a network of terms relating to mind, truth, and knowledge;[10] it consists of a collection of steps that will provide order to thinking and inquiry. The concept of a path suggests movement, from point A to point B, from ignorance to knowledge, from question and doubt to certainty and truth. There is an assumption from the start that we can know the truth of things—unlike the "que sçay-je" of Montaigne. Certainly Descartes acknowledges a certain degree of motion, flux, and fluidity in the nature of thought. The verbs in the title, *conduire* and *chercher*, reinforce this sense of movement, of going somewhere, but they also bring a sense of direction, of bringing or accompanying our sequences of thoughts on a goal-driven journey.[11] They indicate a quest of discovery, an exploration of the unknown, the hunt for something hidden or elusive, a truth that will ultimately be found at the end of the path. Reason is the vehicle that carries us along the path, but method is the guide, the navigator, the conscious will that selects which of the universe's infinite number of paths we should follow. In this sense reason and method exist, even in the title of the text, in a strange, paradoxical relationship, simultaneously connected to one another while at the same time distinct and separate entities.

Descartes' exploration of the relationship between reason and method is one of the first points to capture the reader's attention in the *Discours*. Like Montaigne, Descartes recognizes that all men believe they have the fullest measure of reason that any man can have: "Le bon sens est la chose du monde la mieux partagée: car chacun pense en être si bien pourvu, que ceux même qui sont les plus difficiles à contenter en toute autre chose n'ont point coutume d'en désirer plus qu'ils en ont" (Common sense is the most shared thing in the world: for everyone thinks he is so well provided with it, that even those who are the most difficult to content in all other areas are not in the habit of desiring more of it than they already have, 29). A similar idea is found in Montaigne's essay "De la praesumption" (On Presumption, book 2, chapter 17, 712–48):

> Nous reconnaissons ayséement és autres l'avantage du courage, de la force corporelle, de l'experience, de la disposition, de la beauté; mais l'avantage du

jugement, nous ne le cedons à personne: et les raisons qui partent du simple discours naturel en autruy, il nous semble qu'il n'a tenu qu'à regarder de ce costé là, que nous les ayons trouvées. (741–42)

(We easily recognize others' advantages in courage, physical strength, experience, disposition, and beauty; but the advantage of judgment we concede to no one: and as for the logic that derives from the simple natural discourse of others, it seems to us that we would only have had to look at things from the same angle and we would have found it ourselves.)

As for the "simple discours naturel," I have indicated that Montaigne sees reason as an interior discourse, and Thibaudet interprets the phrase here as referring to "le bon sens" (in Montaigne, 742n1). The one difference between Montaigne and Descartes in this reference to common sense is that Montaigne is skeptical as to whether all men actually do have the same "bon sens"—in fact the title of his essay makes this clear—while Descartes affirms that such a common belief indicates that all men do, in fact, share common sense. However, Descartes also makes it clear that "le bon sens" is simply not enough to make progress on the path to truth:

la puissance de bien juger, et distinguer le vrai d'avec le faux, qui est proprement ce qu'on nomme le bon sens ou la raison, est naturellement égale en tous les hommes; . . . la diversité de nos opinions ne vient pas de ce que les uns sont plus raisonnables que les autres, mais seulement de ce que nous conduisons nos pensées par diverses voies et ne considérons pas les mêmes choses. Car ce n'est pas assez d'avoir l'esprit bon, mais le principal est de l'appliquer bien. (29)

(the power of judging well, and distinguishing the true from the false, which is correctly named common sense or reason, is naturally equal in all men; . . . the diversity of our opinions comes not from some being more reasonable than others, but only from the fact that we conduct our thoughts by different routes and do not consider the same things. For it is not enough to have a good mind, the main thing is to apply it well.)

In this passage Descartes conflates the terms of common sense, reason, and judgment. Each of these is considered to be nothing more than a different name for one and the same faculty, giving a sense of unity to the mind.[12] It is this unified faculty that allows man to recognize, affirm, or deny the existence of things and relationships in reality; to have opinions and draw conclusions on those things and relationships; and to distinguish between propositions and expressions that conform or do not conform to the nature of reality. By the act of distinguishing, we erect a hierarchy of relative intellectual values, with truth at the top, falsehood at the bottom, and varying degrees of probable doubt and certainty in between. These conflated terms constitute more, however, than a simple unified intellectual capacity. They are the glue that binds the human race together in a single unified identity based on intellectual substance—man the thinking animal.[13] Thinking is a common ability of all individuals provided by nature, rather than artifice, inborn rather than acquired, that in its very essence presents no quantitative or qualitative difference from one person to the next.

Yet the very conflation of these terms and the commonality and unity they denote also paves the way for divergence and fragmentation. Alongside the notion of unity, Descartes highlights the opposition of the common and the distinct among individual intellects. The act of distinguishing, rooted in the principle of commonality, is a process that in itself sets apart individuals from among the group. Some are better than others at distinguishing the true from the false, thereby establishing a parallel hierarchy in which those who better succeed in the task of epistemological distinction occupy a privileged place at the top of an intellectual scale, while those less skilled occupy a place at the bottom. If truth is of the highest value, so too is the ability to root it out. Descartes here explicitly identifies the path, suggested etymologically in the title of his work, as the source of the divergence of quality in human conclusions and judgments. The means of approaching problems of the mind are what separate one thinker from another. If human logic, our conceptual activity leading to discursive knowledge, is universal among men, what is not universal is the *manner* of thinking, the particular form that our intellectual process takes, or the technique and procedure of our reasoning. The issue of *manner*, which Montaigne identifies stylistically as what provides the individual and unique among men, the source of their identity, is taken up by Descartes on an intellectual rather than aesthetic level for the same purpose, as the factor that distinguishes one individual from another in the realm of reason.

This emphasis on manner ties the concept of intellectual distinction, and individual intellectual identity, to a variety of new oppositions—that of substance versus application, of content versus form—and above all returns to that of the natural versus the artificial. Taken together, in terms of the operation of the human mind, application, form, and the artificial are privileged by Descartes over substance, content, and the natural. Substance, content, and nature are burdened lexically by Descartes with an associated insufficiency ("ce n'est pas assez"), while the issues of application, form, and artificiality are granted the qualification of being essential, and again of being situated higher in an ascending scale of values.

The esteem that Descartes shows for the artificial over the natural represents something of a change from the late sixteenth-century line of thought of Montaigne, who insists on natural reason and simple common sense. Some in the seventeenth century, such as the writers of the *Logique* (1662) of Port-Royal, would argue straightforwardly that common sense is not at all so common as its name implies. Descartes straddles these opposing positions, admitting that everyone has natural reason while maintaining that it simply is not as good as artificial, methodical reason.

The privileged elements of application, form, and artfulness as situated in the framework of the path of method are the core of what Descartes intends to expose in his *Discours:* "je serai bien aise de faire voir, en ce discours, quels sont les chemins que j'ai suivis, et d'y représenter ma vie comme en un tableau, afin que chacun en puisse juger, et qu'apprenant du bruit commun les opinions qu'on en aura, ce soit un nouveau moyen de m'instruire, que j'ajouterai à ceux dont j'ai coutume de me servir" (I will be pleased to show, in this discourse, which are the routes I have followed, and to represent my life as in a painting, in order that all may judge it, and learning from the general rumors of the opinions held of it, this will be a new means for me to instruct myself, that I will add to those that I am in the habit of using, 31). Descartes insists on the image of the "path" with the term *chemins*, underscoring the elements of movement, objectives, linearity, and sequentiality, the means or manner of attaining a goal. What is new here, though, is that the image of the path is equated with the author's life, his identity as an individual. Descartes presents his work, much like Montaigne does, as a reproduction of the facts and events that constitute what he is, as a reconstruction of the traits that define his existence. He claims to offer the reader a detailed evocation of his total self, equated to thought and thought process.

At the same time his discourse is, by its very nature, an instructional text. It has the obvious intent of exposing a particular manner of exploring the world to the readership. Yet this passage also indicates that the instructive nature of the discourse is envisioned as a two-way street. Descartes identifies the readership as a collective community with a voice of its own, a community capable of opinions and judgments, of drawing conclusions that will be communicated back to the author. These conclusions in turn are a manner of forming the mind and the personality of the author, of acquiring new knowledge, of augmenting his understanding, of modifying his methodical thought.

If the method of learning or the manner of acquiring truth and knowledge constitutes individual identity as Descartes suggests, then there is a continuous flow of identity from individual to community and back. The identity of the author flows into that of the readership, as that of the readership flows back into that of the author. Again there is a parallel with the flow of identity seen in Montaigne's work, though once more Descartes stresses the manner of intellectual processes rather than the manner of expression, privileging reason over expressive articulation, mind over language.

The superiority of reason to expression is indicated explicitly as Descartes continues to sketch out the history of his own education:

> J'estimais fort l'éloquence, et j'étais amoureux de la poésie; mais je pensais que l'une et l'autre étaient des dons de l'esprit plutôt que des fruits de l'étude. Ceux qui ont le raisonnement le plus fort, et qui dirigent le mieux leurs pensées, afin de les rendre claires et intelligibles, peuvent toujours le mieux persuader ce qu'ils proposent, encore qu'ils ne parlassent que bas breton, et qu'ils n'eussent jamais appris de rhétorique. (34)

> (I appreciated eloquence, and I was in love with poetry; but I thought that they both were gifts of wit rather than the fruits of study. Those who have the strongest lines of reasoning, and who best direct their thoughts, in order to render them clear and intelligible, can always better persuade others of what they propose, though they speak only low Breton, and though they had never learned any rhetoric.)

Descartes takes the distinction between reason and expression to an even more fundamental level, that of thought and emotion. He qualifies the arts of language, poetry, and eloquence with complements rooted in sentiment—he *feels an appreciation* for eloquence and *feels love* for poetry. In contrast to these forms of affinity (emphasized with a striking "mais"), he then expresses a second opinion when he tells us what he *thinks* about them.

What Descartes thinks about them is founded in another opposition of mind versus study. The acts of entertaining or persuading through a discursive harmony that appeals to the heart and the senses are set on a lower level of human faculties just like the natural mind. They are gifts from God or nature, and as such they are inborn, like "le bon sens" or undirected reason that has never found the path of method. Of greater significance for Descartes are the products of study, of the methodical application of the mind seeking to understand and learn, rather than simply to reproduce. This view of the discursive arts modifies the fundamental contrast between thought and emotion in that thought, in its natural form, falls close to the emotions and sensation. Natural reason is only slightly superior to feeling. However, methodically applied reason is superior to all natural productions of the mind, be they emotive, perceptive, or rational.

The superiority of *étude,* or the methodical application of mind, is brought into relief as Descartes posits that ordered reason outstrips even rhetoric at its own game, the task of persuasion. The direct line of logic is capable of better developing and exposing the relationships between objects, things, and ideas. Logic becomes, for Descartes, a manner of expression in its own right. If the structure of discourse respects fully the structure of methodical thought, then that discourse will render its objects less ambiguous and confused and more easily seized and comprehended by the mind of the listener. By doing so this discourse of the mind acquires a greater efficacy and potency in transforming the opinions of others than a more traditional rhetoric ever possessed.

Descartes essentially outlines a rhetoric of methodical reason as an alternative to a rhetoric of feeling. The distinction between mind and emotion in the art of persuasion was commonplace in Descartes' time and was espoused by numerous thinkers, though their opinions on the elements opposed in this distinction varied. For example, at one extreme the Port-Royal *Logique* held the very concept of rhetoric—much as Montaigne had done—in extremely low esteem, arguing that it was nothing more than a source of falsehood and the greatest of all vices (29).[14] At the other extreme was a larger body of texts—including Pascal's *Esprit géométrique* (1658), Lamy's *Art of Speaking* (1675), and Hobbes's *Briefe of the Art of Rhetorique* (1637)—which acknowledged that an appropriate appeal to the emotions could help convince an audience provided that equal attention were given to presenting the truth in a rational manner.[15] In effect these thinkers argued for a rhetoric that consisted of a balanced fusion of logical and emotional elements.[16]

Descartes' stance is somewhat different in that while he does not denigrate the rhetoric of emotion absolutely, he also does not propose a synthesis. For him, one can persuade through logical argumentation or through emotional appeal. Descartes argues optimistically that the former will always trump the latter. In manner of discourse the technique that always carries the greater legitimacy is the discourse founded on the method of thought. Manner as thought process must become manner of expression; logical method must be the source of discourse.[17] When this occurs, manner of expression simply takes care of itself, and choice of language elements becomes a secondary concern.

It may even be that certain languages have inherent flaws that in some ways leave them inferior to others; Descartes' own reference to "bas breton" with the denigrating "ne . . . que" marking its linguistic inferiority underscores this point. Nevertheless whatever linguistic deficiency a tongue may have, that tongue will not be persuasively inferior provided that the manner of expression parallels that of methodical reason. Indeed in this way even the "inferior" languages can achieve superiority over the most highly esteemed languages, and an author such as Descartes can raise a "lesser" language such as French to prominence in philosophy and metaphysics over languages traditionally considered "better suited" to such pursuits, such as Latin.[18]

Aiming then to get at the core of a methodical application of mind, both for its own sake in seeking out truth and for communicating that truth to others, Descartes indicates that at the end of a long education and many travels, he one day took "la résolution d'étudier aussi en moi-même, et d'employer toutes les forces de mon esprit à choisir les chemins que je devais suivre" (the resolution to study also within myself, and to employ all the strength of my mind toward choosing the paths I should follow, 37). The fundamental dissatisfaction expressed toward his previous education serves as the spark to begin a new education, a new "formation" of the self in both senses of the term in French—to instruct himself but also to form again or remake himself, linking the notion of thought process once more to the individual's identity. The first stage of this new formation is centered on two basic concepts: will and reflection.[19]

In a sense Descartes is working in parallel with Pascalian ideas on this point, for Pascal claims in his *Esprit géométrique* that the two main manners in which opinions enter the soul are through "entendement" and "volonté" (592). For Descartes, though, reflection and will are more than simple conduits for the entry of knowledge or ideas into the intellect; they are part of the formation of the self. In the case of will, it is a question of selecting which of many intellectual paths the thinking subject will take, and more importantly, as suggested by the term *résolution,* it is a question of making this choice upon reflection. The concept of reflection is evoked in more than one sense in this passage as well. There is first the idea of applying the mind to the acquisition of knowledge, revisiting yet again the symbolic image of the path and the idea of conforming the activity of the mind to the directing line of the path. At the same time we see reflection in the grammatical sense. For example, the thinking subject chooses the path the thinking subject will follow—in other words, the thinking self is both leader and follower. Additionally, as was the case with Montaigne, the thinking entity is both the subject and the object of study: Descartes' "je" studies his "moi-même." So necessarily inherent to the formation (again in both senses of the term) of the self, with its implied identity, is the conflation of the two concepts of reflection and will.[20]

The importance of the association of the will to the thinking self is one of the primary characteristics underlined by Descartes in the second part of the *Discours,* as he metaphorically details the two basic types of educations from which a person has to choose:

> je m'avisai de considérer que souvent il n'y a pas tant de perfection dans les ouvrages composés de plusieurs pièces, et faits de la main de divers maîtres, qu'en ceux auxquels un seul a travaillé. Ainsi voit-on que les bâtiments qu'un seul architecte a entrepris et achevés, ont coutume d'être plus beaux et mieux ordonnés que ceux que plusieurs ont tâché de raccommoder, en faisant servir de vieilles murailles qui avaient été bâties à d'autres fins. Ainsi ces anciennes cités, qui, n'ayant été au commencement que des bourgades, sont devenues, par succession de temps, de grandes villes, sont ordinairement si mal compassées, au prix de ces places régulières qu'un ingénieur trace à sa fantaisie dans une plaine, qu'encore que, considérant leurs édifices chacun à part, on y trouve

souvent autant ou plus d'art qu'en ceux des autres; toutefois, à voir comme ils sont arrangés, ici un grand, là un petit, et comme ils rendent les rues courbées et inégales, on dirait que c'est plutôt la fortune, que la volonté de quelques hommes usant de raison, qui les a ainsi disposés. Et si on considère qu'il y a eu néanmoins de tout temps quelques officiers, qui ont eu charge de prendre garde aux bâtiments des particuliers, pour les faire servir à l'ornement du public, on connaîtra bien qu'il est malaisé, en ne travaillant que sur les ouvrages d'autrui, de faire des choses fort accomplies. (39–40)

(I thought it wise to consider that often there is not as much perfection in works composed of many pieces, and built by the hands of several craftsmen, as there is in those upon which only one man had worked. Thus we see that those buildings undertaken and completed by a single architect are typically more beautiful and better ordered than those that several have attempted to rebuild, using remnants of old walls made for other ends. Thus these ancient towns, which began as only small villages and became through the course of time great cities, are ordinarily so poorly laid out, compared to those regular spaces traced at an engineer's will upon an open plain, that although in considering their edifices one by one, we may often find as much or more art in these as in the others; nevertheless, to see how they are arranged, here a large one, there a small one, and how they render the streets curved and unequal, one would say that it was fortune, rather than the will of men employing reason, that disposed them thus. And if one considers that there have been, throughout history, officers charged with the renovation of private buildings to have them serve for public decoration, one will easily recognize that it is quite difficult, adapting only the works of others, to execute anything very skillfully.)

Descartes' double metaphor represents education as architecture and consists of two semantic networks, one relating to a city constructed by multiple architects (an education provided by multiple and diverse instructors) and the other to a city constructed by a single architect (an education provided by a single instructor, or more specifically, self-education). The city constructed by multiple architects can be qualified as baroque, while its counterpart can be identified as classical in nature.[21] Education by a single instructor produces a mind and a self with these same qualities. Descartes' preference for a classical mind and self over the baroque mind and self is obvious. The classical mind's perfection consists of its organization and methodical thought, of its simplicity and unity. The ideal thinking self for Descartes stands in opposition to the intellect described by Montaigne, with its baroque meanderings and metamorphoses. The Cartesian mind does not waver.

It moves, but only in a forward direction and in a straight line from ignorance to knowledge, progressing rather than wandering, advancing rather than shifting and sliding.

Furthermore its *ouvrages*—taken either simply as thoughts and thought processes or in a more literal and literary sense—must also consist of the same qualities. Clarity, logic, order, and unity are the characteristics essential not only to successful thought but also to the successful accomplishment of the writer's work. Like du Bellay, using the image of architectural ruins employed as the foundation for creation, Descartes posits metaphorically that we cannot successfully build anything—a mind, a self, a text, or any other form of work—using the remnants of others' productions. The being, the thinker, the writer must carve out his own path to create anything of worth.

Herein, of course, lies a problematic question. Descartes proposes independence of thought and emphasizes his own self-education. However, he does so in a didactic work, intended specifically to instruct others.[22] Indeed the metaphor he has selected—that of the construction of a city and the numerous population implicit in that image—is suggestive of community. So how can one reconcile the notion of autodidactism and individuality of the thinking self with the aspect of community inherent in Descartes' image of the individual? How does Descartes reconcile himself as a de facto architect of the community of individual methodical reason? The most likely resolution to this question resides in the relationship of Descartes to the prevailing Scholastic system of education. The Scholastics offered, in essence, a corpus of knowledge and a logical means for justifying that knowledge, which was assumed to be true on the basis of authority and tradition. In contrast to this, Descartes offers, in his *Discours,* not a corpus of knowledge, not a building or city to replace that of the Scholastics, but rather a technique for building one's own edifice or town. He is offering a how-to guide to building rather than a prefabricated house. In a way he is less an engineer than a vocational trainer. In addition, rather than offering a technique justifying what is assumed to be true, as was the case with the Scholastics, he is proposing vocational training in finding truth and in distinguishing truth from falsehood in the first place, with nothing assumed to be true from the outset beyond the idea that truth exists. He offers process rather than substance.

The privileging of process over substance is at the heart of method as an intellectual construct. Many other thinkers of Descartes' era would emphasize this concept as well. Rather than ask "*what* do I know?" as Montaigne or Sánchez had done, the seventeenth-century thinkers asked "*how* do I know?" The Port-Royal *Logique,* for example, recognizes Descartes' role in the formation of such a method (Arnauld and Nicole, 21) and additionally presents its own rules both for reasoning and for the formulation of discourse (306–8). Pascal's *Esprit géométrique*

The Mind/Identity Complex and Human Language

employs as its basis a definition of geometric method (579) and presents, in its turn, its own set of rules for reasoning (597–98), as does Malebranche's *Recherche de la vérité* (1674) somewhat later (1:55).

Descartes describes at length how he has gone through the process of rejecting the existing opinions and knowledge inculcated into him and rationally justified after the fact (41–42). He then proceeds to describe in detail the technique for directing his own mind that he created for rebuilding the edifice of his own corpus of knowledge:

> Et comme la multitude des lois fournit souvent des excuses aux vices, en sorte qu'un État est bien mieux réglé, lorsque, n'en ayant que fort peu, elles y sont fort étroitement observées; ainsi, au lieu de ce grand nombre de préceptes dont la logique est composée, je crus que j'aurais assez des quatres suivants, pourvu que je prisse une ferme et constante résolution de ne manquer pas une seule fois à les observer.
>
> Le premier était de ne recevoir jamais aucune chose pour vraie, que je ne la connusse évidemment être telle: c'est-à-dire d'éviter soigneusement la précipitation et la prévention; et de ne comprendre rien de plus en mes jugements que ce qui se présenterait si clairement et si distinctement à mon esprit, que je n'eusse aucune occasion de le mettre en doute.
>
> Le second, de diviser chacune des difficultés que j'examinerais, en autant de parcelles qu'il se pourrait et qu'il serait requis pour les mieux résoudre.
>
> Le troisième, de conduire par ordre mes pensées, en commençant par les objets les plus simples et les plus aisés à connaître, pour monter peu à peu, comme par degrés, jusques à la connaissance des plus composés; et supposant même de l'ordre entre ceux qui ne se précèdent point naturellement les uns des autres.
>
> Et le dernier, de faire partout des dénombrements si entiers, et des revues si générales, que je fusse assuré de ne rien omettre. (45–46)

(And as the multitude of laws often furnishes an excuse for vice, such that a State is better regulated, when, having only a few laws, they are very strictly observed; thus in place of the great number of precepts of which logic is composed, I believed that I would have enough with the four following principles, provided that I took a firm and constant resolution to never fail a single time to respect them.

The first was to never receive anything as true, unless I recognized it as being evidently so: which is to say, to avoid precipitation and haste; and to never include in my judgments anything more than that which would present itself so clearly and distinctly to my mind, that I had no occasion to place it in doubt.

The second, to divide each of the difficulties I would examine into as many parcels as possible and as necessary to better resolve them.

The third, to conduct my thoughts in an orderly way, beginning with the simplest and most easily understood objects, then rising, little by little, step by step, to an understanding of the most composite ones; and supposing order even between those that did not proceed naturally one from another.

And finally, to everywhere make so complete an accounting, and so general a review, that I was sure to omit nothing.)

Descartes prefaces his four precepts with a reprise of the simplicity/complexity dichotomy. The method he seeks is regular, straightforward, and defined by moderation and rigor. There is a minimalist quality to his method, restricting the mind to the most elementary formula possible. Descartes proposes his simplified method in conscious contrast to established, traditional logic taught in the schools, with its "baroque" accumulation of excessive, confused, and convoluted rules whose multiplicity and complexity lead only to error, defect, and ineptitude. The classical mind instead must operate on the principle of simplicity. Its minimalist formula is sufficient to the task of seeking truth provided that the mind is disciplined and stays within the limits set by the formula. This latter requirement is again an act of the will, which must remain unshakable and stable in its resolution to stay on the path—the term "resolution" here being a term of will while at the same time being echoed in the four precepts as the means of resolving the problems and conundrums arising in intellectual inquiries.

Within the four rules of Descartes' method proper, the first principle is that of doubt. Unlike Montaigne's systematic doubt (the doubting of everything to the end of doubting everything), Descartes' doubt is methodical (the doubting of everything that is not obviously true, to the end of eliminating doubt and arriving at additional truths).[23] Indeed at the heart of Cartesian doubt is, paradoxically, the belief in an objective truth and the belief that we are capable of knowing that truth with certainty. Descartes even supposes that some truths are evident in and of themselves and are not subject to doubt. Again the concept of discipline comes into play within the realm of doubt, in the form of patience and self-control. The great danger in moving from doubt to certainty is excessive haste. We must limit our conclusions to those thoughts that are self-evident truths, or else to which methodical reasoning leads us with such clear and distinct proof that we can no longer hold those conclusions in doubt.

The key to this deliberate movement from doubt to certainty lies in the concept of order, an order rooted in the principle of simplicity. The problems that understanding reality poses to the mind are in and of themselves complex. The method that Descartes recommends imposes simplicity upon that complexity. The complex problems of reality are broken down, separated into their constituent parts until each small fragment of the problem is in the most elementary form possible. These simplified fragment problems are then resolved individually—a resolution not possible without the simplification process and the ordering of ideas by degree of simplicity. Subsequently resolution (in both senses) takes place as the mind intentionally creates order in the disposition of its ideas based on this simplicity principle and then applies that order to the execution of the problem-solving task, uncovering intelligible relationships between the simplified elementary portions of the problem to be solved and giving a regular succession to the linear flow of ideas from point A to point B, from doubt to certainty.

The linear succession constitutes an additional form of order, that of a hierarchy, as the mind moves "upward" and "by degrees," step by step, from the most fundamental ideas (both in the sense of simple and in the sense of foundational in the structure of knowledge) to more difficult ones, a movement of increase in the quantity and value of ideas. In essence the mind forms new truths by adding together previous truths, creating a new harmonious whole (in itself a simple entity) out of the fragmentary elements previously examined. The complexity of the problem leads to the simplicity of resolution and, equally, to the simplicity of truth, regardless of how composed and convoluted the initial question was. The movement from doubt to truth is inherently a movement from the complex to the simple at all levels, either through the processes of analysis (reordering by breaking down a complex question into simplified constituent parts) or through that of synthesis (reordering by constructing a new harmonious whole out of the artificially fragmented elements).

The play of the fragment and the whole, of the simple and the complex, is found in the very structures and functions attributed to the mind by a number of seventeenth-century thinkers. For example, the Port-Royal *Grammar* (1660) distills the intellect's operations into three basic faculties—conception, judgment, and reasoning—that comprise the totality of what we consider to be "mind" (Lancelot and Arnauld, 27–28). The Port-Royal *Logique* takes things a step further and to the first three functions adds the fourth operation of "ordering"—not terribly far removed from the synthetic Cartesian operation of "reordering" (Arnauld and Nicole, 36–38). Ultimately, in the footsteps of Descartes' *Discours,* Locke's *Essay* (1690), though it argues against the French philosopher's basis of intellectual activity in the conception of innate ideas, would nevertheless adopt a similar reorganizational play of the simple and complex ideas that Locke held to be derived from sensation (57–59, 91–93).

Of course, this process of reordering is based on a supposition that Descartes enunciates explicitly, namely the supposition that order actually exists in reality and that among all the objects to which we turn our intellectual processes there is an intelligible relationship, a disposition that makes sense, which is just waiting for the mind to uncover it. This is an enormous supposition in that Descartes holds to it even, as he says, with respect to objects or conclusions that do not appear to proceed from one another naturally. This underlying order of all thoughts and all things is derivative of the ancient concept of Logos, a term supercharged with meanings but all of which are applicable to Cartesian thought. Logos is the order of the universe; it is the will (divine or otherwise) that organizes reality; it is reason and logical thought; and Logos is language—and the importance of this final point to Cartesian thought will be seen shortly.[24] For the moment the notions of order, will, and reason, which are part of Logos, and how these three elements form a unity of reality are of greater importance than the linguistic element. In the end, for Descartes, unity is the highest form of simplicity in the hierarchy of intellectual values implied by his four precepts. It constitutes the final step in the construction of new truths global, general, and coherently whole.

Having outlined this method, Descartes then proceeds to engage the reader in its application—in general to all of the sciences but first and foremost to philosophy, from which all other sciences borrow their principles (49). Beginning with a universal doubt, Descartes brings into question everything that he knows or has ever known, everything that he believes or has ever believed to be true, in an effort to arrive at a first, fundamental, self-evident truth as the basis for his new philosophy, according to the first of the four precepts of his method. Doubting everything, he makes the following realization:

> Mais aussitôt après, je pris garde que, pendant que je voulais ainsi penser que tout était faux, il fallait nécessairement que moi, qui le pensais, fusse quelque chose. Et remarquant que cette vérité: *je pense donc je suis,* était si ferme et si assurée que toutes les plus extravagantes suppositions des sceptiques n'étaient pas capables de l'ébranler, je jugeai que je pouvais la recevoir, sans scrupule, pour le premier principe de la philosophie que je cherchais. (62)

> (But immediately after, I recognized that, while I wanted thus to think that everything was false, it was necessarily true that I, who was thinking this, was something. And remarking that this truth: *I think therefore I am,* was so firm and sure that all the most extravagant suppositions of the skeptics were not capable of undermining it, I judged that I could accept it, with no hesitation, as the first principle of the philosophy that I was seeking.)

Descartes' first self-evident truth is enunciated as an awareness of his own existence, a consciousness of his sense of self. This consciousness constitutes a reaffirmation of the connection between thought and being, coupling the exercise of mental faculties with first-person existence, through a relationship of contingency. In a turn of logical dependency, Descartes evokes the idea that one cannot actually observe or be aware of being as such, although one can observe and be aware of the mind's thought processes. Since thought is contingent on being (obviously one cannot think, or do anything for that matter, if one does not exist), then the thinking entity, the first-person self, must exist. Even if the first-person self attempts to disprove his own existence or to bring it into doubt, this very act proves with necessary logical certainty that the first-person self exists.

This line of reasoning may seem on the surface, at least to the modern mind, to be a frivolous statement, but its significance lies in its context. It is a line of reasoning that destroys any possibility of a pure skeptical position. To a Socrates who claims that "all I know is that I know nothing," Descartes answers, "false, you at least know that you are." To a skeptic arguing that "I don't even know if I exist or not," Descartes replies, "wrong, you do." To a Montaigne who inquires "que sçay-je?," Descartes responds, "well, at least you know that you exist." With this first self-evident truth Descartes definitively unravels any argument for the fundamental and absolute unknowability of self and reality. He transforms such notions as Montaigne's systematic doubt from hypothesis to mere rhetoric, and worse, from rhetoric to fiction, from fiction to unreasoned foolishness. In contrast to Montaigne's idea of knowledge and reality in continual flux, the Cartesian "je pense donc je suis" proves not just the existence of the first-person self but, more importantly, the possibility of a reality that is solid, stable, and unshakable, and a knowledge of that reality.

Operating on his own supposition that there is order and regularity to the universe and to human understanding of it, Descartes refuses to see this first truth as merely an isolated and irrelevant occurrence. He poses it as the "premier principe" of his philosophy, the redundant nature of the expression acting as a redoubling mechanism, emphasizing the idea that this unshakable truth about reality is merely the first in a succession of similar truths that he (and potentially others) will uncover through the process of methodical thought.

From the perspective of the present study's goals, the Cartesian "je pense donc je suis" is of additional importance. Descartes follows up this first truth with an important corollary. He hypothesizes that he might, for example, pretend that he has no body, that there is no world, that there is no place in which he exists. Despite this he cannot pretend, given his first truth, that he does not exist. On the one hand, as just shown, by doubting the truth of everything, he proves that he exists; on the other hand, if he stopped thinking, while all the rest of reality might very well be true, he would have no reason at all to suppose that he actually existed, such that: "je connus de là que j'étais une substance dont tout l'essence ou la nature n'est que de penser" (I knew thereby that I was a substance whose whole essence or nature was only to think, 62) and that the part of his being that thinks is that by which "je suis ce que je suis" (I am what I am, 62). In this Descartes finally and explicitly defines the self's substance, essence, and nature.[25]

As a substance he exists in and of himself and is not contingent upon anything other than his own thoughts. The term "substance," in the philosophical context in which Descartes employs it, implies that which is not subject to change. It is in this way that he can speak of his permanent essence as opposed to changeable accidents or attributes, or that he can speak of *his* nature (which is stable) as opposed to nature in a more general sense (which is in flux). The faculty of thinking is the essence of his substance, the very matter of his being. Thought is the one quality proper to the Cartesian self, the one quality necessary to it, the quality that serves as its defining characteristic. It is innate to the self, inseparable from it. In a phrase, it *is* the self. Anything other than thought is not part of the self but only superficially attached to it. Thought, to the complete and utter exclusion of all other possible qualities, characteristics, or elements, constitutes Cartesian identity.[26]

If it is the case, as Nuri states, that "'je,' c'est d'abord 'je pense' ou 'je parle'" ("I," is before all else "I think" or "I speak," 77), then the question remains of how language fits into the issue of thought as identity in Descartes' *Discours*. The answer becomes apparent as Descartes addresses the difference between man and animals. Animals, for Descartes, are merely machines or automata. For example, Descartes argues that if there were machines that had precisely the same internal and external mechanisms, materials, structures, and appearance of a monkey or of any other animal without reason (for Descartes, all animals other than man are without reason), then we would have no way of distinguishing them from the real thing. The monkey is equal to the sum of his parts—reconstitute precisely the parts, and you have a monkey, no different in any way, shape, or form from his natural counterpart. However, if there were machines

> qui eussent la ressemblance de nos corps, et imitassent autant nos actions que moralement il serait possible, nous aurions toujours deux moyens très certains, pour reconnaître qu'elles ne seraient point pour cela de vrais hommes. Dont le premier est que jamais elles ne pourraient user de paroles, ni d'autres signes en les composant, comme nous faisons pour déclarer aux autres nos pensées. (85)

> (who resembled our bodies, and imitated our actions as much as would be morally possible, we would always have two very certain means to recognize that they were not for all that true men. The first of which is that they could never use words, or other signs, composing them as we do to declare our thoughts to others.)

An examination of manlike machines for Descartes would reveal a tension of identity and distinction. There would be elements of identity between man and machine—similitude of physical appearance and composition of constituent material parts, as well as reproduction of attitudes, behaviors, actions, and gestures. However, these elements of identity are exceeded by factors of distinction. The most important by far is language. Though Descartes indicates a second factor of distinction, which is that these machines "n'agiraient pas par connaissance, mais seulement par la disposition de leurs organes" (would not act through understanding, but only through the disposition of their organs, 86), he devotes far more space and discussion to the language question.

In fact the language distinction and the rational distinction between man and animal can be seen as one and the same in much of seventeenth-century thought. For example, the Port-Royal *Grammaire* defines grammar thus: "La GRAMMAIRE est l'Art de parler. Parler, est expliquer ses pensées par des signes, que les hommes ont inventez à ce dessein" (GRAMMAR is the Art of speaking. Speaking, is to explain one's thoughts by signs, which men have invented to that end, Lancelot and Arnauld, 5).[27] It thus conflates speaking and thinking and even underlines the thought component of speech: "On peut considérer deux choses dans ces signes: La première; ce qu'ils sont par leur nature, c'est à dire, en tant que sons & caracteres. La seconde; leur signification; c'est à dire, la manière dont les hommes s'en servent pour signifier leurs pensées" (Two things can be considered in these signs: First; what they are by their nature, which is to say, as sounds and characters. Second; their signification; which is to say, the manner in which men use them to signify their thoughts, 5), such that language is partially made of thought.[28] The English philosopher Locke is quick to indicate that the role of articulate sounds is to express thought and nothing else (225), while the rhetorician Lamy underlines the spiritual (thought) component of language that necessarily accompanies the corporal (sound) component (180–81). The use of language, and the reason it appears to necessarily imply, is for many of the thinkers of Descartes' era, such as the Grammarians of Port-Royal (Lancelot and Arnauld, 4, 27), Locke (89, 225), and Leibniz (273), the key distinguishing factor between man and animal and an idea that stands in pointed contrast to Montaigne's ideas on animal reason.[29]

For Descartes this means of differentiating between humans and other living creatures is as certain as the statement "je pense donc je suis," and it cements the relationship between language, thought, and identity. In the *Méditations* Descartes states that in addition to thinking or conceiving either "je suis" (I am) or "j'existe" (I exist), the phrase "est nécessairement vraie, toutes les fois que *je la prononce*" (is necessarily true, every time *I pronounce it*, 415–16, emphasis added). Language is at one and the same time a means of defining the self and an absolute indicator of identity and difference. It allows us in no uncertain terms to distinguish between an "us" (who can speak) and a "them" (who cannot); it includes and it excludes. In Descartes' terms, it does this not just by expressing thought but also by expressing the order and organization of thought. Signs not only express individual ideas and concepts but, like thoughts, can be broken down, reordered, restructured, and put back together again in a variety of configurations. What we produce semiotically is a reflection of our methods of thinking.

This is particularly important if we reconsider Descartes' first truth, "je pense donc je suis." In the case of Descartes' first principle, thinking was the proof of the first-person self's existence. However, this starting principle does not prove the existence of any self other than that of the first person, since one person cannot directly perceive the thoughts of another, so deductive evidence is required. In parallel with the first truth, Descartes' continuation suggests that while I cannot perceive your thoughts, I can perceive your speech. In addition, since thought is a necessary antecedent to speech and existence is a necessary antecedent to thought, it follows that existence of the thinking self is necessary to the production of speech. Therefore once you and I have communicated, I can declare that "we speak therefore we are."[30]

This idea of a link between community and language is not far removed from the Port-Royal *Grammaire*'s notion of the invention of various types of words, indicating that the first-person pronoun was the first pronoun invented by man, since "il estoit souvent inutile & de mauvaise grace de se nommer soy-mesme" (it was often useless and graceless to name oneself, 59), and that the second-person pronoun was immediately invented thereafter "pour n'estre pas aussi obligé de nommer celuy à qui on parle" (to not be obliged to name the person to whom one is speaking, 59). This suggests that two of the earliest words invented by man are those designating—or identifying—speaker and listener, I and you, which combined make "us," thereby simultaneously denoting both individual and communal identity. Similarly other thinkers, such as Locke, saw the communal or social element of language as being its key characteristic: "God, having designed man for a sociable creature, made him not only with an inclination and under a necessity to have fellowship with those of his own kind, but furnished him also with language which was to be the great instrument and common tie of society" (225). However, Locke adds further that one of the errors in language use among human beings is that men "suppose their words to be the marks of the ideas in the minds also of other men," which for Locke they are not (229).

For Descartes, the words we use clearly are marks of the ideas not only in our minds but in others' minds as well. Without this very real equivalence, the communal identity inherent to the Cartesian view of thought and language cannot exist. Language binds us together. However, at the same time we cannot ignore the differentiation Descartes made earlier between the individuals' manner of thought. In this sense language separates us. For if expression reflects thought, then it is necessarily implied that manner of expression reflects manner of thought. This last point takes the identity question inherent in Cartesian thought on language beyond the mere inclusivity/exclusivity relative to human beings and imaginary automatons or actual animals. It also links language to the issues of self-identity derived from everything Descartes associates with the mind in general, such as reason, method, order, being. In making this link it is possible to see the potential for a view of language as a distinguishing factor within the broader "us" of humanity, based on a hierarchy of mental ability—never overtly stated but clearly readable in passages from the *Discours* such as the following:

> on peut aussi connaître la différence qui est entre les hommes et les bêtes. Car c'est une chose bien remarquable, qu'il n'y a point d'hommes si hébétés et si stupides sans en excepter même les insensés, qu'ils ne soient capables d'arranger ensemble diverses paroles, et d'en composer un discours par lequel ils fassent entendre leurs pensées; et qu'au contraire, il n'y a point d'autre animal, tant parfait et tant heureusement né qu'il puisse être, qui fasse le semblable. Ce qui n'arrive pas de ce qu'elles ont faute d'organes, car on voit que les pies et les perroquets peuvent proférer des paroles ainsi que nous, et toutefois ne peuvent parler ainsi que nous, c'est-à-dire, en témoignant qu'ils pensent ce qu'ils disent. (86)

(one can also know the difference between men and beasts. For it is quite a remarkable thing, that there are no men so dazed and so stupid, even including the most insane, that they are incapable of arranging together different words, and of composing with them a discourse by which they make their thoughts understood; and contrarily, there is no other animal, however perfect and happily born he may be, that can do the same. Which is not through any lack of organs, since we see that magpies and parrots can proffer words as we do, and nevertheless cannot speak as we do, which is to say, in demonstrating that they think what they say.)

In the man-animal or man-automaton oppositions, the difference is qualitative. Human beings have reason; animals and automatons do not.[31] However, within the human "community," while there are no qualitative differences ("le bon sens" is a shared characteristic), there are nevertheless quantitative differences. The "si" repeated twice in the passage above underlines the difference in degree from one individual human being to the next. While all human beings have intellectual faculties, some suffer from a relative heaviness or inertia of these faculties, lack the same vivacity of intelligence found in others, or are even downright irrational, as opposed to animals and automatons, who are arational. Nevertheless all humans have the ability to give some order, if only a bad, erroneous, or insane order, to their thoughts, and this order becomes evident through the order of elements in their communication.

We have already seen that Descartes' text suggests a hierarchy of minds, in terms of those that grasp truths about reality better than others do. What the language element adds to the equation is evidence. Just as articulate speech becomes the evidence by which we can be sure that other individuals have thought similar to that of the first-person self, articulate speech—composing diverse elements into a more or less coherent whole—also becomes evidence of the degree to which individual minds apply method to their own thinking processes. If the path or method the mind follows defines the identity of the self, so too then does the language employed by the thinking individual serve as evidence of the identity of another's self. In other words, we come to know the thoughts and therefore the identity of the other through his language and the structure of his discourse.

Even discourses outside the mainstream play this role, as in the case of "deaf-mutes,"[32] for example:

> les hommes qui, étant nés sourds et muets, sont privés des organes qui servent aux autres pour parler, autant ou plus que les bêtes, ont coutume d'inventer d'eux-mêmes quelques signes, par lesquels ils se font entendre à ceux qui, étant ordinairement avec eux, ont besoin d'apprendre leur langue. (Descartes 86–87)

> (men who, born deaf and mute, are deprived of the organs that others use to speak, as much or more than animals, are able to invent some signs themselves, by which they make themselves understood by those who, being with them regularly, need to learn their language.)

Unable either to hear human speech or to produce articulate sounds,[33] they are neither deprived of intelligence nor deprived of the means of producing evidence of intelligence. They form their own gestural language as a function of their social group, consisting of other deaf-mutes and those who interact with them. Thus they have thought, and their thought has order, as evidenced by *their* language, which they employ "to make themselves understood," demonstrating will, providing them with all the elements necessary to be a truly thinking self. The only question would be where, in the hierarchy, this language would stand. Descartes' qualification of their language as being merely "a few signs," thereby encompassing little of the grand order of reality, suggests that he would view their language as relatively low on the hierarchy of languages implied by his text. Thus their intellect, for him, would be comparatively low on the hierarchy of intellects also suggested in his work.

This hierarchy of intellects is reflected in Descartes' overall choice of language for writing the *Discours:* "si j'écris en français, qui est la langue de mon pays, plutôt qu'en latin, qui est celle de mes précepteurs, c'est à cause que j'espère que ceux qui ne se servent que de leur raison naturelle toute pure, jugeront mieux de mes opinions, que ceux qui ne croient qu'aux livres anciens" (if I write in French, which is the language of my country, rather than in Latin, which is that of my teachers, it is because I hope that those who use their natural reason alone will be better judges of my opinions than those who believe only in ancient books, 105). Descartes steps beyond the simply theoretical and in practical terms associates French, not Latin, with common sense, thought, and judgment. For a matter in which reason is paramount, French is the better choice. Latin, locked in ancient texts, is the language of authority and tradition, while the vernacular in this passage is stylistically connected with "natural reason alone" and "better judgment." The choice of the vernacular is rooted in cognition and identity. If the self is thought and if French is better suited to expressing pure thought, then French is also better suited to an authentic representation of the thinking self. With or without method French serves in this capacity more effectively than does Latin, which is corrupted by a tradition that divorces it from unfettered mental activity.

The impact of this hierarchy of intellects detectable through the structure of language has implications relative to the context of Cartesian thought and mind as a whole. Descartes distinguishes himself from Montaigne by positing the fundamental knowability of reality and the self. The essence of the Cartesian self is to think, to seek out the truths that the mind can acquire and by so doing realize the self. All other pursuits are "accidental" and not part of the self's essence. So Cartesian identity is defined and qualified by the manner and degree to which the self pursues and finds truth, by the level of order in the mind. The order of the mind's processes is crucial in this definition of identity.

There is a basic supposition in Cartesian thought that the universe has order, which can be defined as Logos in all of its meanings. The organization of the universe, the processes of logical thought, and the language that expresses these two orders are interlocked in a series of parallel hierarchies that are superposed by Descartes upon everything: the hierarchy of truth/doubt/falsehood; that of methodical reason/natural reason/feeling; and finally that of language—explicitly those idiolects that reflect (or not) degrees of method in thought that not only allow us to know the world but also define the thinking self. Language—and in particular idiolect—becomes the evidence of reason in a third Logos-based hierarchy of the self: one of the methodical/rational/irrational/arational self. One can easily read in Descartes the idea that all selves are not equal, although this is not stated explicitly. There is an ideal self, which Descartes strives to become and to which he urges the reader to aspire as well. If Descartes declines to use a classical language as a means of expressing the self, it is nevertheless true that the ideal Cartesian self is still "classical" in its substance. It is balanced, simple, straightforward, regular, stable, ordered, unified, and therefore beautiful and perfect. It knows and can be known, defines and can be defined. Any language, including modern vernaculars such as French, can effectively express that self and the reality in which it exists by maintaining those same characteristics.

With language acting as evidence for reason and recognition of the self and its identity, a whole host of philosophical possibilities open up for post-Cartesian thinkers. While du Bellay argues that no language is inherently inferior to any other by nature, Descartes, by suggesting that some manners of expression are superior to others, opens the way to the possible argument that some languages as a whole could be considered superior to others by art—that is, by their superior adherence to a methodical manner of expression based on the ideal of methodical thought. While Montaigne posits that one can know the manner reflective of one's identity but not the substance as such, Descartes' thinking fuses manner and substance, arguing that manner of thinking is substantive in and of itself, that the manner or form of the thinking self is inseparable from its substance and therefore inseparable from its identity. To know one is to know the other. These concepts of identity, the superiority of an individual or group identity over others, and the reflection of this identity in means of expression, all subsumed in the question of a linguistic hierarchy, pave the way for the thinking of Claude Vaugelas.

Four

⚜

Vaugelas' *Remarques*
Language, Quality, and Communal Identity

Claude Favre de Vaugelas (1585–1650) served as chamberlain of the Duke of Orléans and personal tutor to the children of Thomas of Savoy. Best known as a grammarian, he authored the *Remarques sur la langue françoise,* published in 1647. Linguists and linguistic historians remember him as having contributed above all to the standardization of the French language in the seventeenth century.[1]

Although his work does not constitute a systematic grammar of the French language as such, it nevertheless presents the linguistic historian with an important, albeit scattered and miscellaneous, collection of observations and formulas for the correct use of language, which boiled down, to a large extent, to the usage of polite Parisian society.[2] For the historian of ideas and the philosopher of language, his preface to those diverse observations is a treasure trove of ideological notions underlying the principle of polite usage.

For a better understanding of the ideological underpinnings expressed in Vaugelas' preface, it should be noted that Vaugelas' text is part of a tradition toward a prescriptive *bon usage,* a tradition that, as Trudeau has pointed out, extends at least as far back as R. Estienne's *Traicté de la Grammaire françoise* (1557) and includes such notable works as Estienne Pasquier's *Recherches de la France* (1560), Ramée's *Scholae Grammaticae* (1559), Henri Estienne's *Hypomneses* (1582), and the famous commentaries of François Malherbe (Trudeau, 64–65, 56, 107–8, 125–27, 141–56). All these works express in one form or another, as Trudeau indicates, the concept of "the best French" (64), legitimate or "pure" language (86), the opposition of court usage and general usage (127), and the "tyranny" of one or both of these types of usage (141).

The tensions inherent in such "tyranny" would spill over into seventeenth-century debates on the French language. Streichler's classic work *Commentaires sur les* Remarques *de Vaugelas* outlines how the question of linguistic oppression evolves into a debate between the camp of prescriptive purism—including Vaugelas along with Bouhours, Patru, Conrart, Chapelain, Cassagne, and Andry—and a camp espousing the freedom of a more general usage—including Marie de Gournay, La Mothe le Vayer, Scipion Dupleix, and Gilles Ménage. The era as a whole ultimately leaned more toward the former, with the rise of what is often referred to as the "ideology of the standard," which was certainly helped along by institutions both social, such as the salons, and political, such as the Académie française. In both of these particular institutions Vaugelas figured prominently.

Vaugelas was a regular at the famous Hôtel de Rambouillet, originally conceived as a space for a "new kind of sociability" (Kale, 4). In Madame de Rambouillet's salon, "men and women with diverse interests and congenial manners met to discuss language, science, literature and music. Participants had to adhere to her code of correctness for speech and conduct or face expulsion" (Ojala and Ojala, 30–31). Indeed, "the art of talk was the most important of the courtly skills" (Goldsmith, 6) refined in the salons, where participants "learned to use courtesy codes in refashioning their social selves" (Goldsmith, 4). Eventually, and perhaps inevitably, an excess of such refinement arose—*la préciosité*—which "became associated with the salons, and the female habituées who accepted the marquise's strict code were labeled *précieuses*" (Ojala and Ojala, 31).[3] Nevertheless, Burke has indicated that "the précieuses may well have had the last word. Although they wrote little . . . on the subject, the role of aristocratic women in the purification of the language should not be underestimated. As sociolinguists have often pointed out, women in many societies are more polite than men, as well as displaying a tendency to hypercorrectness" (*Languages,* 100).[4] This tendency toward hypercorrectness is one way in which salon culture redefined "the criteria for inclusion and exclusion" and created a "grand monde purifié" (Goldsmith, 7) that "proposed to discover new definitions of what it meant to be 'naturally' superior" (Goldsmith, 9). Regular contact with this milieu was undoubtedly linked to Vaugelas' association of correctness of language with polite society and the notion of superiority attached to identification with the language of that milieu.

Just as important in contextualizing Vaugelas is the Académie française. The academy was founded by Cardinal Richelieu in 1635, and Vaugelas was one of the original members.[5] The academy's primary mission was to standardize and codify the French language and to assure its purity. To this end it was decreed that the academy would compose a dictionary, a grammar, a rhetoric, and a poetics. The concern over standardizing, purifying, and maintaining the French language was not envisioned as a strictly linguistic endeavor in a narrow sense, which is to say an entirely grammatical and lexical endeavor; a grammar and a dictionary alone would have sufficed to take care of that. Oratory and literary production are seen in the academy's original charter as being central to the institution's mission, and thus the linguistic domain is viewed in a broad sense. It is a shame that only the dictionary was completed. As it turns out, however, Vaugelas worked on the dictionary for fifteen years, from the founding of the institution in 1635 until his death in 1650. Unfortunately the two-volume dictionary would not be finished until 1694, long after Vaugelas' passing. Nevertheless this experience too is closely connected to the movement toward purism previously mentioned and is manifest in Vaugelas' desire to codify what he saw as the most correct French in his *Remarques*.[6] The ideological underpinnings of the *Remarques,* as we shall see, are not limited to the grammatical and the lexical but extend, in line with the academy's philosophy, to the rhetorical and the literary.

The preface of the *Remarques* opens with an explicit discussion of Vaugelas' intentions in writing his book:

> Ce ne sont pas icy des Loix que je fais pour nostre langue de mon authorité . . . l'Usage . . . [est] le Maistre & le Souverain des langues vivantes. . . . Mon dessein n'est pas de reformer nostre langue, ny d'abolir des mots, ny d'en faire, mais seulement de monstrer le bon usage de ceux qui sont faits, & s'il est douteux ou inconnu, de l'esclaircir, & de le faire connoistre. (n.p.)
>
> (These are not Laws that I make here for our language of my own authority . . . Usage . . . [is] the Master and Sovereign of living languages. . . . My object is not to reform our language, nor to abolish words, nor to make them, but only to show the good usage of those that presently exist, and if it is doubtful or unknown, to clarify it and make it known.)

Focused primarily on the question of authority, Vaugelas' book will consist of rules and prescriptions derived from a sovereign principle. Being "sovereign," these rules will have, by definition, a general, comparatively permanent, and imperative quality. Vaugelas makes a point of defining the source of the authority from which these rules emanate. The grammarian, perhaps surprisingly, is not that source. Although the grammarian is a specialist in all aspects of language, it is not for him to dictate linguistic values to the linguistic community. Instead, Vaugelas places the concept of usage in this role.

References to usage in the seventeenth century are not uncommon. A substantial amount of grammatical discussion in the period centers on identifying the true place of usage in linguistic correctness.[7] Some maintain that usage is everything, as is the case with Bouhours in his *Remarques nouvelles sur la langue françoise* (1675), where he indicates that he will not even present a traditional preface to his own work since it would be a waste of time after "la belle Préface de M. de Vaugelas. Comme elle donne les veritables idées que nous devons avoir de nostre Langue, & qu'elle n'omet rien de ce qui se peut dire sur l'usage" (the beautiful Preface of M. de Vaugelas. As it provides the proper ideas that we should have about our Language, and as it omits nothing that can be said on usage, n.p.).

Others, contrarily, seek a more rational (one might say Cartesian) emphasis on rules and method. This is the case, for example, in Chiflet's *Essai d'une parfaite grammaire de la langue françoise* (1659), which claims that the flaw in the work of contemporary grammarians is that "il y en a quelques-uns qui s'embroüillent, en cherchant le vray point de l'étenduë & des limites de la Regle qu'ils veulent establir: & aprés s'estre bien debatus, desesperant d'en voir le fond, ils vous renvoyent à l'usage" (there are some who get mixed up, in seeking the true extent and limits of the Rule they wish to establish: and after much struggling, despairing to see the bottom of things, they direct your attention to usage, 3), suggesting the inadequacy of usage as the sole mechanism of linguistic correctness. Chiflet does not necessarily suggest that usage is an entirely bad thing but rather that a rational set of rules must be involved in the process of determining correct usage. Vaugelas, however, by focusing so strongly on usage, represents a position separate from that of a "Cartesian" grammar such as that of Port-Royal. While not necessarily its polar opposite—Ayres-Bennett has in fact effectively argued that we should be "wary of trying to make a simple contrast between 'Vaugelas' school' and 'the Port-Royal school'" ("Usage and Reason," 235)—the focus on usage goes in a somewhat different direction that becomes more and more discernible through the course of his preface, as will be seen.[8]

In the most general sense, for Vaugelas, the authority of usage is rooted quite simply in the age and frequency of linguistic behaviors. These two characteristics give the grammatical rules derived from usage an imperative quality, turning habits into norms, transforming the descriptive into the prescriptive, and guiding the practice of linguistic realization within society as a whole. Employing a political metaphor, Vaugelas paints usage as having dominion over expression, as having an absolute power in all matters grammatical and lexical wherever living languages are concerned. Vaugelas' highlighting of living languages, as opposed to dead ones, is significant. If he defines usage as the ruling element in linguistic correctness, it is because he feels a dissatisfaction with traditional views of grammarians derived from the study of dead languages. There is no usage in dead languages since people do not speak them anymore. In such languages the only indicator of correctness is authoritative prescription, as derived from textual artifacts and dictated by the grammarian. However, as has been seen in the thinking of du Bellay, this approach to language—the attempt to reconstruct an ancient language from its ruins—was generally thought to be inadequate. Vaugelas' thinking on this matter suggests that a similar grammatical approach to modern languages is also doomed to inadequacy. The grammarian-as-dictator method for understanding ancient languages, while insufficient in du Bellaysian conceptions of language, is for Vaugelas a necessary evil for those idioms. There is, as implied in Vaugelas' text, no other means of approaching dead tongues. The grammarian-as-dictator approach is the best (or only) option available. Vaugelas implies as well, however, that the same approach to a living language is not the best option, though early in the preface he does not give any indication as to why this is the case.

Vaugelas does insist, in sticking with the semantic network of the political power and authority analogy, that the grammarian has no "legislative" powers in the sense of reforming, abolishing, or making rules. Vaugelas' idea here, again, is a point of contention with grammarians such as Chiflet, who argues that linguistic specialists do have a prescriptive role, suggesting that they, and other more learned grammarians than themselves, have the responsibility to "former les Regles du langage plus exactement & plus judicieusement" (form the Rules of language more exactly and judiciously, Chiflet, 2). Even while acknowledging a debt to Vaugelas, Chiflet also underscores that "Je ne suis pas pourtant tellement idolatre de ses opinions que je n'en aye dit mon jugement, quād j'ay creu qu'il s'estoit mesconté " (I do not however so idolize his opinions that I have failed to give my own view, when I believed that he was in error, 4).

The idea that the grammarian establishment should set down rules is also taken up later by the academy in its *Observations sur les Remarques de M. de Vaugelas* (1705), which essentially consists of Vaugelas' *Remarques* retouched and corrected and which underlines that the academy's republication of the work focuses on "regles & de preceptes pour se perfectionner sur les endroits les plus difficiles de la Langue Françoise" (rules and precepts for perfecting oneself in the most difficult points of the French Language, Académie, 4). Furthermore the academy underlines its own grammatical-legislative authority by pointing out that many of Vaugelas' remarks have generated controversy and debate, and that their present observations were intended to "dissiper les doutes, & . . . fixer le Public sur l'usage des phrases & des mots" (dissipate doubts, and . . . fix the Public on the usage of sentences and words, Académie, 6). In addition, having "bien voulu passer en revûë devant elle les *Remarques* de Monsieur de Vaugelas, elle a decidé pour ou contre, après quoi il faut mettre le doigt sur la bouche, n'étant plus permis d'en appeler" (been willing to pass in review the *Remarques* of Monsieur de Vaugelas, we have decided for or against, after which we place a finger on our lips, prohibiting all appeal, Académie, 6). Such is the authority of the academy that its word ends all discussion.

For Vaugelas, however, it is decidedly not the task of the grammarian to remake, destroy, replace, or create linguistic structures and concepts. Instead the power of the grammarian is quite limited. If he were to be given a role at the "court" of the sovereign of language, he would be a scribe and a chronicler observing, recording, and revealing to the eyes of a speaking and writing public how things are, and have been, said and written. He might also be considered an adviser of sorts, instructing and making clearer and more comprehensible linguistic ambiguities. While not making the rules, he is responsible for helping to shape what can be defined as good usage, in the same way that a royal adviser does not make royal laws and policies but may help to formulate them.

The term "good usage," of course, implies its opposite, a point upon which Vaugelas quickly elaborates:

> il est necessaire d'expliquer ce que c'est que cet Usage, dont on parle tant, & que tout le monde appelle le Roy, ou le Tyran, l'arbitre, ou le maistre des langues; . . . Il y a sans doute deux sortes *d'Usages, un bon & un mauvais.* Le mauvais se forme du plus grand nombre de personnes, qui presque en toutes choses n'est pas le meilleur, & le bon au contraire est composé non pas de la pluralité, mais de l'élite des voix, & cest veritablement celuy que l'on nomme le Maistre des langues, celuy qu'il faut suivre pour bien parler, & pour bien escrire. (n.p.)

> (it is necessary to explain this Usage, of which so much is said, and which everyone calls the King, or the Tyrant, the arbiter, or the master of languages; . . . There are without doubt two types *of Usages, a good and a bad.* The bad is formed by the majority of people, which in almost all things is not the best, and the good on the contrary is composed not of the plurality, but the elite of voices, and this is in fact the one which is called the Master of languages, the one which must be followed in order to speak well and to write well.)

Vaugelas keeps his discourse in the realm of the sovereign metaphor in addressing the concept of usage. In parallel with the differing views one can have of the role of a sovereign power, Vaugelas outlines different manners in which usage can be viewed: king, arbiter, tyrant, and master. Apart from the image of the master, certain of these terms suggest colored views of usage. The image of the king, for instance, presents usage as hereditary—in keeping with the inherent concept of tradition in the notion of usage—and divinely authorized—providing usage with a dignity, an unquestionable imperative to obey, and even an inherent goodness. The image of the arbiter, in its turn, implies agreement, justice, balance, and rationality. The tyrant presents a clearly negative image of usage. It represents popular origins (suggestive of the "unclean masses" and also suggestive of the vulgar—as a linguistic concept and as a social concept), usurpation and illegitimacy, destruction of free expression, and arbitrariness. So in a general way usage might be thought of, at first glance, to be good or bad depending on one's perspective.

Vaugelas, however, takes this base concept as a starting point to suggest that there is not simply one usage that is good or bad according to perspective but in fact two distinct and unrelated types of usage—good usage and bad usage—and the existence of these two distinct entities is the source of these varying views. Seen as separate entities, good usage and bad usage can be viewed only as they are inherently and absolutely, regardless of perspective. Good usage is always good. Bad usage is always bad. There is no relativism possible on this count.

Vaugelas defines the opposition of good usage and bad usage according to elements still derived from the lexical network of sociopolitical constructs. On the bad side of the balance sheet are plurality and majority, the tyranny of the masses, and the usurpation of linguistic authority by the popular and vulgar elements of society. Corrupt and illegitimate, this usage, as Vaugelas states rhetorically, "n'est pas le meilleur," by which he in fact means that it is the worst. It lacks quality, both in the normal sense of "goodness" and in the social sense of "nobility." It is also painful and harmful—painful to the ear and harmful to the purity and correctness of the language. On the good side of the balance sheet are the "élite des voix," where "voix" can simultaneously be read in the social sense of "those who have a say" and in the simple linguistic sense of "those who speak." The concept of an elite represents the opposite of everything that the plurality of bad usage brings to the table—the concepts of a minority, of quality (again in both senses of the term), of legitimacy, prestige, culture, and merit—all of which confer on good usage the right to set the tone and even dictate the rules of expression. Indeed, in the sociopolitical sense, the elite voices carry more weight and do so to such an extent, despite their minority, that they outweigh the majority, representing the superiority of social quality over demographic quantity. At the same time, in the literal, vocal sense, the elite voices are presented as expressing themselves with a higher quality, in terms of linguistic correctness.

Like Descartes, Vaugelas establishes a hierarchy of language, though on a clearly different basis. Where Descartes' hierarchy is based on language as evidence of reason, Vaugelas' hierarchy is based on language as evidence of social standing.[9] One is a better person, a person of quality, through breeding and/or education, and this superior quality is demonstrated through language. Language becomes a marker of belonging to, or exclusion from, a higher social class. It is the sign of one's social identity. By conforming one's speech and writing to the dictates of the elite voices, one indicates one's own belonging to that circle. Failure to meet this necessary requirement results in exclusion, which is why you cannot rely just on the usage of your nursemaid or your servants in order to speak and write properly, or to merit a place within the higher echelons of social status. Language is a manifestation of one's social self in a range of higher or lower social identities.

This fundamental distinction between good and bad usage leads Vaugelas to formulate his celebrated definition of good usage:

> Voicy donc comment on definit le bon Usage. *C'est la façon de parler de la plus saine partie de la Cour, conformément à la façon d'escrire de la plus saine partie des Autheurs du temps.* Quand je dis *la Cour,* j'y comprens les femmes comme les hommes, & plusieurs personnes de la ville où le Prince reside, qui par la

communication qu'elles ont avec les gens de la Cour participent à sa politesse. (n.p.)

(Here is how good Usage is defined. *It is the manner of speaking of the best part of the Court, in accordance with the manner of writing of the best part of the Authors of the time.* When I say *the Court,* I include women as well as men, and several persons of the city where the Prince resides, who by the communication they have with the people of the Court share its politeness.)

Good usage is a question of expressive manner. Just as manner of expression was implicated in individual identity in Montaigne's and Descartes' works, it is implicated here in social identity. Proper manner of expression occurs in two linguistic media represented by two social groups. First there is the medium of the spoken word that is the province of the court.[10] The court can be understood as those individuals of aristocratic quality who form the entourage of the prince and also can be understood simply as the place where the prince resides. Alongside the court there are the authors who, vocationally or avocationally, produce literary works of artistic quality or merit. This emphasis on merit, just as with the specification of "people of quality," is crucial in that in both cases, with respect to the court and to the body of authors, Vaugelas is interested only in "la plus saine partie."

The term *saine* is heavily weighted with signification. It suggests health and freedom from alteration or contamination. It represents a language and a social group with no anomalies and no vices and which can be considered good, normal, balanced, coherent, lucid, and pure. The value of these portions of the court, and of the literary profession, consists of a fusion of all these qualities, and their manner of expression exhibits this fusion. The sum total of these characteristics defines both the quality of expression and the quality of the group and its identity.

The court, for linguistic purposes, is more broadly defined by Vaugelas than one might expect. First, with a nod to the *salonnières* of his time, he stresses the role of both men and women in the formulation of this pure form of language—which suggests that the salons, however separate these entities may be from the court in reality, are considered for his linguistic purposes to be part of the court. Second, he does not limit his use of the term "court" strictly to individuals of noble birth in the prince's entourage. He includes certain members of the financial and administrative class, who have a status and wealth that bring them into frequent and substantial contact with the court proper. Such contact "communicates" the quality of speech and manner to this upper middle class both in the linguistic sense and in the sense of involuntary transmission or "rubbing off." In essence there is a transference through conversation. While the upper middle class is not inherently as polished, well-mannered, and well-educated as the "true" members of the court, this quality is passed on to them.

Thus what Vaugelas is implying is that the best manner of expression comes from the "plus saine partie(s)" of society as a whole and is composed not only of people of quality as such (those who govern politically) but also of the bourgeoisie (who "govern" financially) and the literary elite (who "govern" taste and aesthetics). In a "geographical" sense the best manner of expression is not limited to the physical location of the prince but extends to domains such as the salon, which by its very nature brings these three subgroups together and creates a milieu of communication in all the manners just mentioned.

In this same vein and despite its dominant role, the court is not capable of creating good usage all by itself: "Toutefois quelque avantage que nous donnions à la Cour, elle n'est pas suffisante toute seule de servir de reigle, il faut que la Cour et les bons Autheurs y concourent, & ce n'est que de cette conformité qui se trouve entre les deux que l'Usage s'establit" (Nevertheless whatever advantage we give to the Court, it is not sufficient by itself to provide regulation; it is necessary that the Court and the good Authors converge and it is only from this conformity between the two that Usage establishes itself, n.p.). For Vaugelas, the strength of the system resides in the principles of concurrence and conformity among the court and the authors.[11] Linguistic correctness can be found where the usages of the court and of the authors coincide. Vaugelas considers language through two different but parallel perspectives, speaking and writing. Each is the special province of one of the two primary subgroups: speaking belongs to the court; writing belongs to the authors. It would be surprising if they, as parallel domains, did not exhibit a certain identity—both through linguistic resemblance (speaking identically) and through sense of self (social identity)—as far as manner of expression is concerned. Both groups represent the flower of expression in their respective media. So as a rule, this identity of usage should be perfectly natural—it should not be contrived or forced but should typically happen on its own without any intentional effort to make it come into existence.

This comparative identity of expressive manner does not, however, make the court and the authors equals:

> Ce n'est pas pourtant que la Cour ne contribuë incomparablement plus à l'Usage que les Autheurs, ny qu'il y ayt aucune proportion de l'un à l'autre; Car enfin la parole qui se prononce, est la premiere en ordre & en dignité, puis que celle qui est escrite n'est que son image, comme l'autre est l'image de la pensée. Mais le consentement des bons Autheurs est comme le sceau, ou une verification, qui authorise le langage de la Cour, & qui decide celuy qui est douteux. (n.p.)

(This is not to say however that the Court does not contribute incomparably more to Usage than the Authors, nor that there is any equality between them;

For in the end the word that is spoken is the first in order and dignity, since that which is written is but its image, as the other is the image of thought. But the consent of good Authors is like the seal, or a verification, that authorizes the language of the Court, and that decides when it is doubtful.)

Vaugelas explicitly grants higher status to the court than to the authors. There is a difference not simply of degree but of nature as well, a quantitative difference in their impact on language based on a qualitative distinction. This qualitative distinction is reflected linguistically in the relative value of the respective domains of the two cultural groups, speaking and writing. Inscribing his text in a tradition that runs at least as far back as Aristotle's *De Interpretatione,* Vaugelas presents the articulations of the voice as primary.[12] This primacy takes two forms, again reflecting the qualitative and quantitative distinctions between the court and the authors. The primacy is quantitative in that speaking is the first linguistic medium to exist chronologically, the first in temporal succession. It is qualitative in that the spoken word for Vaugelas is also the first in "dignity," carrying within it an intrinsic value above and beyond that possessed by the written word. The spoken word is substance, while the written word is a "mere" representation of it. In seventeenth-century social terms one is led to think of noble family bloodlines, where the first in succession, the person who is a direct descendant, is of higher dignity than he or she who is related but further removed from the original noble ancestor.[13] Vaugelas therefore confers value, prerogative, rank, and respect upon spoken language in preference to the written word.

The reflection of language media in terms of social structures does not end there. The difference in quality between the two groups is suggested in their analogy with different branches of the French monarchy. If the members of the court are the royalty of language and play the primary role in dictating the laws of good usage, the authors have a role as the "parliamentarians" of language.[14]

This is not to say, of course, that Vaugelas is in any way favoring the actual language of real-life parliamentarians. On the contrary, he explicitly points out the lack of grace in the "barreau" (n.p.). However, the basic elements of the politico-legal system do, by parallel, clarify the relative relationship and standing of the speakers of the court and the best authors of the era. For example, the parliament, while beneath the royal court in power and status, nevertheless has certain of its own political prerogatives, and in particular the inscribing of royal edicts and ordinances, along with the enunciation of remonstrances against certain edicts and ordinances deemed inappropriate and in need of correcting. Just as the support and consent of the parliament are politically necessary (or at least useful) to the sovereign in the effective promulgation of laws, so too does the corpus of good authors confer authorization on the linguistic dictates of court usage.

Vaugelas extends the analogy with the metaphor of "le sceau" (n.p.), or the parliamentary seal, in a way legitimizing the usage of the spoken word of the court by way of the inscription of that usage in writing by authors, who thus grant their approval, creating the overall conformity and concurrence necessary for the establishment of the more general concept of good usage.

Furthermore those cases where court usage and literary usage do not match can be viewed as metaphorical forms of linguistic parliamentary remonstrance. In such cases the usage is considered neither bad nor good but doubtful: "il y a un bon *& un mauvais Usage; &* j'adjouste que *le bon* se divise encore en *l'Usage declaré*, & en *l'Usage douteux*. . . . *L'Usage declaré* est celuy, dont on sçait asseurément, que la plus saine partie de la Cour, & des Autheurs du temps, sont d'accord, & par consequent *le douteux* ou *l'inconnu* est celuy, dont on ne le sçait pas" (there is *a good and a bad Usage;* and I add that *good Usage* is divided yet again between *declared Usage* and *doubtful Usage*. . . . *Declared Usage* is that of which it is known for certain that the best part of the Court and the Authors of the time are in agreement, and consequently *doubtful Usage* or *unknown Usage* is that of which the same is not known, n.p.). The question of uncertainty leads Vaugelas to break down good usage still further into declared usage and doubtful usage. In a very literal sense, to declare something is to affirm it orally or in writing, or in specifically Vaugelasian terms, to affirm it *both* in speaking and in writing, to the extent that both the speakers of the court and the writers of literature render usage certain due to the fact that their respective manners of expression coincide. However, when the monarch-parliament system of language breaks down, we are left with the same tension we have seen in Montaigne and Descartes, that of the known versus the unknown, the certain versus the uncertain—though instead of reflecting an epistemological question, the issue for Vaugelas becomes purely linguistic.

However, unlike Montaigne and in keeping with a Cartesian attitude, Vaugelas considers the state of doubt unacceptable. Almost by definition good usage is declared usage—it is firm, solid, evident. It represents a unanimity of minds and wills, the stability of a system of rules, a tranquillity of linguistic structure based in an order that maintains a stylistic status quo, an untroubled expressive conservatism. Thus the doubtful elements must be eliminated, and so a third branch of linguistic government—what one might call a linguistic judicial branch—is required for the maintenance of good usage. This consists of commentators or what Vaugelas refers to as "les gens sçavants en la langue" (people learned in the language):

> Il est vray que d'ajouster à la lecture, la frequentation de la Cour & des gens sçavants en la langue, est encore toute autre chose, puis que tout le secret pour

acquerir la perfection de bien escrire & de bien parler, ne consiste qu'à joindre ces trois moyens ensemble. Si nous l'avons fait voir pour la Cour & pour les Autheurs, l'autre n'y est gueres moins necessaire, parce qu'il se presente beaucoup de doutes & de difficultez, que la Cour n'est pas capable de resoudre, & que les Autheurs ne peuvent esclaircir, soit que les exemples dont on peut tirer l'esclaircissement y soient rares, & qu'on ne les trouvent pas à point nommé, ou qu'il n'y en ait point du tout. (n.p.)

(It is true that to add to reading the frequenting of the Court and people learned in the language is something altogether different, since the whole secret to acquiring the perfection necessary to write well and to speak well consists only of joining these three means together. If we have demonstrated this for the Court and for the Authors, the other group is hardly less necessary, because many doubts and difficulties present themselves which the Court is not capable of resolving, and which the Authors cannot clarify, either because examples from which one might obtain clarification are rare and cannot be found readily, or because such examples do not exist.)

All three parts of linguistic government are necessary for Vaugelas in the regulation of one's speech and writing. This idea is echoed by other commentators of the era. For example, Chiflet indicates that correctness in French is "fondé sur l'usage de la Cour, sur celuy des Maistres de la Langue, & sur celuy des bons Écrivains" (founded on the usage of the Court, on that of the Masters of the Language, and on that of good Writers, 4). Bouhours points out that his own *Remarques* are based on his observations of "l'usage," consultation with "les personnes les plus habiles dans la Langue" (those persons most skilled in the Language), and "le témoignage des bons Auteurs" (the example of good Authors, n.p.).

For Vaugelas, this three-pronged source of expressive truth is the foundation of good language, its hidden mechanism, which can be accessed only by the initiated—in this case those who are reading Vaugelas' book.[15] This is a significant point, in that Vaugelas' book serves then in part as an initiation into the community of a linguistic elite. Vaugelas implies that one can develop purity and perfection of expression. Correctness is an acquired skill, something that one can come to possess through application and effort, through contact with the court, reading of selected authors, and consultation with language experts such as himself. In essence by possessing these three elements, one becomes a part of the linguistic elite. Adapting du Bellay's concept of imitation of ideal literary models, Vaugelas transforms linguistic imitation into a mechanism of individual social progress and the tool for transforming individual identity.

The notion of linguistic correctness and purity as a doorway to elite status is also evidenced in Bouhours' *Remarques,* though with some degree of limitation on how large a social leap made through language can be: "Comme elles [les *Remarques*] sont faites particuliérement pour regler le stile, elles regardent moins le peuple, que les personnes qui se meslent un peu d'écrire" (As they [the *Remarks*] are made especially for regulating style, they have less to do with the common people than with those persons who have occasion to write, n.p.). While style can be improved, this is only a question for those belonging to a relatively educated class, and any possibility of improvement is denied the masses. Similarly the later *Observations* of the academy would also underscore the limited possibility of an upward shift in social status through the acquisition of more precise expression, stating that its book "servira aux François qui ne parlent point exactement leur Langue maternelle" and that "encore aujourd'hui il fait les delices de tous ceux qui aiment à écrire et parler poliment" (will serve those Frenchmen who do not speak their maternal Language with precision" and that "even today it delights all who enjoy writing and speaking politely, 4–5). The point here, of course, is that perfection of language, a polishing of expression, can be acquired and that, if the Vaugelasian view of speech and writing as markers of social identity holds true, some degree of shift in social identity, however small, can be acquired.

For this to happen at all, however, there must be a pure and perfected language as a whole to which people can aspire. The three elements underlined—court, authors, and linguistic commentators—must all come into service and fulfill their respective functions in order for such a language to exist. Furthermore if, in the purification of language as a whole, it is the role of the court to perfect speech and that of the authors to perfect writing, it is the role of the third group, the commentators, to judge in all cases of doubtful usage where the court and the authors disagree. Through a process of analysis and reflection, the commentators are charged with finding solutions to linguistic difficulties, with rendering the knowledge of usage clearer and more intelligible. Indeed their role sounds very Cartesian in the semantic network employed by Vaugelas to define their work and centered on the resolution of difficulties.[16] However, while the Cartesian ideal proper is to reject authority in favor of analysis and reflection, the Vaugelasian ideal admits of such a process only when authority fails, when there exists no precedent to indicate good usage, since precedent is the fundamental principle on which all good usage is based. So when there is no clear model set by the royal court or the parliament of authors, it becomes the role of the judiciary of the commentators to make the determination.[17]

There are a number of examples given by Vaugelas as to the cause of such doubtful usage. For example, pronunciation, which precedes writing, is not always indicative of spelling. There is also the question of rarity of usage in a particular case, such that there might not be a sufficient number of examples to go on. In some other cases one may read or hear something written or said in different ways.

At one time there may simply be exceptions to general rules of usage. At another time the careless pronunciation of certain constructions may make it difficult to know how to write them. In all such instances the commentator must settle the issue.

Vaugelas proceeds to explain how commentators go about resolving these issues:

> Certainement ils ne s'en sçauroient esclaircir, que par le moyen de *l'Analogie,* que toutes les langues ont tousjours appellée à leur secours au defaut de l'Usage. Cette *Analogie* n'est autre chose en matiere de langues, qu'un Usage general & estably que l'on veut appliquer en cas pareil à certains mots, ou à certaines phrases, ou à certaines constructions, qui n'ont point encore leur usage declaré, & par ce moyen on juge quel doit estre ou quel est l'usage particulier, par la raison & par l'exemple de l'Usage general; ou bien *l'Analogie* n'est autre chose qu'un usage particulier, qu'en cas pareil on infere d'un Usage general qui est desja estably; ou bien encore, c'est une conformité qui se trouve aux choses desja establies, sur laquelle on se fonde comme sur un patron, & sur un modelle pour en faire d'autres toutes semblables. (n.p.)

> (Certainly they would not be able to clarify them except by means of *Analogy,* which all languages have always called to their aid for want of Usage. This *Analogy* is nothing more in the matter of languages, than a general and established Usage that is applied in similar cases to certain words, or to certain sentences, or to certain constructions, which do not yet have their usage declared, and by this means it can be judged what should be or what is the particular usage, by reason and by the example of general Usage; or otherwise stated *Analogy* is nothing more than a particular usage, which in a similar case is inferred from an already established general Usage; or said still another way it is a conformity already established between certain things, used as a pattern and as a model for establishing others just like it.)

If Vaugelas implicates reasoned analysis and reflection in his resolution of linguistic difficulties, it is clearly in a very different spirit from Cartesian reason, despite the utilization of Cartesian terms noted earlier. At the core of Vaugelas' hinted-at reason is the principle of analogy. Analogy is a concept based on relationships of resemblance between different things subjected to comparison and found to have common traits or characteristics. In other words, it suggests—just as in the case of the simple, declared, good usage—an element of conformity and correspondence, which in turn evokes, paradoxically, the very concept of authority and tradition that appeared to be lacking in cases of doubtful usage in the first place. After all, in putting analogy into context, Vaugelas highlights that analogy is a principle "which all languages have always called to their aid."

So the act itself of resorting to analogy is in its very essence based on tradition and the authority of commentators past, and as such it reinforces Vaugelas' definition of analogy as a type of "general usage." In other words, it is a manner of speaking and writing that is habitually or normally observed by the members of the court and literary communities in the majority of other specific cases that despite their specificity nevertheless have elements of similarity to the doubtful case. This usage becomes, in effect, a "universal usage," based on the idea that conformity trumps doubt. An assumption is made that there is, in fact, always a wider usage in place, fixed and well established, that can be utilized when there is no specific usage governing the particular case. The particular is defined and resolved by the general, which serves as a default framework, a template, to which all uncertain cases must conform.[18]

Ultimately particular usage is best, while the universal usage of analogy is second best. Method must never take precedence over tradition; and when method is employed, the method itself must be a variation on the theme of tradition and authority, not a method of reason. In fact, Vaugelas explicitly states that one must not criticize forms of usage that are contrary to reason, "car la raison n'y est point du tout considerée, il n'y a que l'Usage & l'Analogie" (since reason is not at all considered in them, there being only Usage and Analogy, n.p.). So in the end, although Vaugelas talks of "analysis and reflection," there really is no application of reason at all, at least not in the sense of breaking away from authority as Descartes, for example, would have employed the term. Vaugelas presents instead a bizarre transformation of analysis and reflection, an analysis and a reflection that are not analysis and reflection at all. First, tradition is an authority more important than method. Second, when there is no traditional authority to rely on, one must be methodical to get at the "truth" of things. Third, though, the method itself is nothing more than systematic reversion to another broader, more general form of the authority of tradition.

The point of this discussion is not to criticize or denigrate Vaugelas. After all, on what else would one base the resolution of doubtful cases of usage? In spite of its lack of Cartesian reason, Vaugelas' method is in its own way the most logical approach to resolving issues of usage. What is rather important in highlighting the lack of a specifically Cartesian reason in Vaugelas' thinking is the set of ideological underpinnings holding up the principle of analogy and their correspondence to other aspects of Vaugelas' thinking involving hierarchy, superiority, and conformity with the sociolinguistic status quo as established and fixed by authority. It is this important ideological point that leads Vaugelas to argue against the employment of reason in the determination of usage.

For example, Vaugelas points out that things which are contrary to reason "non seulement ne laissent pas d'estre aussi bonnes que celles où la raison se rencontre, que mesmes soüvent elles sont plus elegantes & meilleures que celles qui sont dans la raison, & dans la reigle ordinaire, jusques-là qu'elles font une partie de l'ornement & de la beauté du langage" (not only turn out to be as good as those where reason is found, but oftentimes are even more elegant and better than those which follow reason and ordinary rules, to such an extent that they form a part of the ornamentation and beauty of the language, n.p.). Vaugelas equates quality of usage not with reason or with clarity but rather with aesthetics.[19] He finds aesthetically oriented language superior to rationally oriented language. Grace and harmony of form and disposition provide language with a delicacy and distinction not possessed by rational discourse. The decorative embellishment of discourse raises language above the lowly level of the purely functional where reason resides. Figures of style and tropes, however divorced from reason they might be, provide a value added to language that it would not have otherwise.

Here again the question of quality enters the equation, as Vaugelas separates this value-charged means of expression as being not only above purely rational and pragmatic expression but also above common usage, the lower rules of speaking of average people, that can be equated with the rational to the extent that such expression is again limited to the purely practical. To Descartes' statement that reason is the most shared attribute among men, one can easily imagine Vaugelas responding that indeed this is why their speech is common, and it is the aesthetic concerns of the courtly and literary class that set their discourse apart.

The distinction between rational principles and good usage leads Vaugelas to enunciate another of his famous pronouncements that "l'Usage fait beaucoup de choses *par raison,* beaucoup *sans raison,* & beaucoup *contre raison*" (Usage does many things *by reason,* many *without reason,* and many *against reason,* n.p.). Three different prepositions define simultaneously the relationship between language and logic. Each comes into play depending on the specific point of usage in question. At times reason corresponds to the choices made by usage. At other times reason is simply absent, and at still others reason pulls against usage. The combination of these three aspects of usage and reason suggests that there is not an opposition of reason and usage in Vaugelas' mind, but rather a complete and total dissociation—in other words, reason may or may not coincide with usage, but whether it does so or not, the presence, absence, or resistance of reason is purely coincidental and means absolutely nothing. It does not alter what usage is, nor does it in any way add to or detract from the authority of good usage.

The total dissociation of reason from language is the main ideological difference between the Cartesian grammar approach of, for example, the thinkers of Port-Royal and the usage-based approach of Vaugelas.[20] For the former, as noted previously, reason is the model on which all language is based, and Logos—as the natural order of the world, the natural order of thought, and the natural order of language—is the glue that holds the language triangle of reality, mind, and speech together. Order is of paramount importance, and some, such as the editor of d'Aisy's *Génie de la langue française* (1685), would point out that despite their merits authors such as Vaugelas, Bouhours, and Ménage neglect the concept of order to a fault:

> ce qui fait de la peine à ceux qui étudient la pureté & la netteté de nôtre Langue, c'est que ces Auteurs n'ont observé aucun ordre dans leurs Remarques ou Observations. . . . Dans cette veuë, l'Auteur de ce nouveau Livre [d'Aisy] a crû qu'il obligeroit le public, s'il formoit un dessein dont la methode pût rendre l'étude des Remarques plus facile, & mettre en leur jour plusieurs Decisions qui paroissent obscures, parcequ'elles sont separées les unes des autres, quoyqu'elles ayent un rapport & une dependance naturelle. . . . L'Auteur de ce livre a tâché de prendre le sens de ces Maîtres de nôtre Langue, & de l'expliquer, quelquefois dans les mêmes termes, quelquefois d'une maniere qui le rend plus intelligible. Il pouvoit y ajoûter quelques Reflexions; mais. . . . Il s'est contenté de donner un Abregé de la Grammaire Françoise, qui sert de fondement aux Remarques, & qui estoit necessaire pour les bien entendre. Cet Abregé est dans un ordre trés-methodique. (n.p.)

> that which causes difficulty for those who study the purity and the clarity of our Language, is that these Authors have not observed any order in their Remarks or Observations. . . . Given this, the Author of this new Book [d'Aisy] believed he would well serve the public, if he formed a plan whose method would render the study of his Remarks easier, and bring to light several Decisions which seem obscure, because they are separated from each other even though they are related and naturally interdependent. . . . The Author of this book attempted to take the sense of these Masters of our Language, and to explain it, sometimes in the same terms, sometimes in a manner which renders it more intelligible. He could have added some Reflections; but. . . . He satisfied himself with giving an overview of French Grammar, which serves as a foundation for these Remarks, and which was necessary to understand them well. This overview is in a very methodical order.)

It is striking that d'Aisy, given a choice, would have Vaugelas' and the others' "Remarks" on language presented in a more methodical way, since for him there *is* an underlying reason (the question of "dépendance naturelle") between them, reflecting a fusion between the opposing usage and reason positions. In addition, as a necessary antecedent to understanding the remarks themselves, an orderly, methodical, rational grammar is needed, as this is the foundation of all the remarks on usage.

Vaugelas, however, was not to acknowledge the underlying strength or necessity of reason and the natural order as determining good usage. Instead the dissociation he establishes between reason and usage allows a distinctly different relationship to exist between good usage and the aesthetic qualities of language. Vaugelas places these aesthetic qualities far above reason as a principle of discourse: "Il est indubitable que chaque langue a ses phrases, & que l'essence, la richesse, & la beauté de toutes les langues, & de l'elocution, consiste principalement à se servir de ces phrases-là" (There is no doubt that each language has its expressions, and that the essence, the richness, and the beauty of all languages, and of elocution, consist principally in using these expressions, n.p.). A language is defined by its "phrases," a term that suggests both the usage-based rules for grammatically structuring expression into semiotically coherent units as well as fixed figures or specific manners of rhetorical and poetic expression. These two elements combined, unique to each language, essentially constitute—to return to du Bellay's term—the genius of any given language, a genius that contributes infinitely more to an appreciation of the subtleties of usage than any conceived universal rational order could.

As a language's essence, this genius makes the language what it is and constitutes the language's ideal nature. This ideal nature of any given language is associated by Vaugelas with the complexity, abundance, and variety of already existing expressions—for Vaugelas is not overly fond of neologisms—allowing for a vast array of nuances of signification. On the one hand, this genius manifests itself in a simply communicative fashion, and on the other hand, it presents itself in the capacity of a language to appeal to the senses and the emotions, thereby evoking an aesthetic reaction beyond the mere communicative capacity of its words. Herein lies a paradox, in that where previously we saw that, for Vaugelas, aesthetics determines good usage, we see in this excerpt that at the same time good usage determines aesthetics. All beauty in a language derives from the proper use of existing, declared means of expression.

For Vaugelas, deviation of any sort from declared usage will never produce an aesthetically pleasing effect. You are permitted, he argues, to invent new phrasing but only if there is no existing expression already in usage. Those writers and speakers who neglect or intentionally disobey this precept "pensent enrichir nostre langue d'une nouvelle phrase; mais au lieu de l'enrichir, ils la corrompent" (think to enrich our language with a new expression; but instead of enriching it, they corrupt it, n.p.). In effect Vaugelas equates neologism with corruption and equates established "authorized" language with purity. The rules for grammatical structure and fixed rhetorical and poetic expression are not to be tinkered with. Doing so changes the natural state of the language and renders up bad usage. Innovative composition for Vaugelas is really a *de*composition, a rotting away of the language, a sickness, that weakens the language and reduces its value both in terms of precision of expression and in terms of its beauty. The only form of "enrichment" of the language permissible is the filling in of gaps where no set manner of expression is already in use. For Vaugelas, the enrichment of language should mean the fixing and completion of the language, not the evolution of the language into something else.

Here Vaugelas' idea of enrichment, equated with stabilizing the language rather than causing it to evolve, appears self-contradictory. Or perhaps Vaugelas simply unwittingly acknowledges the impossibility or futility of the task of completing and fixing the language. Indeed the ambitious but never accomplished projects of the Académie française are concrete examples of this potential impossibility and futility with which Vaugelas was intimately acquainted. The dictionary of the academy was ultimately published, but it was quite some time in coming, and the other three books never saw the light of day. Or perhaps Vaugelas was simply acknowledging the historical reality of the French language and of all languages in general, for he admits that languages do change and that one day even his own *Remarques* will no longer be valid. French will have changed to the point that his rules will no longer apply. The awareness that such change occurs appears at least as early as the *Essais* of Montaigne, who had observed that the French language would not be the same even fifty years after the writing of his book (1100–1101). Even in Vaugelas' own era Ménage, like Montaigne had done, would highlight in his "Parnasse alarmée" (1649) the futility of trying to concretize the language in its present state:

> O! nos chers Maistres du langage
> Vous sçavez qu'on ne fixe point
> Les langues en un mesme point:
> Tel mot qui fut hier à la mode,
> qui ce jourd'huy n'est pas commode,
> Et tel qui fut hier descrié,
> Passe aujourd'huy pour mot trié
> ... Laissez vostre Vocabulaire
> Abandonnez vostre Grammaire,
> N'innovez ny ne faites rien,
> En la langue, & vous ferez bien. (14–16)
>
> (Oh! our dear Masters of the language
> You know that one cannot freeze
> Languages in a particular moment:
> Such a word as was yesterday in style,
> Is today no longer in fashion

>And such as yesterday was condemned,
>Passes today for refined
>. . . Leave your Vocabulary
>Abandon your Grammar,
>Do not innovate or do anything
>With the language, and you will do well.)

In effect for Ménage as well, language change is inevitable. Since the fixing of language is futile, and since he holds it to be neither good nor bad, he proposes a laissez-faire economy of language.

Vaugelas, however, is unwilling to acknowledge the neutral nature of this language change. It is, for him, fortunate that such alteration occurs so slowly as to be imperceptible. He states, in what might strike the reader as an exceedingly odd statement, that the imperceptible nature of this change is crucial, in that "si l'on avoit esgard à ce changement . . . il n'y auroit point de Nation qui eust le courage d'escrire en sa langue, ny de la cultiver" (if we took into account this change . . . there would be no Nation with the courage to write in its language, or to cultivate it, n.p.). For Vaugelas, the transformation or modification of language is a linguistic horror that would strike fear into the stoutest of souls. No author would have the will to go on writing in his vernacular if he realized that what he writes is doomed to be eventually lost and forgotten in some future era when his language would no longer be understandable to the readership. Vaugelas appears to suggest that the vernacular writer is doomed to literary death, that glorious literary immortality is a myth. Ironically only the dead languages, presumably unwavering, could possibly provide a mechanism for literary permanence.

Additionally, and again ironically, Vaugelas hints that authors are at fault for the fluctuations in the French language, for their task when writing, much as du Bellay had suggested, is to cultivate their language. However, the notion of cultivation can be read in two distinctly different manners. In the first place, cultivation indicates the maintenance and exploitation of a language, as it currently exists, toward utilitarian or aesthetic ends—this would correspond to what Vaugelas has outlined as the primary role of authors in the promotion of good usage. In the second place, the concept of cultivation more often implies the principle of growth, the propagation of new branches, new flowers, new fruit—to use du Bellay's imagery—which takes the language in question toward a superior state, toward a development of its qualities and the elimination of its weaknesses.

These two differing perspectives on cultivation lead to a tension in the role of the author in Vaugelas' preface. The author is charged with two contradicting and mutually incompatible offices. He is tasked, in the ideal, with ratifying, fixing, and solidifying usage, but at the same time the author is inevitably the agent of linguistic change *because* of his very role in providing a carved-in-stone model.

When speaking individuals deviate from good usage, their deviations do not crystallize so easily since their divergences are not transmitted and diffused to a wide public. When authors make such deviations, the same cannot be said, as their alterations of the language are transmitted to the entire literate segment of society. The deviation, as imperfect as it may be in Vaugelas' eyes, is set permanently in print, right alongside the examples of good usage, and then is inevitably taken up by society as a whole, first and foremost by that selfsame "plus saine partie de la cour" who is supposed to be in the role of setting down the rules. In effect, as authors influence the court, what occurs is a corruption of social order, which results in a corruption of the language by way of a literature-driven evolution.

Strangely enough the idea of such a corruption leads to a final tension seated in the binary relationship between change and stability. Vaugelas closes his preface by addressing the long, arduous process by which the French language had to evolve in order to reach its present state of perfection. In a preface such as his own, Vaugelas states, an eloquent man could have talked about many things that he opted not to discuss himself:

> descendant du general au particulier de nostre langue, ne l'eust-il pas consideré en tous les estats differens où elle a esté? N'eust-il pas dit depuis quel temps elle a commencé à sortir comme d'un Caos, & à se deffaire de la barbarie, qui l'a tenuë durant tant de siecles dans les tenebres . . . ? N'eust-il pas représenté nostre langue comme en son berceau, ne faisant encore que begayer, & en suite son progrés, & comme ses divers âges, jusqu'à ce qu'en fin elle est parvenue à ce comble de perfection, où nous la voyons aujourd'hui? Il eust bien osé la faire entrer en comparaison avec les plus parfaites langues du monde, & luy faire pretendre plusieurs avantages sur les vulgaires les plus estimées. Il luy eust osté l'ignominie de la pauvreté, qu'on luy reproche, & parmy tant de moyens qu'il eust eu de faire paroistre ses richesses, il eust employé les Traductions des plus belles pieces de l'Antiquité, où nos François égalent souvent leurs Autheurs, & quelquefois les surpassent. Les Florus, les Tacites, les Cicerons mesme, & tant d'autres sont contraints de l'avoüer, & le grand Tertullien s'estonne, que par les charmes de nostre eloquence on ayt sceu transformer ses rochers & ses espines en des jardins delicieux. Il ne faut donc plus accuser nostre langue, mais nostre genie ou nostre paresse, & nostre peu de courage, si nous ne faisons rien de semblable à ces chef-d'œuvres. . . . il n'y a jamais eu de langue, où l'on ait escrit plus purement & plus nettement qu'en la nostre. (n.p.)

> (descending from the general to the particular in our language, would he not have considered it in all the different states through which it has passed? Would he not have told of the time it began to emerge as from a Chaos, and

of how it shook off its barbarity, which held it for so many centuries in the shadows . . . ? Would he not have represented our language as it was in its cradle, still only stammering, and then as it progressed and through its diverse ages, until in the end it came to the summit of perfection where we see it today? He would have dared to compare it to the most perfect languages in the world, and even attributed to it several advantages over the most esteemed vernaculars. He would have removed the ignominy of the poverty for which it has been reproached, and among all the means that he would have had to display its riches, he would have employed Translations of the most beautiful works of Antiquity, whose original authors are often equaled by our Frenchmen and sometimes even surpassed by them. A Florus, a Tacitus, a Cicero even, and so many others would be forced to admit it, and the great Tertullian would be dazzled, that by the charms of our eloquence we have been able to transform his rocks and thorns into delightful gardens. No one must any longer accuse our language, but our genius or our laziness, or our insufficient courage, if we create nothing to equal these masterpieces . . . there has never been a language in which anyone wrote more purely and more precisely than in our own.)

Vaugelas states that he did not speak in detail about all of these things because they would have required a volume rather than a preface, and being a task beyond his force, this should be undertaken by someone else. Yet even this outline of items that he opts not to discuss illuminates certain key points and suppositions inherent to Vaugelas' view of language and of language change. For example, he underlines the reality and, strangely enough, the importance of linguistic change by his briefest of sketches of the evolution of French. Vaugelas underscores the different states through which French has passed and points out the progress the language has made. Not merely transformation for transformation's sake, the movement of the French tongue has been forward, a movement of growth and advancement toward an ideal end.

The importance of this evolution is evident in the brief indicators he gives of the qualities of different stages in that transformation. Vaugelas presents us with a nearly biblical "in the beginning," speaking of a language that came out of the chaos, an immense nothingness, an infinite darkness preceding creation, a vast emptiness and shadow into which light and being of language enter only with divine intervention—an intervention that will ultimately lead to the French language being divine.

However, if French would one day reach that point, it is nevertheless the case for Vaugelas that in its earliest stages the French language was barbaric. It was primitive, uncivilized, and uncultured. It was a language of ignorance that lacked coherence, order, and refinement and therefore was an inferior tongue. It moved into infancy and grew stronger, still stammering but nevertheless communicating articulately, aging, growing up, improving from its modest beginnings to the present, in which it has achieved maturity.

For Vaugelas, this maturity represents the summit of linguistic plenitude both in quantitative and qualitative terms, a state in which French has arrived at the highest levels of values in all areas, such as structure, expression, sonority, and harmony. Taking as a basis for comparison the languages of the ancients, regarded traditionally as the models of linguistic perfection, Vaugelas finds French in no way lacking and indeed considers it often surpassing its forebears, in addition to surpassing its contemporaries. For Vaugelas, this budding superiority of the French tongue is due to its purity and clarity. No language for him has ever been freer from corruption, contamination, and degradation, so whole and uniform. No idiom has ever been more precise and distinct in its manner of expression, more exempt from incertitude, confusion, and ambiguity.

These two elements of progress and maturity are the foundation of what essentially constitutes, in the final pages of Vaugelas' preface, his own version of a defense and illustration of the French language. Concerning defense of the language we see expressions such as "osté *l'ignominie* de la *pauvreté*, qu'on luy *reproche*," or the fact that one should not "*accuser* nostre langue." In illustration we see the insistence on making evident "ses *richesses*" and even, in translation of the ancients, the idea that the French language has achieved such a level of greatness that these conversions of Roman and Greek texts into French are an improvement on the originals.

In fact, this one-sentence illustration of the French language closes on a return to an image of the garden borrowed from du Bellay. Du Bellay's "ronces et épines" (25) are here echoed in Vaugelas' "rochers et épines," which are associated with a transformation of a different sort from that indicated by du Bellay. Where du Bellay's "ronces et épines" were a starting point for a change in the French tongue, an escape from its own barbarity, Vaugelas' "rochers et épines" represent the impact of the French tongue on other cultures, taking the *other* civilization out of *its* relative barbarity and bringing its artifacts into the light of an eloquence that can be provided only by French. This revised image of linguistic and cultural transformation leads to another vision of Eden: the image of "jardins délicieux," again both similar to and different from the one present in du Bellay's garden metaphor. Du Bellay's Eden was a promise for the future. Vaugelas' is, for him, a reality of his present. It is the manifestation of the utility and beauty of his language as it is.

As for the future of that Eden, this too falls on the shoulders of writers of quality. If the French do not excel in literature now, it is not the fault of their language but rather of their literary aptitude, their mental and creative faculties, their willingness (or unwillingness) to labor and craft works of literature in their own tongue, their strength of will and heart in producing such works in the face of the razor-edged path of the author, the tightrope on which linguistic creation and maintenance must balance one another above the chasm of linguistic corruption. Herein lies the trick that the author is obliged to execute: to harness the creative energy behind the evolution of the language and now employ that same energy to instead fix and concretize it.

For Vaugelas, the usage of society's elite is the foundation of linguistic correctness and purity. There is inherently good usage, inherently bad usage, and doubtful usage—which is, by default, bad but which can ultimately be determined and made good. Vaugelas' sociopolitical analogy is the mechanism by which usage is determined. The court makes laws of usage, authors take on the parliamentarian role of approving and inscribing the laws, and the commentators act as judges in cases of doubtful usage where discrepancies exist between the usage of the court and that of the authors. In processing such cases of doubtful usage, the tool to be employed by the commentators is analogy, a broader, general, universal usage. Reason is not employed as it is, for Vaugelas, completely unconnected with usage. Aesthetics are the real driving force behind good usage. Aesthetic sense is what distinguishes quality of expression from mere efficacy and distinguishes good usage from bad.

Vaugelas' text was intended as a guide for provincials and others not familiar to the court to learn the language of the court and thus avoid embarrassment by "fitting in." Good usage in language therefore is not just a "linguistic" concept as such; it is an identity issue. You are how you speak, and your identity, as an individual or as a member of a community or social subgroup, is equated with your manner of expression. Language "communicates" identity—both in terms of indicating who you are and in terms of forming who you are. The identity of others may rub off on you—be communicated to you—through linguistic transmission. Linguistic quality can be, to some degree at least, acquired.

Aesthetics are the driving force not just behind good usage but also behind the general genius of a language. This connection, in turn, associates good usage with the broader identity of the nation. Languages begin in a primitive, "barbaric" state but gradually grow out of it. The authorial class has the responsibility of cultivating the language. Enrichment of the language becomes the purview of the authors. This process of enrichment enables language to rise from the depths of barbarity to the heights of perfection. However, at some point in time the brakes must be put on, for once the state of perfection has been reached, any further transformation becomes a form of corruption. In the state of perfection the enrichment of the language changes focus. Enrichment then consists of completing and fixing language in its perfected state, to the extent that this is possible, rather than attempting to accelerate its transformation.

These lines of thinking in Vaugelas' *Remarques* reveal a number of philosophical tensions that are difficult to resolve. There are evident stresses between higher and lower, past and present, certainty and doubt, stability and progress, creation and preservation, and aesthetics and reason. If the higher quality of usage is related to a higher-quality person and the lower quality of usage is connected with the common vulgar classes of society, both determined by the innate quality of bloodlines, then how is it possible to acquire better usage? More importantly, how is it possible for good usage to evolve? When the general usage of analogy is the only tool for addressing questions of doubtful usage, how can there be any certainty at all, since every case of usage is based on precedent? If the language of the past was inferior to that of the present, then it would seem impossible for a useful precedent to exist. If creativity is the mechanism by which past progress has been made in the language, if it has been the perfecting agent of the language, then how can creative originality be the corrupting agent of today's language? What makes it possible for the same force that brings about transformation to also bring about concretization? How can aesthetics be divorced from reason? If a language's artifacts are beautiful, must this not be due to a harmony between aesthetics and reason? Would not a total dissociation of the aesthetic from the rational create expression that does not mean anything?[21]

Above all, despite the primary role explicitly assigned by Vaugelas to the courtly class for creating usage and the judgmental role assigned to the commentators for resolving the tensions of doubtful usage, it appears that the group that suffers from these tensions most is the nation's authors. They are the ones who in all instances must walk the fine line between these oppositional elements, as they are the ones who diffuse aesthetics; who communicate usage on a large scale; who operate specifically in the field of aesthetics, creativity, and originality; who are responsible both for the past progress and the present need for stability of the language.

Again what is important here is that for Vaugelas, none of this seemed illogical, contradictory, or oppositional, which tells us something of the underlying assumptions of the era. Vaugelas presents us with a perfect example of the Sainte-Beuvian view of the classical—the vision of the writer as being perfectly happy and in total accord with the milieu (the era, the state, the society) in which he was born (Sainte-Beuve, 15:369). However, the self-satisfaction derived from having acquired a certain level of social taste and refinement, and the natural desire to maintain that contentment, harmony, and satisfaction, lasts only as long as the social and economic conditions creating that milieu continue to exist. The changing environment of seventeenth-century France, from prosperity to poverty, from pleasure to austerity, from relative freedom to relative oppression, inevitably brings such wide-eyed optimism to an end and reopens the floodgates of critical thinking. The tensions arising from several of the elements in Vaugelas' text—the innate and the acquired, the question of preservation, the dissociation of reason from aesthetics—would be seen from a very different perspective in the century that followed. Others would be maintained and adapted—usage based on traditional authoritative analogy will become usage based on rational analogy, perfection will become perfectibility, and the superiority of one part of French society to other subgroups of French society would transform into the general superiority of the French nation to other nations as a whole.

Five

Condillac's *Essai*
Language, Analytical Method, and Identity

Étienne Bonnot, abbé de Condillac (1714–80), was a sensualist and a theoretician of language. He was a rarity among the thinkers of the French Enlightenment in that he was less a philosophe, in the eighteenth-century French understanding of the term—a freethinker and an agent and advocate of social change—and more a traditional philosopher. This is not to say that he was divorced from the movement of *les lumières*. He was a personal acquaintance of many of the philosophes, and most, if not all, of them had read at least some of his works. For example, in the early days of their careers he, Diderot, and Rousseau had regular weekly dinners together at the Panier Fleuri, where the three of them discussed the main philosophical topics of the day. It was, in fact, Diderot who convinced the bookseller Durand to print Condillac's first book, *Essai sur l'origine des connaissances humaines,* in 1746. Some years later Rousseau, in his *Discours sur l'origine de l'inégalité* (1755), explicitly credited Condillac with providing the basis for many of his own ideas on thought and language. Even Voltaire was no stranger to the abbé. When some of Condillac's sensualist theories began in some quarters to generate accusations of materialism and heresy, Voltaire invited Condillac to stay with him at les Délices and to write a revised, consolidated edition of his existing works. Condillac turned down the invitation, undoubtedly thinking that an association with Voltaire was not what he needed while being accused of impiety.[1]

In any event the accusations could not have been terribly serious or well founded, for nothing ever came of them. Even though Condillac did leave the country, it was only to take an establishment-oriented job, serving as tutor to Louis XV's grandson, the Prince of Parma. This was hardly a position to be awarded to someone subverting the authority of church and state. Such subversion was never Condillac's intention, and this is what makes him a philosopher rather than a philosophe, despite the fact that many of his ideas ultimately lent themselves well to subversive uses by the philosophes. All that interested Condillac was an honest intellectual inquiry into the truth of the human mind and how it works, without regard for parties, politics, and cabals.

Condillac's inquiry into human cognition is composed of two primary components: Lockean sensualism and the role of language in human thought. Many modern sources emphasize only the sensualist aspect of Condillac's philosophy and his support of Lockean cognitive theories founded on sensory perception. These sources often cite Condillac's *Traité des sensations* (1754) as his most representative work. This, however, is misleading and unfortunate. The *Traité des sensations*, while certainly of historical and philosophical value, is arguably not the most interesting and original of Condillac's works.[2] The vision of Condillac's contribution to philosophy consisting only of a rehash of Lockean ideas probably has its roots in Thomas Nugent's subtitle to his 1756 English translation of Condillac's *Essai*, which qualifies the French abbé's work as being merely "A Supplement to Mr. Locke's Essay on the Human Understanding."[3] Ever since then much of the English-speaking world has seen Condillac as primarily concerned with developing Lockean philosophy and as having little independent merit.

However, this all-too-common assessment is unfounded. Although sensualism plays an extremely important part in Condillacian philosophy (and will be discussed in this chapter), it is nonetheless in the second component of Condillac's cognitive philosophy—his theories of language—that he truly shines. While not particularly original in the realm of sensualist philosophy, Condillac is the single most significant eighteenth-century theoretician of language—undisputedly so in France and quite possibly in all of Europe. Even if Condillac adopts a Lockean perspective as his cognitive foundation, he nevertheless breaks away dramatically from the English philosopher in his treatment of reason and language—a recurrent theme that occupies an essential role in nearly all of his works other than the *Traité des sensations*.[4] Ideas may come from the sensation, but true thought is created by language. Language is, for Condillac, the source of all conscious, analytical reasoning.[5]

In general terms these two points are fundamental to understanding Condillac. Condillac ultimately attempts to explain the human mind without resorting to any innate capacity. For this reason he borrows Locke's sensualism to combat Descartes' innate ideas. Locke, however, had simply divided thought into two basic faculties: perception and reason; and while Lockean perception destroys Cartesian innate ideas as an inborn *content* of the mind, Lockean reason still sits in the mind as an innate *faculty*. Condillac therefore emphasizes the role of language in creating human reason in order to remove even this last vestige of innatism, by demonstrating a natural origin of language parallel to that of perception as the natural origin for ideas.

In the more specific terms of the present study, Condillac's thinking is significant in that it dialogues with both Descartes and Vaugelas with respect to mind, language, and identity. Where Descartes implies a hierarchy of mind or reasoning of which language is but the reflection, Condillac's basic premise implies the possibility of a similar hierarchy of which language is the cause. Where Vaugelas suggests language as a marker in a hierarchy of group identities, Condillac's structuring of the language-mind relationship ultimately allows for a similar hierarchy of identity groups for which, again, language is the foundation.

Condillac's *Essai,* rather than later books, will be the focus of this chapter for two reasons. First, the *Essai* is, of all of Condillac's works, the best and most thorough treatment of his principles of language and mind. Therefore only occasional references are made to later texts whose qualifications or alterations of theories expressed in the *Essai* are relevant to the present study. The second reason for examining the *Essai* is that it makes the clearest and most direct connection between language, mind, and identity on individual, communal, and even specifically national levels. The goal here is to show that Condillac's thinking becomes a focal point that fuses together the majority of the preoccupations and concerns of the thinkers examined previously. In so doing, Condillac serves as a catalyst for lines of thinking on language and identity in the middle eighteenth century that will become the foundation on which Rivarol ultimately builds his arguments for the universality of the French language as the century and the early modern era draw to a close.

At the start of his *Essai,* Condillac states that his inquiry is a metaphysical one, and he proceeds to distinguish between two types of metaphysics. The first is a Cartesian metaphysics of the soul, while the second is a Lockean metaphysics of the mind (7–8). From there Condillac indicates:

> Notre premier objet, celui que nous ne devons jamais perdre de vue, c'est l'étude de l'esprit humain: non pour en découvrir la nature, mais pour en connoître les opérations; observer avec quel art elles se combinent, et comment nous devons les conduire, afin d'acquérir toute l'intelligence dont nous sommes capables. Il faut remonter à l'origine de nos idées, en développer la génération, les suivre jusqu'aux limites que la nature leur a prescrites; par-là, fixer l'étendue et les bornes de nos connoissances, et renouveller tout l'entendement humain. (9)

> (Our primary objective, of which we must never lose sight, is the study of the human mind; not to discover its nature, but to know its operations; to observe with what art they combine with one another, and how we should conduct them, in order to acquire all the intelligence of which we are capable. We have to go back to the origin of our ideas, develop their generation, follow them as far as the limits nature has prescribed for them; in so doing, to determine the extent and the boundaries of our knowledge, and to renew all of human understanding.)

Like Descartes, Condillac will explore the principles of human thought and reflection, human psychological and intellectual faculties, even questions relating to identity and self. However, Condillac breaks this exploration into an opposition of nature versus operation. Unlike Descartes, Condillac will not be interested in the mind as a hidden, immaterial source of intellectual activity, a supernatural essence that defines us in some abstract and mystical manner. Instead, Condillac intends only to address the activity of intellectual functions, the actions of the mind that we can perceive every time we think. In opposition to Cartesian existence as *being*, Condillac from the outset establishes existence as *doing*.

The abbé's initial enunciation of existence as doing is formulated as an enumeration of mental actions—the art of combining operations, of conducting them, of acquiring intelligence. His focus is on technique, the means and the manner of associating and assembling relationships between various mental functions, how the mind guides the execution of those functions, how our brains take possession of and organize thoughts and ideas to form a larger understanding of the world.

To this end he establishes a line of investigation based on the concept of an evolutionary process, making the supposition that thought has not always existed as it exists now and that it is a teleological phenomenon. His point of departure is the instant in which, for the individual or for the species, human thought occurs for the first time. From there he will proceed to lay out chronologically and in detail the production, formation, and gradual filiations in the development and organization of human ideas up to their current state. This in turn, he suggests, will be the beginning of a new step in the evolution of the mind, as a new faculty of understanding will be attainable and will potentially replace the epistemological field currently in place.

The evolution of mind from some primitive beginning is, in effect, the only remedy to what Condillac views as the defect of the doctrine of innate mental capacities in either the Cartesian or the Lockean sense. If there is a categorical difference between human and animal intellects and if there is no intellectual evolution, there can be no other explanation for mind beyond the concept of a divine gift, as many of Condillac's predecessors had suggested.[6] The evolutionary principle grows significantly in popularity in the eighteenth century, with philosophers such as La Mettrie applying it from a scientific perspective or Rousseau adopting it in sociopolitical discussions.[7] Condillac's approach, however, precedes these two and serves as a cognitive framework not only for them but also for Maupertuis, Turgot, and Maine de Biran, who engage in a more direct discussion with Condillac's text by focusing on the same theoretical cognitive field. While they do not agree with Condillac on all points, they do all adopt the fundamental assumption that man's mind was not always what it is now.

Cartesian principles could never have led to an evolutionary vision or to the theoretical possibility of a future revolution in human thinking, since Descartes bases his philosophy on reflection rather than on the empiricism promoted later by Locke. Empiricism makes all the difference for Condillac:

> Ce n'est que par la voie des observations que nous pouvons faire ces recherches avec succès; et nous ne devons aspirer qu'à découvrir une première expérience, que personne ne puisse révoquer en doute, et qui suffise pour expliquer toutes les autres. Elle doit montrer sensiblement quelle est la source de nos connoissances, quels en sont les matériaux, par quel principe ils sont mis en úuvre, quels instrumens on y emploie, et quelle est la manière dont il faut s'en servir. J'ai, ce me semble, trouvé la solution de tous ces problêmes dans la liaison des idées, soit avec les signes, soit entre elles. . . .
>
> On voit que mon dessein est de rappeller à un seul principe tout ce qui concerne l'entendement humain, et que ce principe ne sera ni une proposition vague, ni une maxime abstraite, ni une supposition gratuite; mais une expérience constante, dont toutes les conséquences seront confirmées par de nouvelles expériences.
>
> Les idées se lient avec les signes, et ce n'est que par ce moyen . . . qu'elles se lient entr'elles. (9)

(It is only by following the path of observation that we can perform this research with success; and we must aspire only to the discovery of a first experience, that no one can call into doubt, and which will be adequate to explain all others. It must show clearly the source of our knowledge, the materials of which that knowledge consists, by what principle they are brought into operation, which instruments are therein employed, and in what manner they must be used. I have, I believe, found the solution to all these problems in the connection of ideas [*la liaison des idées*], either with signs, or with each other. . . .

It can be seen that my purpose is to reduce to a single principle all that concerns human understanding, and this principle will be neither a vague proposition nor an abstract maxim, but a constant experiment, all of whose conclusions will be confirmed by new experiments.

Ideas connect themselves with signs, and it is by this means alone . . . that they connect with each other.)

On the one hand, the importance of Lockean methodology over Cartesian methodology is relentlessly hammered upon by Condillac, who stresses the need for an empirical approach to the mind, repeating in this brief passage the word "experiment/experience" as well as stressing the need for observation. On the other hand, his process still maintains Cartesian overtones. In response to a Cartesian first principle, Condillac seeks a "first experience." As for Descartes, this first element of Condillac's new philosophy must be an idea that defeats all possible occasions of doubt, and it must also be capable, like Descartes' first principle, of serving as the starting point for an entire philosophical system.

Here then, in its broadest lines, lies the problem that Condillac lays out for himself: to essentially "Lockify" Cartesian philosophy. To do this, again in keeping with Cartesian methodology, Condillac will break down the larger problem into several smaller, more manageable parcels, constituting the details of the teleological perspective he previously announced. These will include not only the origins of human thought but also several specific elements of their development and generation: the material elements that enter into the construction and composition of our ideas and mental faculties; the study of the intellectual equipment and tools we use to process those materials; the active causes that enable us to put those tools, materials, and techniques into motion; and the manners and methods by which we funnel those causes and techniques into the production of new, more complex ideas and epistemological systems.

To all of these problems the abbé offers a single, elegant solution, which will be the focus of his work—the *liaison des idées*. Every difficulty in understanding the human intellect can be resolved by understanding the manner in which we join and combine our ideas, the fashion in which we create continuity and cohesion between them in order to make sense of the world around us. In this concept the original element of Condillac's thinking appears. This fundamental principle of the human mind, the *liaison des idées,* occurs through the use of signs. These signs can be taken in the largest semiotic sense, as any material representation (figure, image, gesture, sound, graphism, and so on) that has a natural or conventional value beyond itself or that, in other words, has meaning. The abbé will treat numerous types of signs through the course of his *Essai*. However, the most prominent of all, the most commonly encountered, and the one most responsible for the progress of the human mind is the linguistic sign, and much of the *Essai* revolves around the function of the linguistic sign in the *liaison des idées*. In one way or another, though, all intellectual activity beyond the mere immediate perception of things around us is rooted in some form of signification. The abbé's insistence here that "les idées se lient avec les signes, et ce n'est que par ce moyen . . . qu'elles se lient entr'elles" echoes throughout his work.

Condillac explains that to achieve his objective he will explore not only the origins and development of thought as such but also the origins and development of signs of all types, and in particular those of language, as a necessary component to understanding the processes and evolution of the human mind. On the one hand, he examines the evolution of mental faculties, while "d'un autre côté, j'ai commencé au langage d'action. On verra comment il a produit tous les arts qui sont propres à exprimer nos pensées; l'art des gestes, la danse, la parole, la déclamation, l'art de la noter, celui des pantomimes, la musique, la poésie, l'éloquence, l'écriture et les différens caractères des langues" (on the other hand, I begin with the language of action. I show how it produced all the arts connected with our first thoughts; the art of gesture, dance, speech, declamation, the art of notation, that of pantomime, music, poetry, eloquence, writing, and the different characters of languages, 9).

For Condillac, just as for Locke, all human thought has its origin in sensation, in *per*ception as opposed to Cartesian *con*ception. From this first point Condillac outlines a progression of increasingly complex mental faculties that run as follows: perception, attention, reminiscence, imagination, contemplation, memory, reflection, distinction, abstraction, comparison, composition/decomposition, analysis, affirmation/negation, judgment, reasoning, conception, and finally the overall blanket combination of all of these faculties, understanding (20–47). The *liaison des idées* is, for Condillac, formed by the faculty of attention, and it engenders contemplation and memory (30). In other words, only three faculties of the mind —perception (the reception of a sensation), consciousness (the awareness of a stimulus acting on the senses), and attention (the drawing of our focus onto a particular stimulus, due to its greater impact on our senses than other stimuli)—do not require any form of signification to function. Everything else, the abbé claims, inherently involves some form of connection between multiple ideas and, being thus anchored in the *liaison des idées,* requires the use of some form of signification (though not necessarily language).

In response to any possible objection that the *liaison des idées* might resemble Locke's innate faculty of reason, Condillac explains where these connections come from:

> La liaison de plusieurs idées ne peut avoir d'autre cause que l'attention que nous leur avons donnée, quand elles se sont présentées ensemble: ainsi, les choses n'attirant notre attention que par le rapport qu'elles ont à notre tempérament, à nos passions, à notre état, ou, pour tout dire en un mot, à nos besoins; c'est une conséquence que la même attention embrasse, tout à la fois, les idées des besoins et celles des choses qui s'y rapportent, et qu'elle les lie. (31)

(The linking of several ideas can have no other cause than the attention which we have given to them, when they present themselves together: thus, things attract our attention only through the relationship they have to our temperament, our passions, our state, or in a word, to our needs; consequently this very operation of attention embraces, all at once, the ideas of needs and of the things to which they are related, and connects them.)

Derived from attention, a faculty that does not require the *liaison des idées* in order to operate, these initial ideas connect themselves through the mere fact of existing one beside the other in time and/or space. They also connect to one another through the naturally existing cause-and-effect relationships they have to our needs. They represent things of which the human body naturally feels (or perceives) a lack—food, water, and so on. These needs may be related to a variety of accidents of our existence. For example, they may relate to the particularities of individual body structure, the constitution of our organism, its "humors," or autonomous reactions of the neural system. They may be related to psychological and emotional states produced by the so-called "animal spirits" of the Cartesians, detached from all will or intentionality. Or these connections can be related to the specifics of our situation, the time and place in which we exist. In all cases what is common to all of these forms of need is that in no case is there any intellection, no act of reason, no voluntary connecting of one idea to another. Attention simply absorbs natural ties between ideas based on our needs (perceptions/feelings) and the things that cause and/or relieve them.

Condillac emphasizes the role of need in the creation of more and more elaborate *liaisons d'idées:*

> Tous nos besoins tiennent les uns aux autres; et l'on en pourroit considérer les perceptions comme une suite d'idées fondamentales, auxquelles on rapporteroit tout ce qui fait partie de nos connoissances. Au-dessus de chacune s'éleveroient d'autres suites d'idées qui formeroient des espèces de chaînes. ... À un besoin est liée l'idée de la chose qui est propre à le soulager; à cette idée est liée celle du lieu où cette chose se rencontre; à celle-ci, celle des personnes qu'on y a vues; à cette dernière, les idées des plaisirs ou des chagrins qu'on en a reçus, et plusieurs autres. On peut même remarquer qu'à mesure que la chaîne s'étend, elle se soudivise en différens chaînons; ensorte que, plus on s'éloigne du premier anneau, plus les chaînons s'y multiplient. Une première idée fondamentale est liée à deux ou trois autres; chacune de celles-ci à un égal nombre, ou même à un plus grand, et ainsi de suite.
>
> Les différentes chaînes ou chaînons, que je suppose au-dessus de chaque idée fondamentale, seroient liés par la suite des idées fondamentales, et par quelques anneaux qui seroient vraisemblablement communs à plusieurs; car les mêmes objets, et, par conséquent, les mêmes idées, se rapportent souvent à différens besoins. Ainsi, de toutes nos connoissances, il ne se formeroit qu'une seule et même chaîne, dont les chaînons se réuniroient à certains anneaux pour se séparer à d'autres. (31)

(All of our needs are connected to one another; and we could consider perceptions as a series of fundamental ideas, to which we could reduce all that is part of our knowledge. Above each one extends other series of ideas which would form chainlike structures ... connected to a need is the idea of the thing that will satisfy it; to this idea is connected that of the place the thing can be found; to this idea that of people we have seen there; to the latter, the ideas of the pleasures or chagrins they have caused us, and many other thoughts. We can even see that as the chain extends itself, it subdivides into different links; such that the more we distance ourselves from the first link, the more the links multiply. A first, fundamental idea is attached to two or three others; each of these to a similar or even greater number, and so on.

The different chains or links, which I suppose extending from each fundamental idea, would be connected by the sequence of fundamental ideas, and by certain rings that would be in fact common to several; for the same objects and, consequently, the same ideas, are often related to different needs. Thus, all our knowledge would be formed into one single chain, whose links would join up to certain rings only to separate themselves from others.)

To each of our needs and requirements for survival are attached several other ideas: the object that fulfills our needs; its geographic location; pains and pleasures associated with the need; the object; the place; and so forth. Each of these ideas is attached to other ideas, which are in turn attached to still others ad infinitum, forming a structure that Condillac qualifies with the metaphor of a chain. However, the chain in Condillac's metaphor is a special one in that it is not linear. The sequencing of links, which one would tend to think of as being organized in a linear fashion, takes on the structure of a sort of chain-link mesh. Instead of the links being connected one by one, they are separated into multiple strands. Each strand of links is attached to several other strands of chain as well.

Even the first link (the original need) is not unique. The primary rings, related to fundamental, basic ideas, are linked among each other as well as with various secondary strands or clusters of chain that have their origins in other fundamental ideas or other primary links. Thus all ideas are connected directly or indirectly to every other idea. Any idea can be traced to any other idea or group of ideas. The structure is multiple, reversible, and potentially infinite. This never-ending, multidimensional chain is the basis for all thought and, as will be seen, expression.

In essence every connection between two or more ideas of any sort constitutes, in and of itself, signification in the most simple and general sense. A sign, in its most basic form, is any thing that evokes another thing. In the case of Condillac's chains and strings of needs and the objects that cause and relieve them, one idea suggests another; thus each idea becomes a sign for something else. The feeling of hunger becomes a sign for a piece of fruit. The sensation of the sun's heat becomes the sign for a shaded pond with cooling waters. Causes and effects, needs and solutions are simply physical characteristics of the universe that, in a prelinguistic existence, form themselves on a visceral level, with no rational input from our minds. We are simply the passive receivers of these basic, natural signifiers and signifieds. They are nature's products, rather than our own.

These fundamental connections, however, are the source of all higher thinking that will come with more and more sophisticated systems of signification. Without these *liaisons d'idées*, without these basic signs, there can be no higher thought. Condillac indicates quite clearly that "l'usage des signes est la vraie cause des progrès de l'imagination, de la contemplation et de la mémoire" (the use of signs is the true cause of the progress of imagination, contemplation and memory, 33). The use of signs brings about the progress in lower- and middle-echelon mental faculties, which in turn brings about increased sophistication in signs. Ultimately such progress leads to the most sophisticated form of signs of all, linguistic signs. Only once these signs have evolved into actual language can the mind have anything resembling truly human reason.

Condillac presents a variety of examples of the necessity of linguistic signs for the formation of rational thought. To cite one instance, linguistic signs are essential in the creation of complex ideas. While we can, without language, imagine simple figures just by picturing them in our heads, such as a triangle or a square, this is not possible with more complex figures: "si je pense à une figure de mille côtés, et à une de neuf cent quatre-vingt-dix-neuf, ce n'est pas par des perceptions que je les distingue, ce n'est que par les noms que je leur ai donnés. Il en est de même de toutes les notions complexes. Chacun peut remarquer que, quand il en veut faire usage, il ne s'en retrace que les noms" (if I think of a thousand-sided figure, and of one with nine hundred ninety-nine sides, it is not through perception that I distinguish between them, it is only through the names I have given them. It is the same with all complex notions. Anyone can see that, when he wants to access such ideas, he only thinks of their names, 28). This activity is the faculty of abstraction, Condillac's ninth operation in his hierarchy of sixteen mental functions. While some form of natural sign is required for everything above attention, the linguistic sign becomes necessary to go anywhere above the halfway point of the abbé's list of intellectual activities.

To take a second case of the importance of linguistic signs, one level higher in Condillac's hierarchy of thought, the abbé argues that language is crucial for reasoning, beginning with the operation of comparison:

> Quand nous comparons nos idées, la conscience que nous en avons nous les fait connoître comme étant les mêmes par les endroits que nous les considérons, ce que nous manifestons en liant ces idées par le mot *est*, ce qui s'appelle *affirmer*: ou bien elle nous les fait connoître comme n'étant pas les mêmes, ce que nous manifestons en les séparant par ces mots, *n'est pas*, ce qui s'appelle

nier. Cette double opération est ce qu'on nomme *juger.* Il est évident qu'elle est une suite des autres.

De l'opération de juger, naît celle de raisonner. Le raisonnement n'est qu'un enchaînement de jugemens qui dépendent les uns des autres. (46)

(When we compare our ideas, the awareness that we have of them makes us see that they are similar from the perspective of our consideration, which we manifest by connecting these ideas with the word *is,* which is called *affirming:* or, it makes us see that they are not similar, which we manifest by separating them with the words, *is not,* which is called *negating.* This double operation is what is named *judging.* It is evident that this operation is derived from the other two.

From the operation of judging is born that of reasoning. Reasoning is nothing more than a chain of judgments that depend one upon the other.)

The act of comparison involves seeking out aspects of two simultaneously considered states or objects that are or are not held in common between those states or objects. However, the author of the *Essai* specifically qualifies the functioning of such judgment as a linguistic process. It requires the formulation of a statement indicating the truth or falseness of qualities belonging to a particular object or situation. Creating a relationship between the subject and possible attributes is done only through language—indeed it is a linguistic process because the tracing of a relationship between the two situations or objects (or associating the ideas of the two situations or objects) depends on their being linked through the use of a word: the verb "to be." The lack of language would obviously make such an attachment impossible. Indeed, as Auroux has stated, "l'affirmation réside dans la *prononciation* du verbe substantif. Autrement dit, il n'y a pas d'acte de l'esprit qui soit une affirmation, c'est un *acte de langage*" (affirmation resides in the *pronunciation* of the substantive verb. In other words, there is no act of the mind that can be called an affirmation, it is an *act of language,* "Condillac," 159).[8]

This point can reasonably be considered Condillac's largest divergence from the thinking of his predecessors. By basing reason entirely on language, he stands in contrast to Descartes, the writers of Port-Royal, and Locke, who all hold that language was merely the manifestation of rational thought. However, this latter view of language expressing thought did not simply die out just because Condillac chose to invert it. On the one hand, many philosophers who arrived in Condillac's wake still insisted on the more Cartesian view that thought comes first. Beattie holds to the idea that language expresses thought, as do Horne Tooke, Monboddo, and Court de Gébelin, who kept this perspective alive late into the century.[9] On the other hand, a substantial wave of writers including La

Mettrie, Rousseau, Maupertuis, Diderot, Turgot, Herder, and Condorcet would express the necessity of language for thought on some, if not all, levels.[10] Herder in particular goes to the extreme in adopting the Maupertuisian principle of words as cognitive distinguishing marks to suggest that the primary and original function of language is not communicative but rather cognitive (116).

While Condillac will not go quite that far—maintaining that language begins only through communication—he is the first thinker to truly popularize the notion of language as thought. In this sense his conception has more impact than Montaigne's view of thought as internal discourse. Additionally Condillac elaborates on the idea much more fully than Montaigne does. Taken together the two examples above of the dependence of thought on language enable the abbé to argue that language, through both its lexical and syntactic properties, is a necessary tool in the construction of upper-echelon intellection, both from the standpoint of the mere formation of complex ideas and from the perspective of the creation of linear—or analytical—thought. This combination allows Condillac to account for all of Cartesian, or for that matter Lockean, reason.

The next hurdle that Condillac has to jump is the question of where language originates, since, without explaining that, all he has succeeded in doing is transforming Locke's innate capacity for reason into an innate capacity for speech. The trick will be to explore the origins of language in order to demonstrate that language is not inborn.

In tackling the second question, of origin and progress, Condillac opens a whole new inquiry into language. Prior to the publication of Condillac's *Essai*, the most widely accepted line of thinking on language was that it was of divine origin—a doctrine maintained to a degree even in the eighteenth century in the works of such men as Beattie and Court de Gébelin.[11] The Bible is clear on such matters as God granting Adam the power to name all the animals and the diversification of human language at the tower of Babel. Beattie's discussion is fairly elaborate and is interesting in that it goes beyond merely accepting biblical accounts. He makes an actual argument for the divine origin of language on two fronts: first, if humans could have lived at all without language in their past, they would have had no impulse to invent it; and second, he simply finds the idea of animal language as the source of human language to be too degrading to accept (Beattie, 301–6). It must be admitted that while the first part of the argument is worth considering, the logic of the latter part is specious. Yet it is this type of thinking that inspired others—in reaction to the natural and animalistic origins proposed by Condillac—such as Monboddo or Herder, who were unwilling to accept either a supernatural account of language or the bestialization of mankind, instead to dignify humanity and its special place in the cosmos by insisting that language was an invention of human reason—a theory that presupposes the existence of reason prior to that of language.[12] Obviously either supposition—a supernatural origin or the necessity of a preexisting reason—would not suit Condillac's needs, and so he, like Rousseau and Maupertuis after him, assumes a natural language derived from animal communication.[13] Only in this way can it possibly make sense for language to serve as the non-innate framework for a non-innate reason.

Still, the abbé was not imprudent, and to avoid stepping on the toes of the church authorities, Condillac posits a postdiluvian landscape as the setting for his naturalistic theory. At some point after the great flood two children, who as yet do not know how to speak, wander off and get lost in the wilderness (99).[14] The operations of the children's minds, as long as they live separately, have very little scope. Each has perceptions, awareness, and attention. Each also has some small degree of reminiscence (involuntary memory) when the circumstances connected with some other feeling or object recur, acting as the simplest of natural signs to trigger recollection. Finally each child possesses enough imagination to "see" ideas triggered in this manner in his or her head. Without living together there can be no language and therefore no thought beyond these most primitive of functions. Certainly there is no abstraction or attribution, and thus no reason. However, everything changes once the two children encounter each other and begin living together:[15]

> Quand ils vécurent ensemble, ils eurent occasion de donner plus d'exercice à ces premières opérations; parce que leur commerce réciproque leur fit attacher aux cris de chaque passion les perceptions dont ils étoient les signes naturels. Ils les accompagnoient ordinairement de quelque mouvement, de quelque geste ou de quelque action, dont l'expression étoit encore plus sensible. Par exemple, celui qui souffroit, parce qu'il étoit privé d'un objet que ses besoins lui rendoient nécessaire, ne s'en tenoit pas à pousser des cris: il faisoit des efforts pour l'obtenir; il agitoit sa tête, ses bras et toutes les parties de son corps. L'autre, ému à ce spectacle, fixoit les yeux sur le même objet; et, sentant passer dans son ame des sentimens dont il n'étoit pas encore capable de se rendre raison, il souffroit de voir souffrir ce misérable. Dès ce moment, il se sent intéressé à le soulager; et il obéit à cette impression, autant qu'il est en son pouvoir. Ainsi, par le seul instinct, ces hommes se demandoient et se prêtoient des secours. Je dis *par le seul instinct,* car la réflexion n'y pouvoit encore avoir part. L'un ne disoit pas: *il faut m'agiter de telle manière, pour lui faire connoître ce qui m'est nécessaire et pour l'engager à me secourir;* ni l'autre: *je vois à ses mouvemens qu'il veut telle chose, je vais lui en donner la jouissance:* mais tous deux agissoient en conséquence du besoin qui les pressoit davantage. (100–101)

> (When they lived together, they had occasion to more readily exercise these first operations; because their reciprocal commerce made them attach to the

cries of each passion the perceptions of which they were the natural signs. They ordinarily accompanied the cries with some movement, some gesture or some action, whose expression was even more appreciable. For example, one who suffered, because he was deprived of an object required to satisfy his needs, did not limit himself to crying out: he made efforts to obtain it; he shook his head, his arms and all the parts of his body. The other, moved by this spectacle, fixed his eyes upon the same object; and, feeling in his soul sentiments for which he could not rationally account, he suffered to see the other poor devil suffer. From that moment, he felt an interest in relieving the other one; and he obeyed this feeling to the extent that it was in his power. Thus, by instinct alone, these men asked for and offered aid. I say *by instinct alone* since reflection could yet have had no part in it. The one did not say: *I must make such a motion, to make him see what I need and to encourage him to help me;* nor the other: *I see by his movements that he wants such and such a thing, I will help him obtain it:* rather, both acted as a consequence of need which pressed them ever more strongly.)

Human language begins with natural signs. To the natural connections previously mentioned regarding the *liaison des idées,* Condillac specifically adds and focuses on instinctive sounds emitted under the influence of emotions and sensations. However, these natural outcries connected with the instinctive reactions of the mind are not sufficient in and of themselves to form real language as such. They are the forceful, brutish cries of animals and are technically not, for Condillac and others of his era, part of actual human language.[16] While natural signs are the source of human speech, only with the development of what Condillac calls "accidental" signs (derived from the natural) does anything resembling true language begin to emerge.

The accidental sign is, for Condillac, anything that comes to represent another thing through circumstance or situation (34). In the case of the two children, various natural cries, just by chance or by the reflexive act of grasping for whatever object is needed, couple their vocal productions with some form of activity in one or more body parts. This concrete activity coinciding with the cry, the attempt to perform some act, to *do* something, renders the vocal cry all the more meaningful, increases and focuses its expressive value, and makes more manifest the feelings, needs, and states of *being* behind the act. So again doing underlines and defines being. This superior degree of signification occurs only through sensation: the expression only becomes "plus sensible," more apt to be perceived and understood (only as a perception) by the other, through what Condillac calls the *langage d'action,* which by definition is a language of doing.

The catalyst in this increase in significative value is the concept of sympathy. The "speaker" *moves,* while the "listener" *is moved* by the other's plight. The "listener" feels a sympathetic internal movement, like a sympathetic vibration, in response to the "speaker's" external movement. The needs and emotions of the other cause the "listener" to *sentir des sentiments* (to feel feelings)—an intentional redundancy that underscores the importance of sensation in this process (as opposed to reason) and the fact that feelings, in the emotional sense, are part and parcel of our physical sensations.[17] So the sympathetic pains of the "listener," who suffers to see the other suffer, work in tandem with his being moved by the other's movement. The physical and emotional coincide, such that a parallel suffering occurs.[18] The "listener" feels the same needs, pains and pleasures as the "speaker." In this way the accidental sign is formed on the same basis as the simplest *liaison des idées*. The most basic connections of ideas cause the "listener" to shift from "taking an interest" in the other to developing a "vested interest in" helping the other. The feeling of urgent need is "communicated" (both "expressed" and "transferred") from the "speaker" to the "listener." For the "listener," easing the distress of the "speaker" becomes an act of easing his own distress.[19]

Condillac emphasizes that reason is not a factor by insisting that the "listener" has no capacity to "rationally account for" what is going on in his primitive mind. He is not in control. Neither interlocutor makes any reflection, or as Condillac equivalently underlines, neither *says* "I must cry out and move this way" or "I see what he needs and must help." Reflection and saying are equivalent, after all, in Condillacian theory. Instead we see only natural activity in the wake of need, the logical (from our outside perspective only) follow-up to circumstance. In a word, it boils down to instinct, which Condillac defines in his own unique way. Instinct is simply that activity or those actions acquired through repeated, habitual circumstances and situations.[20]

This Condillacian form of instinct is the driving force behind the final step needed by the abbé to explain the creation of human language. The last element consists of demonstrating, in the *Essai,* how these natural signs, and the accidental signs of the *langage d'action,* become the institutional, or voluntary, signs of true language:[21]

> Cependant les mêmes circonstances ne purent se répéter souvent, qu'ils ne s'accoutumassent enfin à attacher aux cris des passions, et aux différentes actions du corps, des perceptions qui y étoient exprimées d'une manière si sensible. Plus ils se familiarisèrent avec ces signes, plus ils furent en état de se les rappeller à leur gré. Leur mémoire commença à avoir quelque exercice; ils purent disposer eux-mêmes de leur imagination, et ils parvinrent insensiblement à faire avec réflexion ce qu'ils n'avoient fait que par instinct. . . . L'usage de ces signes étendit peu à peu l'exercice des opérations de l'ame; et, à leur tour, celles-ci ayant plus d'exercice perfectionnèrent les signes, et en rendirent l'usage plus familier. (101)

(However, the same circumstances could not be often repeated, without them making a habit of attaching to the cries of each passion, and to the different actions of the body, the perceptions which were expressed thereby so markedly. The more they became familiar with these signs, the better they were able to recall them at will. Their memory began to get called into practice; they were able to control their imagination themselves, and they managed imperceptibly to do by reflection that which they had done only by instinct. . . . The use of these signs extended little by little the exercise of the mind's operations; and in turn, these operations, being more practiced, perfected the signs and made their use more familiar.)

Foreshadowing Pavlov and his dog, Condillac emphasizes, on a linguistic level, the reiteration and reproduction of secondary stimuli (signifiers) that accompany primary conditions or phenomena (signifieds). The habitual co-occurrence of these stimuli and phenomena provokes a proportional and concordant increase in the creation of accidental signs and in the ability to retain them in the mind, giving them an ever more permanent status, a degree of stability equivalent to that of the natural signs. Once the accidental signs of the *langage d'action* arrive at such a level of permanence, their use becomes just as "natural" to human beings as the use of natural signs.

This latter point, however, adds a twist to the character of these fully assimilated accidental signs. While being as "natural" to produce and understand as actual natural signs, they are nevertheless not truly natural. This means that to use them involves an act of will, a conscious choice on the part of the user. In effect Condillac simply adopts the Cartesian equivalence of reason and will. However, paradoxically, in the Condillacian scheme of the origins and evolution of language, willful choice in the use of signs is *accidentally imposed* upon the primitive mind.[22] Man does not choose to choose. He instead has choice thrust upon him by outside circumstance. A mind previously incapable of any act of free will now has the capacity to exercise its will because of the situational acquisition of a significative capacity not natural to it. This allows the primitive mind to arrange signs, and therefore ideas, in a free and arbitrary order and to be able to do so from then on, strangely enough, without being forced to through outside stimuli.[23]

This cognitive-linguistic progress is so gradual, so slow and occurring in such tiny and widely spaced increments, that it is imperceptible to those undergoing it. It takes, according to Condillac, many generations. However, he insists, little by little feeling and habit are replaced by reason and free will. Once the first institutional signs are formed, the capacity to produce more has been seeded in the brain. After this the gradual progress of language leads to the gradual progress of the mind, which in turn leads to more and more sophisticated signification, which then provokes additional progress of the intellect, and so on in a continual and mutual cycle of evolution in both language and intelligence.

Other writers who deal with the origins of language also tend to follow Condillac's lead and insist on the lengthy, slow, mutual cycle of evolution between language and intellect. Maupertuis, for example, emphasizes the mutual dependence on linguistic and intellectual development, though he allows for a more rapid pace than Condillac does.[24] Rousseau and Monboddo do the same and, like Condillac, allow for a ponderous cognitive-linguistic evolutionary process.[25]

Of particular interest, however, in Condillac's discussion of the language development time line is that in these early stages of linguistic and mental development we see also the slow beginnings of an additional relationship of language and mind to questions of identity. In the first place, there is a glimpse of this in the formation of the *langage d'action*. If one primitive individual "suffers to see suffer" another individual, it is because he *identifies* with the other individual. In other words, on a natural, instinctive level he equates himself with the other. So it can be said that in parallel with the natural ideas of perception, and with the natural signs produced by the primitive voice, there is a form of "natural identity" already beginning to emerge in the primitive mind. However, like mental and linguistic activity at this early stage, it is an unconscious and unrefined sense of identity. Furthermore identity can also be seen on an accidental level. It exists only as a communal construct and therefore will be dependent—like accidental signification—on the individuals with whom one is associated. Being part of a different community, one would have a different sense of identity, by identifying in the previously mentioned sense with individuals who have different temperaments, passions, states, and needs. Consequently the same parallel factors that establish identity on a natural and an accidental level will, by analogy, produce identity-related effects on an institutional level.[26] The effects of institutional identity are even more clearly pronounced than those of the natural and accidental sort. It is in the evolution of institutional language and identity that Condillac's ideas will begin to dialogue with those of Vaugelas.

A substantial portion of the second part of Condillac's *Essai* is devoted to demonstrating how the development of institutional language occurs beginning with the *langage d'action* and continuing through the invention and evolution of various arts such as dance, music, poetry (all three of which reproduce in one way or another the movement of the *langage d'action*), painting, hieroglyphs, and alphabetic writing (all three of which parallel the preceding arts in a transition from the most natural to the most abstract). All of these arts contribute to the slow, incremental increase of linguistic sophistication, finally resulting in the refinement of language through oratory eloquence and the stylistic perfection of literature, which ultimately produce the different characters of languages (101–56).

This latter concept, the character or genius of languages, serves to illustrate the impact of language-mind evolution on the implied notion of institutional identity. As a prelude to discussing the character of languages, Condillac points out four causes that contribute to the development of talents in the various arts noted above and in particular of the arts relating to language (163–64). First there is the "climate," or the overall environment in which the particular linguistic community exists.[27] Next there is the necessity of having a fixed and stable government, which sets the character of the nation. Third, the character of the nation provides a character to the language. Finally, once a language is "formed" (that is, no longer in its primitive state), rules of analogy establish themselves.[28] These allow talents to develop and pave the way for the appearance of the great *geniuses* who make progress possible:

> Quand un génie a découvert le caractère d'une langue, il l'exprime vivement et le soutient dans tous ses écrits. Avec ce secours le reste des gens à talens, qui auparavant n'eussent pas été capables de le pénétrer d'eux-mêmes, l'aperçoivent sensiblement, et l'expriment à son exemple chacun dans son genre. La langue s'enrichit peu à peu de quantité de nouveaux tours, qui par le rapport qu'ils ont à son caractère, le développent de plus en plus; et l'analogie devient comme un flambeau dont la lumière augmente sans cesse, pour éclairer un plus grand nombre d'écrivains. Alors tout le monde tourne naturellement les yeux sur ceux qui se distinguent: leur goût devient le goût dominant de la nation: chacun apporte dans les matières auxquelles il s'applique, le discernement qu'il a puisé chez eux: les talens fermentent: tous les arts prennent le caractère qui leur est propre, et l'on voit des hommes supérieurs dans tous les genres. C'est ainsi que les grands talens, de quelque espèce qu'ils soient, ne se montrent qu'après que le langage a déja fait des progrès considérables. Cela est si vrai, que, quoique les circonstances favorables à l'art militaire et au gouvernement, soient les plus fréquentes, les généraux et les ministres du premier ordre appartiennent cependant au siècle des grands écrivains. Telle est l'influence des gens de lettres dans l'état. (164)

(When a genius has discovered the character of a language, he expresses it markedly and maintains it in all of his writings. With this aid, the remaining people of talent, who beforehand would not have been capable of penetrating it themselves, become appreciably aware of it, and, following his example, express it each in his own genre. The language becomes enriched little by little with new expressions, which by the relation they have to its character, develop it more and more; and analogy becomes like a torch whose light grows unceasingly, to illuminate a greater number of writers. Then everyone naturally turns their eyes to those who distinguish themselves: their taste becomes the dominant taste of the nation: each brings, to the subjects to which he applies himself, the wisdom that he received from them: talents flourish: all the arts take on their own particular character, and superior men are seen in all genres. It is thus that great talents, whatever their field, appear only after the language has made considerable progress. This is true to such an extent that, although circumstances favorable to the military arts and government are the most frequent, generals and ministers of the first order belong nevertheless to the century of great writers. Such is the influence of men of letters on the state.)

In this passage Condillac plays with the word "genius." In the first place he uses it to refer to an individual or to a mind that possesses special aptitudes or a natural disposition capable of creation, invention, or enterprises of a superior order.[29] At the same time his use of the term occurs in a chapter entitled "Du génie des langues" (On the Genius of Languages), coming back to genius in the sense in which du Bellay uses it in his *Deffence et illustration,* as the character or the spirit of individual languages that makes each distinct from all others. Scholars such as Trabant have convincingly demonstrated the importance of the genius of language in Condillac's philosophy as "the goal and the end of his theory of language" (in Meschonnic, 83), showing circularity in the evolution of language leading to this genius, which in turn leads to further evolution. Of additional interest, however, is what can be considered a second circularity in Condillac's use of the term, in that genius of one type begets genius of the other type, which in turn begets genius of the first type once more. It is the person of genius who manages to understand and make known the true genius or character of his language, which was previously hidden from the common consciousness of his linguistic community. This individual alone sees the real nature and quality of that system of expression, rendering it more perceptible by his own forceful, intense expression of that character. This forceful and intense expression parallels, across eons of linguistic evolution, the same force and intensity of man's primal emotional cries and his *langage d'action.*

The ability to discover this character of the language constitutes the difference between the creative genius and the merely talented. Those who are talented, whatever their natural or acquired gifts and aptitudes, cannot pierce the mysteries of the language's character. They cannot exceed the limitations of their own cognitive-linguistic impotence. Only the genius with his near supernatural ability to penetrate language's essence truly *creates* new language. He becomes for Condillac a sort of Socratic "name giver" without whose help language would go nowhere.

However, this individual of genius is not just any person of genius; he is specifically a writer. For Condillac, only by expressing the newly discovered character of the language in writing can this discovery be given any stability. The written form of literary composition defends the new expression from the ravages of time and forgetfulness—what du Bellay sought to avoid for French writers and the very shadow that Vaugelas feared would prevent writers from writing if they were aware of its inevitability. Condillac's take, like that of du Bellay and contrary to that of Vaugelas, is optimistic since the author, never actually departing from analogy, does not corrupt the language but only perfects it further and further, with no upper limit to that perfection.

Indeed the idea that there is no upper limit to human progress is one of the key themes of the Enlightenment that distinguish the period from the previous century. While seventeenth-century thinkers tend to talk of perfection as a *state*, as Descartes and Vaugelas do, the eighteenth-century mind views perfection as a *process*. In other words, the eighteenth century thinks of *perfectibility* rather than of what is *perfect*. This is the case not only in terms of language but also in the broader realm of overall human development. Herder, for example, underlines the general idea of human perfectibility, as does Rousseau—though for him, the abstract principle of perfectibility is employed as a construct to demonstrate the actual imperfection of present human society—and the idea eventually finds perhaps its fullest expression in Condorcet.[30]

In the case of Condillac, the notion of a general progress and linguistic progress are intertwined. While the ceilingless progress of a society begins with the literary genius for Condillac, that progress is not limited to language since all progress is analogous for the abbé. Language is for all intents and purposes reason. So the evolution of language is equivalent to an evolution in human understanding, an evolution of analytical method, and an evolution of how we put information together and move forward to new knowledge. It brings about progress in the way we form an epistemology and a worldview. In the hands of the Condillacian language maker, a linguistic community's system of communication becomes more abundant, growing in metaphors, tropes, and figures and thus new words and structures. The literary genius's work may initially appear nothing more than an exercise in linguistic or aesthetic acrobatics, destined only to serve as printed spectacle to entertain a literate public. However, the driving force of analogy takes hold and shows the new modes of expression to be worthy of replication. All individuals of talent in all fields and categories of work or endeavor, having now perceived this adjustment to the language that is their analytical framework, adopt it in their turn.[31]

In highlighting the principle of analogy, Condillac takes a departure from Vaugelas' conception of the term. For Vaugelas, analogy represents pure conformity to established rules of language, an absolute adherence to the existing character or genius of the language. Condillac, though, stresses analogy as an agent of flexibility. Analogy does not regulate the language by preventing change; instead it is the mechanism that regulates change of the language:

> Quoique les grands hommes tiennent par quelque endroit au caractère de leur nation, ils ont toujours quelque chose qui les en distingue. Ils voient et sentent d'une manière qui leur est propre; et pour exprimer leur manière de voir et de sentir, ils sont obligés d'imaginer de nouveaux tours dans les règles de l'analogie, ou du moins en s'en écartant aussi peu qu'il est possible. Par-là ils se conforment au génie de leur langue, et lui prêtent en même temps le leur. (164)

> (Although great men are tied in some way to the character of their nation, they always have something which distinguishes them from it. They see and feel in a manner unique to them; and to express their manner of seeing and feeling, they are obliged to imagine new expressions within the rules of analogy, or at least straying from them as little as possible. In this way, they conform to the genius of their language, while at the same time infusing it with their own.)

Analogy is the means by which the writer negotiates between communal and individual usage, communal and individual thought, communal and individual identity.[32] Condillac stresses the communal by the claim that the individual's fundamental character emanates from that of the language system of the group, which forms his mind and thought process. This semiotic system gives meaning and organization to the world and lays out implicitly the rules of reason by which the world should be interpreted.

At the same time there is a tension in great minds between this fundamental, institutional gravitational pull of the intellect and a natural difference between these individuals in their most basic mental operation, perception. Returning to the dual function of feeling, in the physical sense and the emotional sense, Condillac underscores, in opposition to an institutional commonality, a natural impulse of the individual toward escape velocity. In parallel with Montaigne's concept of manner of expression and with Descartes' principle of manner of thinking, Condillac places individual difference of the great minds in manner of feeling. The stresses between inclusivity and exclusivity necessitate, as a means of releasing the tension, the invention of manners of expression previously unknown and untried. In this way Condillac fuses manner of feeling with manner of expression, which ultimately yields up a new manner of thinking and thus of being, thereby tying together, through his sensualism, the philosophical bases for identity seen in Montaigne and Descartes.

In the process of conflating feeling, expression, and thought, the principle of analogy acts as mediator between the two opposing forces of community and individuality. Each new expression is, by definition, unknown to the community—otherwise it would not be new. However, in order for the expression to be of any use, of any significance, it must still have meaning. Herein lies the problem. On the one hand, if the expression is not new, then it will constitute not a source of progress but merely a Vaugelasian manifestation of the status quo. On the other hand, if the expression pulls too far away from what is known, if it is completely, one hundred percent divorced from established usage, it will be incomprehensible to the community and, again, useless as a source of progress. This why analogy is so crucial. Analogy in its Condillacian definition, which breaks with the definition proposed by Vaugelas, becomes a relationship of *partial* identity between different realities. By following the principle of analogy, by creating new means of expression that are partially similar to and partially different from existing usage, the intellectual or creative genius is able to remain comprehensible to the community despite the individuality of his or her manner of expression.

Analogy therefore is able, for Condillac, to establish a harmony between the old and the new, between logic and feeling, between the communal and the individual, by means of an economy of exchange where both the (distinguished) individual and the community coexist in a cognitive-semiotic give and take. The character of a language and thus the character of a people and the individual's character are determined by the particular balance between these factors blended together by the mechanism of analogy and manifest in their semiotic output on a bell curve, running from extreme reason at one end to extreme imagination at the other and with the ideal sitting on top of the curve in the center:

> Puisque le caractère des langues se forme peu à peu et conformément à celui des peuples, il doit nécessairement avoir quelque qualité dominante. Il n'est donc pas possible que les mêmes avantages soient communs au même point à plusieurs langues. La plus parfaite seroit celle qui les réuniroit tous dans le degré qui leur permet de compatir ensemble: car ce seroit sans doute un défaut qu'une langue excellât si fort dans un genre, qu'elle ne fut point propre pour les autres. (165–66)

> (Since the character of a language develops little by little and in conformity with the character of a people, it must necessarily have some dominant quality. It is therefore not possible that the same advantages be common to the same degree in several languages. The most perfect would be that which unites all advantages to a degree that permits them to work together compatibly: for it would be no doubt a flaw for a language to excel so well in one genre, that it was inept in others.)

The bell curve is essentially a double-sided symmetrical hierarchy of expression. Each language, and by association each linguistic community, can be defined and can have its value determined by its position on this sliding scale. This definition of a language's (or a community's) value is clear-cut in that the sum total blend of imagination and reason corresponds, in a way, to the notion of a numerical value. In the ideal, reason and imagination must equal each other, cancel each other out, and add together as positives and negatives in a relation of mathematical identity creating a sum of zero. Only here will a language sit on the top of the bell curve, and few languages achieve this. Most, if they are lucky, approach this zero sum, making them relatively apt for use in all forms of linguistic expression, from the scientific, to the philosophical, to the poetic, albeit with perhaps some slight advantage in one area and with corresponding deficiencies in other areas. The less lucky will be so skewed to one side or another of the scale as to be considered clearly inferior, achieving greatness in the sciences perhaps but completely lacking in literature, or vice versa. This in turn will stunt future progress even in that language's particular field of excellence.

The perfect language—that rare, perhaps nonexistent entity—is one that has reached a state of plenitude. It excels in all genres of production equally due to its balance, due to the fact that the elements of reason and imagination *compatissent ensemble*. Just as with the two children in the wilderness who created language to begin with, this sympathy of qualities promotes continual progress in the language. Unlike Vaugelas' vision of maintaining a perfect language in a comparatively static state, Condillac's view of the perfect language is one in which the forces of change exist in such precise balance that progress is never ending, a continual process in which science, literature, philosophy, and by semiotic connection all other arts and areas of human endeavor mutually feed each other and grow proportionally to one another indefinitely.

For Condillac, however, the French language has not achieved this level of perfection. It may be near the top of the curve, but it is not at the summit:

> L'analyse et l'imagination sont deux opérations si différentes, qu'elles mettent ordinairement des obstacles aux progrès l'une de l'autre. Il n'y a que dans un certain tempérament, qu'elles puissent se prêter mutuellement des secours sans se nuire; et ce tempérament est ce milieu dont j'ai déjà eu occasion de parler. Il est donc bien difficile que les mêmes langues favorisent également l'exercice de ces deux opérations. La nôtre par la simplicité et par la netteté de ses constructions donne de bonne heure à l'esprit une exactitude, dont il se fait insensiblement une habitude, et qui prépare beaucoup les progrès de l'analyse; mais elle est peu favorable à l'imagination. (166)

> (Analysis and imagination are two operations so different, that they normally act as obstacles to each other's progress. There is only a limited temperament in which they can offer each other mutual aid without detraction; and this

temperament is the happy medium of which I have already spoken. It is therefore difficult for the same language to favor the exercise of these two operations equally. Our language, by the simplicity and precision of its constructions, readily provides the mind with an exactitude which imperceptibly becomes a habit, and which prepares it well for progress in analysis; but it is poorly suited to imagination.)

In the gamut of analytical-ideal-imaginative languages, French leans toward the analytical part of the spectrum. The fact that French is not in the ideal position for Condillac does not mean that the language does not have its qualities and advantages. It consists of a natural and spontaneous manner of expression, avoiding affectation and pretension. Its syntax and usage follow the natural order of things. It is easy to understand and relatively devoid of superfluous elements. French is precise and clear, a language that promotes intellectual acuity and provides a high degree of conformity to reality in its representation of the world. These qualities, for Condillac, nearly but not quite fully compensate for its weakness in the imaginative genres such as poetry.[33]

By Condillac's attempt to explain human cognition without resorting to any innate elements or processes, his sensualist-linguistic epistemology ultimately leads to a linguistic theory of national and cultural identity. In metaphysical opposition to Cartesian existence as being, Condillac establishes existence as doing—doing that takes the form of feeling and speaking. While all human thought has its origin in sensation, the real fundamental principle of the human mind is the *liaison des idées,* which occurs only through the use of signs of some sort, be they natural, accidental, or institutional. All higher thought requires some form of signification to occur, and in particular, language as such is required for complex operations such as the formation of abstract ideas and the creation of linear, analytical thought.

The *liaison des idées* (including the simplest levels of signification) in the most primitive stages of human development derives solely from needs or from accidental associations. Language (or institutional signification) comes into being slowly and only in communities. The driving factor in the transition of signs from an accidental to an institutional use lies in repetition and identity. Identity occurs naturally (through identifying with the other and through sympathetic responses to the other's plight that are the result of this identification), accidentally (through one's habitual associations with a particular set of others), and ultimately institutionally (through the development of a language that provides an epistemological framework to serve as the basis of a common worldview).

Once language, thought, and identity reach the institutional stage, the interplay of the individual and communal, of the sensory-sentimental and the rational, work together through the mechanism of analogy to continually renew and restructure language, worldviews, and identities on both individual and communal levels. This interplay defines both linguistic and national character. The ideal for Condillac lies in an equilibrium between these forces that results in balanced and general levels of excellence in all endeavors within a nation—which establishes even national or cultural identity as doing. Languages, and by extension nations, can be hierarchically scaled according to how close they come to achieving this balance and their ability to do the things that lead to progress and further perfection.

Perhaps the most important element of Condillac's theory is that it prefigures linguistic determinism by over two hundred years. Environment and human needs are the source of language, and language directs how we think and how we view the world. His is a very different take on language, thought, and identity from that of, say, Descartes. While he would agree with Descartes, in contrast to Montaigne, that the world is knowable, it is not for Condillac knowable through mind. The world is knowable through language. In place of Descartes' "I think therefore I am," Condillac, for whom speaking is the source of thinking, could easily have stated "I speak therefore I am" or even more appropriately "We speak therefore we are (what we are)."

This is the root of Condillac's view of the French genius or character. Indeed, French, for him, just as Vaugelas had believed and as du Bellay had hoped, had in his time reached a highly developed state. French by the mid–eighteenth century was viewed as an extremely "logical" language, as having produced great progress in its people and in their arts, science, and philosophy. Its rise to some degree of prominence was viewed as inevitable due to the environment in which it was created and in which it evolved. Yet for Condillac, French had not reached the ideal. While always in the process of perfecting itself, it was not perfect. While good, it was not best since it was not absolutely balanced in the factors contributing to its progress. In contrast, Rivarol, who bases much of his discussion on Condillacian principles, will argue that French is indeed the best of all languages and that it represents not only good linguistic and cultural development but beyond this shows the highest possible level of achievement, leaving behind all other nations, cultures, and languages.

Six

Rivarol's *De l'Universalité*
French Superiority

Antoine Rivarol (1753–1801) was a writer and promonarchy pamphleteer of the revolutionary period.[1] He frequented the salons of his time and had a reputation as a witty conversationalist.[2] Much of his writing was political in nature, and according to Comfort, he "took an active part in the pamphlet skirmishes" at the opening of the French Revolution (iii). His political writings included articles for the *Journal politique national* (1787), the satirical *Petit Almanach des grands hommes* (1787), the equally critical *Petit Dictionnaire des grands hommes de la Révolution par un citoyen actif, ci-devant Rien* (1790), and the *Actes des apôtres*, a counterrevolutionary periodical. Writings such as these forced Rivarol into exile first to London, then to Brussels, and finally to Berlin, where he died in 1801.

Despite the volume of his politically active texts, he is best known for his early nationalistic prerevolutionary discourse on the French language entitled *De l'Universalité de la langue française* (1784).[3] In fact the work can be considered his first truly substantial piece and one which, according to Loiseau, made his reputation overnight (37). In 1783 for its essay competition the Berlin Academy had posed the following questions: "Qu'est-ce qui a rendu la langue française universelle? Pourquoi mérite-t-elle cette prérogative? Est-il à présumer qu'elle la conserve?" (What has made the French language universal? Why does it merit this prerogative? Can we presume that it will maintain it?). The first noticeable aspect of these questions is that the Berlin Academy asked them in French. The second remarkable element is that not one of the three questions inquires *if* French is in fact a universal language. In 1783 the assumption made by the Berlin Academy is that French *is* universal, and the only valid questions are how, why, and whether it will continue to be such. Rivarol's essay won the competition, *ex aequo* with Johann-Christoph Schwab.

The primary characteristic of Rivarol's *Universalité* is patriotic pride:

> Le temps semble être venu de dire le *monde français,* comme autrefois le *monde romain;* et la philosophie, lasse de voir les hommes toujours divisés par les intérêts divers de la politique, se réjouit de les voir, d'un bout de la terre à l'autre, se former en république sous la domination d'une même langue. (1)[4]

(The time seems to have come to speak of the *French world*, as long ago people spoke of the *Roman world;* and philosophy, weary of seeing men always divided by the diverse interests of politics, rejoices to see them, from one end of the earth to the other, join in a republic under the domination of the same language.)

Equating the status of France in his era with the past glory of the ancients, Rivarol parallels the dominion of the French language in terms of both worldwide geographical extent and global social impact with that of Latin. He sets his national language as the foundation of an earth-spanning community and a global identity. However, if the French of Rivarol's time has taken the place of yesterday's Latin, the question of French endurance becomes problematic. If French is what Latin was, does not the natural order of things suggest that French will become what Latin is today, namely a dead language? This, in fact, was how du Bellay had envisioned the ultimate evolution of all languages including French. However, Rivarol does not want to accept the cyclical view adopted by du Bellay, where all languages rise and fall only to be replaced by another, younger language. Instead, Rivarol seeks a solution to the problem of longevity through his approach to defining "le monde français" and the mechanism of its linguistic "conquest," by which he breaks the parallel between the destinies of French and Latin. In defining the French and Roman "worlds" Rivarol underlines two distinct characteristics, philosophy and politics, which constitute the essence of these two languages and cultures.

The Roman world, for Rivarol, was defined by the state, by its power, and by the struggle for power, and this struggle is characterized by separation into parties and cliques, by differences in goals, privileges, advantages, and disadvantages. In the end the internal contradictions and oppositions between factions led the fundamental structure of the Roman world to rot from the inside out. The inherent corruption of the Roman dominion over the world underlines the superiority of the French world and the advantage it will have over its ancient predecessor.

The French world is defined by rational understanding, by knowledge, and by the love of knowledge. The French "conquest" of the world is not based on weapons or power or force but is instead a linguistic conquest, resulting in unifying tendencies rather than divisive ones. French dominion over the world provides joy, pleasure, satisfaction. Its global dominion is formed by the voluntary consent of those who come to adopt French as their language. By this consent they effectively form themselves into a kind of republic—not a republic in the sense that the French Revolution would use the term but rather in the classical sense, as it sometimes appeared in antiquity, as the rule by a plurality of elite voices. In place of the political despotism ultimately imposed by the Romans, the

French are simply, by the majority endorsement of a very Vaugelasian literary and artistic "senate," placed at the head of a Republic of Letters.

So for Rivarol, where the Romans had a physical superiority over other nations, France holds a moral superiority. Rather than imposing, France influences. The voluntary nature of belonging to the French world (with people desperate to get in rather than desperate to get out) provides for unity and oneness among the members of this Republic of Letters. Furthermore, with this republic spanning across national boundaries, it becomes more than a republic; it becomes an empire, a uniform and peaceful Empire of Letters that is stronger and more enduring than Empires of Arms (1). The difference in origins between the Roman and French worlds is what Rivarol holds will prevent the latter from decaying and dying as the former did. Such an empire built upon consent is not inherently rotten and will not collapse under its own weight.

Rivarol then addresses the question of how French in the first place achieved the status it now holds:

cette honorable universalité de la langue française, si bien reconnu et si hautement avouée dans notre Europe, offre pourtant un grand problème: elle tient à des causes si délicates et si puissantes à la fois, que pour les démêler il s'agit de montrer jusqu'à quel point la position de la France, sa constitution politique, l'influence de son climat, le génie de ses écrivains, le caractère de ses habitants, et l'opinion qu'elle a su donner d'elle au reste du monde; jusqu'à quel point, dis-je, tant de causes diverses ont pu se combiner et s'unir, pour faire à cette langue une fortune si prodigieuse. (2)

(this honorable universality of the French language, so well recognized and so highly acclaimed in our Europe, offers however a great problem: it is rooted in causes simultaneously so delicate and powerful, that to unravel them it is necessary to show to what extent the position of France, its political constitution, the influence of its climate, the genius of its writers, the character of its inhabitants, and the success of the language in giving a favorable opinion of itself to the rest of the world; to what extent, I say, so many diverse causes have been able to converge and combine to establish such a prodigious fortune for that language.)

Taking a page from authors such as Condillac, Rousseau, Monboddo, and others who explored the origin and development of language as a general feature of human existence, Rivarol adopts a similar genetic approach to the French language in particular.[5] He highlights the precarious path that the evolution of the French language has followed, a precariousness derived from the opposition of the fragility and strength of the influencing elements of the language's environment, and he underscores the delicate balance between changeability and durability that characterizes the French language. He enumerates the various factors that have contributed to the establishment of this equilibrium: the natural conditions existing in France's geographical location; the body of its laws; the structures and mechanisms of its politics; the intellectual and artistic conditions created by society; the aptitudes and intellectual faculties of its writers, along with their extraordinary creativity; and the distinctive psychological and moral characteristics of its citizens. All of these items are reproduced directly from Condillac's chapter on the "génie des langues."

However, one item in Rivarol's litany constitutes an important original contribution not found in Condillac's work, and that is "l'opinion qu'elle a su donner d'elle au reste du monde." That is to say that Rivarol adds to the mix the transmission of the language and of its character along with a sense of the value of the language and its character, outside of the political and geographical boundaries of France. This key deviation from Condillac's thinking is one of a handful of subtle differences that allow Rivarol to argue in favor of the superiority of French over other languages, where Condillac could not. While Condillac focuses only on the qualities of the language as such, Rivarol focuses additionally on what can effectively be called the "marketing" of the language. Rivarol argues that by promoting the merits of French far and wide, this final ingredient, marketing of the language, provided for the favorable situation and circumstances that French enjoys in his time, thereby driving the French language toward an extraordinary and superior standing among the languages of Europe. Rivarol then presents the reader with a double-thrusted hypothesis as to why French has become universal. He shows that the French language is a "quality product" and further how it has been successfully "marketed" abroad.

As a prelude to this dual demonstration, Rivarol acknowledges that other languages of Europe have had their shot at universality. He gives a lengthy history of European languages and explains why German, Spanish, and Italian failed to become universal. Rivarol argues, for example, that German had no great literature, that with no link to Latin it was too hard to learn, and that its guttural pronunciation shocks the ear of people from other regions of the Continent (4–6). Spanish, he argues, lost too much prestige in Spain's conflicts with Richelieu's France, produced some good literature but not enough to capture the broader European mind, and had an external expressive magnificence that hid an interior linguistic poverty (7–9). Italian, for Rivarol, had great potential as Italy led the way into the Renaissance: Italy had political and commercial domination of the Mediterranean, Galileo's science, and the literature of Dante, Boccaccio, and Petrarch (11–12). However, though Italy had great potential, Italian did not become universal for a variety of reasons. Italian matured too early in history, and other nations were so uncultured and so preoccupied with their own political and cultural growing pains that they took too little notice of Italy's accomplishments. Italy was frequently invaded by others (such as the Germans, Spanish, and French), and these invasions caused that nation to lose political clout. The discovery of new trade routes outside the Mediterranean caused a decline of Italy's economic importance. The combination of these factors led to a corruption of "taste" in Italy, equated with the loss of all Italy's cultural advantage, just at the moment when taste and culture were rising in France (12–13).[6]

The final and principal reason why Italian could not achieve universality, argues Rivarol, lies in the genius of the language:

> le caractère même de la langue italienne fut ce qui l'écarta le plus de cette universalité qu'obtient chaque jour la langue française. On sait quelle distance sépare en Italie la poésie de la prose: mais ce qui doit étonner, c'est que le vers y ait réellement plus d'âpreté, ou pour mieux dire, moins de mignardise que la prose. Les lois de la mesure et de l'harmonie ont forcé le poète à tronquer les mots, et par ces syncopes fréquentes, il s'est fait une langue à part, qui, outre la hardiesse des inversions, a une marche plus rapide et plus ferme. Mais la prose composée de mots dont toutes les lettres se prononcent, et roulant toujours sur des sons pleins, se traîne avec trop de lenteur; son éclat est monotone; l'oreille se lasse de sa douceur, et la langue de sa mollesse: ce qui peut venir de ce que chaque mot étant harmonieux en particulier, l'harmonie du tout ne vaut rien. La pensée la plus rigoureuse se détrempe dans la prose italienne. Elle est souvent ridicule et presqu'insupportable dans une bouche virile, parce qu'elle ôte à l'homme cette teinte d'austérité qui doit en être inséparable. (14–15)

> (the very character of the Italian language is what removed it the most from this universality which the French language obtains each day. The distance which separates poetry from prose in Italy is well known: but what might surprise is that verse there really has more roughness, or to put it better, less preciosity than prose. The laws of measure and harmony have forced the poet to truncate words, and by frequent syncopation, made it a language apart, which besides the boldness of its inversions, has a firmer and more rapid step. But its prose, composed of words whose letters are all pronounced, and always rolling on full sounds, drags with too much sloth; its radiance is monotonous; the ear is wearied by its sweetness, and the tongue by its softness: which is caused by the fact that each word being harmonious individually, the harmony of the whole is worthless. The most rigorous thought falls flat in Italian prose. It is often ridiculous and almost intolerable in a virile mouth, because it takes away from man the tint of austerity that must be inseparable from him.)

The character of any language is the prime determinant of whether that language becomes universal or not, and marketing factors such as political clout, economic power, and exportation of culture are all subordinate to it. If a language lacks a genius that will make it palatable to all, the marketing factors mean nothing. This was Italian's primary impediment to becoming universal.

Rivarol's explanation of the Italian language's impoverished character begins in the contrast between Italian poetry and Italian prose, a point that sheds light on those qualities possessed by French that in turn make it universal where Italian has floundered. Superior to Italian prose, Italian poetry is, for Rivarol, forceful and powerful. This is due to the general aesthetic prescriptions of Italian verse, which provide for a regularity in its metrics, figures, and sonority. These rules give to Italian verse a "masculine" musicality, evidenced in the various elements of Italian poetry that Rivarol praises: the constraints that cut off or suppress what he sees as extraneous portions of Italian words for the benefit of the aesthetic whole; and its "firm and rapid march," which gives it a strength, quickness of execution, and a determined tone. Even the one characteristic of Italian poetry that Rivarol does not like, its "irrational" inversions, is qualified as having a certain boldness.[7] This boldness, strength, force, determination of tone and purpose, Spartan quality of eliminating the nonessential, brusqueness, and rapid dynamism are all reminiscent of Montaigne's preferred linguistic style: "Le parler que j'ayme, c'est un parler simple et naïf . . . un parler succulent et nerveux, court et serré, non tant délicat et peigné comme vehement et brusque . . . hardy . . . plustost soldatesque" (The expression I like is a simple and naive expression . . . a succulent and nervous expression, short and tight, not so much delicate and groomed as vehement and brusque . . . unruly . . . rather soldierly, 207). The Montaignian qualities ascribed to Italian poetry by Rivarol make it a language of its own, separate and distinct from normal, everyday Italian speech and prose.

Contrarily it is the quality of Italian prose that prevented the language as a whole from having a universal character. Rivarol underlines the exaggerated affectation of delicate preciosity, the strained, overdone sweetness of the language. It is not that Italian prose is not harmonious, but rather that it is too harmonious. The harmony of each individual word is overbearing to the harmony of the whole, such that this "micro-harmony" drowns out everything else. The fact that "all the letters are pronounced"—unlike the phonetically truncated French language with all its silent endings, lending it an affinity to Italian poetry—leaves it too luxuriant and voluptuous, too "feminine," just as Estienne had claimed as far back as 1578.[8]

With Rivarol, however, the feminine qualities attributed to Italian are additionally suggestive. As Bullock and Eilderts have pointed out, during the Renaissance "the imagined polarization of manly and unmanly forms . . . is but an echo of the medieval disparagement of the French language in its entirety as a frivolous and effeminate language when compared to its stately, manly progenitor, Latin"

(292). In Rivarol's text it is Italian, the most natural descendant of Latin, that in its commonly written and spoken prose forms the least manly of all the languages competing to take over Latin's role.

For Rivarol, Italian prose "rolls" (suggesting feminine curves), is made up of "full" sounds (again suggesting eighteenth-century ideals of feminine beauty), and is gentle and soft. In contrast to the "Spartan" style of Italian poetry, Italian prose is a language of comfort that drags along sleepily and slowly, basking in the excessive pleasure of its own sound. The linguistic result of these "feminine" characteristics is that Italian prose intoxicates, and its sweet monotony is like a lullaby that sends the minds of the speaker and the listener into dreamy slumber.

This latter point is the crux of the matter. Dulling the mind, Italian prose is presented by Rivarol as incapable of serving as the vehicle of rigorously rational discourse. Rational thought, no matter how strictly analytical it is, is diluted by expression in Italian prose. Italian prose corrupts thought. Ideas expressed in Italian, Rivarol suggests, become laughable and grotesque parodies of reason. For Rivarol, as for Descartes, reason is the one characteristic common to all humankind. Feeling and sentiment can vary from culture to culture, but the potential and the need for reason are universal. Rivarolian reason is inherently masculine in nature.[9] Italian is unsuited to universality because the feminine qualities of Italian speech are not palatable to the "virile mouth" of reason. The thinking mind cannot bear to express itself in a language that takes away the Spartan and manly rigor so essential to the expression of analytical reason. Masculinity, like reason, is equated by Rivarol with universality.

Of course, Rivarol's ideas on the masculinity of reason and on the defects of the Italian language are completely and utterly absurd, for obvious reasons. Indeed they even appear self-contradictory. If the universal quality of virile reason makes the Italian language insufferable to all other nations, it would seem logical that the Italians, who presumably possess just as much of the universal quality of virile reason as everyone else, would find their own language just as horrible and reject it. However, Rivarol anticipates this objection by undertaking to highlight both the general importance of linguistic genius and, eventually, the character of the French language in particular.

With respect to the general importance of the genius of languages, Rivarol states that "on voit le caractère des peuples, et le génie de leur langue marcher d'un pas égal, et l'un est toujours garant de l'autre. Admirable propriété de la parole, de montrer ainsi l'homme tout entier!" (we see the character of a people, and the genius of their language, marching in step, and the one always vouches for the other, 16). The genius of a language parallels precisely the character of a people. If that character and genius, paradoxically, deviate from the general, rational character of humanity, the language cannot become universal. Conversely a language that can best serve as the vehicle of reason will do quite well. These two points will allow Rivarol to explain how other nations such as Italy have for so long been content in speaking "inferior" languages and also why French is able, by its genius, to serve as a universal tongue.

The emphasis on the concept of genius returns Rivarol's reader to the fundamental issue—expressed in Montaigne, Descartes, Vaugelas, and Condillac—of the relationship of language to thought and world:

> Des philosophes ont demandé si la pensée peut exister sans parole ou sans quelqu'autre signe: non sans doute. L'homme, étant une machine très-harmonieuse, n'a pu être jeté dans le monde, sans s'y établir une foule de rapports. La seule présence des objets lui a donné des *sensations,* qui sont nos idées les plus simples, et qui ont bientôt amené les *raisonnements.* Il a d'abord senti le plaisir et la douleur, et il les a nommés; ensuite il a connu et nommé l'erreur et la vérité. Or, *sensation et raisonnement,* voilà de quoi tout l'homme se compose: l'enfant doit sentir avant de parler, mais il faut qu'il parle avant de penser. (16)

> (Some philosophers have asked if thought can exist without speech or without some other sign: certainly not. Man, being a very harmonious machine, could not have been cast into this world without establishing a host of relationships. The mere presence of objects provided him with *sensations,* which are our most simple ideas, and which soon brought in their wake *reason.* He first felt pleasure and pain, and he named them; then he learned and named error and truth. So, man is composed entirely of *sensation* and *reason:* a child must feel before speaking, but he must speak before reasoning.)

Rivarol adopts the Condillacian argument that thought can exist only through language or other signs, and he underscores that this is fundamentally part of material human existence. Taking the man-as-machine premise as his starting point, he posits that the complex combination of organs that constitutes man's internal existence, and the organs' orderly relationships and interactions, is in fact at the very core of our understanding of the world.[10] We automatically and from the start operate on the assumption that there are orderly mechanical relationships in the outside world as well. The world, like the body that provides human sensation, is a balanced, homogeneous whole. Man's perceptions—his first mental operation—lead him naturally to find connections and relationships between the objects producing sensations in him.

Like Condillac, Rivarol subscribes to the importance of language in this process. Sensation leads to reasoning because man immediately begins to name things. He feels pain and pleasure, and he names them.[11] He distinguishes between those ideas that reflect reality and those that do not, and he names them too. By naming these categories he assigns value to them of good and bad, true and false. Thus sensation and reason define the human species as a rational animal, in a very Condillacian sense. Rivarol's statement that sensation creates language, which in turn creates thought may well be the best one-line summary of Condillacian theory ever written.

The fact that Rivarol accepts Condillac's theory as a basis for his argument is significant in that it allows him, on the individual level, to justify a Montaignian view that rational thought is an interior discourse: "si la parole est une pensée qui se manifeste, il faut que la pensée soit une parole intérieure et cachée" (if speech is the manifestation of thought, then thought must be an internal and hidden speech, 17). Additionally, on the societal level, this approach justifies the Vaugelasian/Condillacian view of the genius of a language as representing the group as a whole: "L'homme qui parle est donc l'homme qui pense tout haut; et si on peut juger un homme par ses paroles, on peut aussi juger une nation par son langage" (A man who speaks is therefore a man who thinks out loud; and if we can judge a man by his words, we can also judge a nation by its language, 17). The genius of languages allows us to judge not just those other languages but also other cultures and nations.

Having dispatched Germany, Spain, and Italy on the basis of their defective genius, Rivarol narrows his discussion of the universality question to a competition between two remaining nations, England and France. These two peoples, he states, differ in everything: climate, language, government, vices, and virtues. They are two peoples who have fought for supremacy for over three hundred years, and having done so, "se disputent encore la gloire des lettres, et se partagent depuis un siècle les regards de l'univers" (still vie for the glory of letters, while for a century the universe has looked on, 18–19). Though Rivarol cites politics, armed conflict, and economics as the prime arenas of confrontation in their past, he identifies literature as the principal field of ongoing contention between England and France in the present.

Rivarol lists numerous factors contributing to the differences in the characters of those nations. For example, England lies under cloudy skies, is isolated from the rest of the world, and was once considered the "exile of the Romans." France, in contrast, enjoys a "Greek sky," is open to the rest of the world, and was once considered "the delight of the Caesars" (19). From these fundamental differences derive many others. The isolation and limited resources of a small island require England to depend on imports and war to get what its people need. France has enormous internal resources, so peace is much more in its nature. France provides other nations with what they need, while England takes from them (20). The Englishman is dry and taciturn and is marked by the social timidity of the northern peoples while at the same time being impatient and feeling a "disgust" for all things, often including life itself (22). In contrast, the Frenchman has a certain happiness and joie de vivre. The Frenchman sees life as a comedy, while the Englishman sees it as a drama (25).[12]

A lengthy collage of expressions shows Rivarol's view of France as an intellectual and cultural middle ground in addition to being a geographic one.[13] France's empire is that of taste, since the "exaggerated" opinions of both the northern and the southern nations are adopted and adapted by France and moderated such that they are pleasing to all (21). France possesses neither the excessive subtlety for which the southern nations are reproached nor the excessive simplicity of the northern peoples (22). Paradoxically for Rivarol, "quand on compare un peuple du midi à un peuple du nord, on n'a que des extrêmes à rapprocher: mais la France, sous un ciel tempéré, changeante dans ses manières et ne pouvant se fixer elle-même, parvient pourtant à fixer tous les goûts" (when one compares a people of the south to a people of the north, one has only two extremes to reconcile: but France, beneath a temperate sky, changing in its manners and unable to remain fixed, manages nevertheless to fix all tastes, 23).

It took French, Rivarol tells us, over a thousand years to arrive at maturity. As with France's manners, there were continual changes in the language throughout this time. However,

> à travers ces variations, on voit cependant combien le caractère de la nation influait sur [la langue]: la construction de la phrase fut toujours directe et claire. La langue française n'eut donc que deux sortes de barbaries à combattre: celle des mots et celle du mauvais goût de chaque siècle. (26)
>
> (through these variations, we see nonetheless how much the character of the nation influences [the language]: the sentence structure was always direct and clear. The French language had therefore only two types of barbarism to combat: that of words and that of the poor taste of each century.)

Rivarol distinguishes between manner of doing and manner of being, between the particular forms that cultural processes take (which vary and oscillate over time) and the underlying character of a people (the distinctive traits that make them what they are, that make them unique, and which are constant). For Rivarol, just as for Condillac, the character of the nation determines the character of the language. Diverging from Condillac, however, and taking a position akin to that of Vaugelas, Rivarol suggests that the forces of change (processes) and the forces of stability (character) do not necessarily work in harmony, but they can very well be at odds.

Stability of national character, derived from government, climate, and so forth, is the driving force behind the arrangement of words in the sentence and sentences in larger discourse, according to the rules of usage. The character of the language fixes the essence of all aspects of intonation, grammatical coherence, and the larger creation of meaning. Such is the moderate, balanced nature of the French environment that the French character has a certain classical order and simplicity to it. Consequently discourse in French goes straight to its point without following distorted, winding baroque paths, without covering up or embellishing, and always in a way that is easily and quickly understood.

Legitimate linguistic change is that alteration in the language that respects the existing genius of the language. However, linguistic changes that do not respect this character of the language constitute sources of instability. The forces of instability are qualified by Rivarol as "barbarous," and we come full circle to du Bellay's early preoccupations. Rivarol splits linguistic barbarism into two categories: the semiotic ("barbarie des mots") and the cultural ("barbarie du mauvais goût"). Linguistic enemies number one and two contain between them all that is uncivilized or uncultured, in the sense of being contrary to humanistic norms of intellectual and aesthetic activity. Historically "barbarian" was a term employed by the ancient Greeks for foreigners unable to speak their language. For Rivarol, the term "barbarous" is extended to any practice that does not correspond to the overall moderate and rational character of the French people and any linguistic product that, if adopted into the language, would cause it to veer away from that character. Just as preoccupied with the purity of the language as his predecessor Vaugelas, Rivarol is skeptical of all change that would alter the fundamental genius of the French language, thereby making the language no longer French and altering the national identity. The genius of the language is rooted both in its capacity to represent reality with accuracy and in the aesthetic sensibility that determines it, and which in turn it determines.

In practical terms the "barbarism of words" was a threat posed primarily in the French language's tendency to borrow words from numerous Celtic and Latin sources. However, the rise of a strong central monarchy in France (no doubt thanks to Richelieu, who in reinforcing and raising up that monarchy also founded the Académie française) unified these various linguistic sources, making them conform to the genius of the nation (26–27).

A similar process of centralization of taste—also rooted in the rise of a strong, centralized monarchy—occurred, and an inherently French taste developed with the perfecting of social order. With the strengthening of royal authority, a number of social constructions took more fixed forms: monetary fortunes stabilized; social privileges were confirmed; rights were clarified; ranks were assigned. For Rivarol, the formalization of these specific elements of social life created a happy and respected nation that enjoyed glory abroad and peace and commerce at home (27). People of all stations and ranks mixed in the capital while maintaining the respective distinctions of their ranks and classes, and the population as a whole

commence à distinguer autant de nuances dans le langage que dans la société; la délicatesse des procédés amène celle des propos; les métaphores sont plus justes, les comparaisons plus nobles, les plaisanteries plus fines; la parole étant le vêtement de la pensée, on veut des formes plus élégantes. C'est ce qui arriva aux premières années du règne de Louis XIV. Le poids de l'autorité royale fit rentrer chacun à sa place; on connut mieux ses droits et ses plaisirs; l'oreille plus exercée exigea une prononciation plus douce: une foule d'objets nouveaux demandèrent des expressions nouvelles; la langue française fournit à tout, et l'ordre s'établit dans l'abondance. (27)

(begins to distinguish as many nuances in the language as there are in society; the delicacy of practices brings in its wake that of expression; metaphors are more appropriate, similes more noble, humor more subtle; speech being the garment of thought, people seek more elegant forms. So it came to pass in the first years of Louis XIV's reign. The weight of royal authority set everyone in his place; each better understood his rights and his pleasures; a more practiced ear demanded a gentler pronunciation; a host of new objects required new expressions; the French language offered everything, and order was established in the midst of abundance.)

This is not to say that the process was without difficulties. Rivarol actually accuses du Bellay's Renaissance of pushing French deeper into barbarism rather than out of it prior to this high point of French linguistic and cultural perfection begun under Louis XIV:

contre tout espoir, la renaissance des lettres . . . fit rebrousser [la langue française] vers la barbarie. Une foule de poètes s'élevèrent dans son sein, tels que les Jodelle, les Baïf et les Ronsard . . . ils s'imaginèrent que la nation s'était trompée jusque-là, et que la langue française aurait bientôt le charme du grec . . . les métaphores basses ou gigantesques se cachèrent sous un style entortillé; enfin ces poètes parlaient grec en français, et de tout un siècle on ne s'entendit point dans notre poésie. (28–29)

(against all hope, the Renaissance of letters . . . turned [the French language] back toward barbarism. A host of poets was lifted on its rising tide, your Jodelles, your Baïfs, your Ronsards . . . they imagined the nation had been mistaken up until then, and that the French language would soon have the charm of Greek . . . metaphors from the base to the gigantic were hidden beneath a twisted style; these poets ended up speaking Greek in French, and for a whole century, no one understood anything in our poetry.)

Nevertheless through its entire history French writing managed to charm the whole world by possessing a relative perfection despite its many minor flaws (31).

In contrast Rivarol sees the history of the English language and literature very differently. Rivarol finds nothing of value in English literature apart from Chaucer and Spencer for a period of four hundred years. From Chaucer until Shakespeare and Milton, "rien ne transpire dans cette île . . . et sa littérature ne vaut pas un coup d'œil" (nothing transpires on this island . . . and its literature is not worth even a glance, 32).[14] The charming but imperfect development of French literature continues until the glorious arrival of Malherbe, who "éleva le premier des monuments nationaux" (raised the first national monuments, 33).[15] This opened the floodgates of classical verse and theater seen in Corneille and Racine and in the creative genius of writers such as Voiture, Pascal, Racan, Boileau, Descartes, Bayle, Molière, Fénelon, and La Fontaine (33–36). The works of these great writers led the fight against the barbarism of both words and taste, and they gave to the language a universally palatable character. Like so many before him, Rivarol identifies literature as the principal cause in the establishment and refinement of language, culture, and identity.

With the "product" perfected, the issue comes back to that of exportation and "marketing." Rivarol supplies a narrative underscoring an increase in French industry and exportation during the seventeenth century. French commercial items had no names in the native tongues of the countries to which they were exported, and the people there "furent comme accablés sous l'exubérance de l'industrie française . . . et . . . *pour n'être plus séparé de nous,* on étudia notre langue de tous côtés" (were overburdened beneath the exuberance of French industry . . . and . . . *to no longer be separated from us,* they studied our language everywhere, 37, emphasis added). The French exported not only goods but also the desire to be like the French—an exportation of identity—which was reflected in the desire everywhere of other nations seeking to learn French. Rivarol also explains how this linguistic expansion was reinforced politically. Louis XIV's political and military victories allowed him to establish French as the language of treaties and diplomacy. Later in his reign, when he was defeated militarily, he was "humiliated" in French as the peace documents were drafted in that language (38). The revocation of the Edict of Nantes resulted in the expulsion of French Protestants to other nations, and these exiles took French with them (38).

Ultimately, though, the "marketing" of French abroad, like the purification of French language and culture, comes down more to literature than to any other cause. For Rivarol, Louis XIV was a great king not by politics or commerce but "par goût" (by taste, 37). Even when describing the commercial exports of France, Rivarol hastens to point out that these were accompanied abroad by "nos meilleurs livres" (our finest books, 37). With England being an economic, political, and military powerhouse as well, it is the difference in quality of the two nations' respective literatures that allows France to take precedence over England in establishing French as universal. Even though England near the end of the seventeenth century began, in Rivarol's view, to know its own significant literary success, it was already too late for Britain to catch up. French at that time was already firmly ensconced in the top *literary* position, and there was no room for anyone else, whatever the economic or political conditions might be (39).[16] Even supposing that England had been quicker out of the gate, Rivarol argues that it would not have mattered. English is the daughter of German, and "les défauts de la mère ont passé jusqu'à la fille" (the flaws of the mother were passed on to the daughter, 40). With Latin having been the original universal language, it was only natural that one of Latin's offsprings, French, would take this place of privilege.

This is Rivarol's explanation for how France arrived in its position of linguistic prominence. Having dealt with the issue of past linguistic "marketing" and "product quality," Rivarol turns to address the continued evidence of "product quality" in the present: "si la langue française a conquis l'empire par ses livres, par l'humeur et par l'heureuse position du peuple qui la parle, elle la conserve par son propre génie" (if the French language conquered the empire through its books, through its temperament, and by the fortunate position of the people that speak it, it conserves that empire through its genius, 43). French's universal quality is rooted in the moderate and rational nature of the people who speak it, derived from their environment, and exported to others through its literature. However, it presently maintains its hold everywhere through its genius, which reflects the universal traits of reason and order that mark the French national character. In linguistic terms, reason and order manifest themselves in the "natural" construction of the sentence that other languages fail to respect as scrupulously as does French:[17]

> Ce qui distingue notre langue des langues anciennes et modernes, c'est l'ordre et la construction de la phrase. Cet ordre doit toujours être direct et nécessairement clair. Le Français nomme d'abord le *sujet* du discours, ensuite le *verbe* qui est l'action, et enfin l'*objet* de cette action: voilà la logique naturelle de tous les hommes; voilà ce qui constitue le sens commun. (43)
>
> (What distinguishes our language from other ancient and modern tongues is the order and structure of its sentences. This order must always be direct and necessarily clear. French names first the discursive *subject,* then the *verb* or the action, and finally the *object* of that action: this is the natural logic of all mankind; this is what constitutes common sense.)

Rivarol returns once more to the principles of "directness" and "clarity" as the defining features of the French tongue. These principles are the cornerstones of French sentence structure and follow what many French grammarians of the eighteenth century referred to as the "natural order." As the basis of his natural-order argument, Rivarol adopts the commonly asserted hierarchy of subject-verb-object constructions. The principle was a foundational one of much linguistic thinking in France from at least the seventeenth century onward, being laid down in the works of the grammarians of Port-Royal and others. Additionally Rivarol's own era saw numerous references to this natural order, both inside and outside of France. Diderot, for example, highlights that French has fewer inversions of this natural order than other languages do, a fact that makes the French tongue more suitable than other idioms to the expression of logic and reason.[18] Similarly the articles "Construction" and "Inversion" in the *Encyclopédie* stress this idea as well, and even the German writer Johann-Christoph Schwab adopts the principle.[19]

The notions of a natural order and the superiority of a language that follows it are so widespread that it is difficult to find thinkers who do not adhere to this view. The one notable exception is Condillac, who argues that "ce qu'on appelle . . . naturel varie nécessairement selon le génie des langues. . . . Le Latin en est la preuve; il allie des constructions tout-à-fait contraires, et qui néanmoins paroissent également conformes à l'arrangement des idées" (that which is called . . . natural varies necessarily according to the genius of languages. . . . Latin is proof of this; it allies constructions that are completely contrary, and which nevertheless appear to conform equally to the arrangement of ideas, 150). Of course, having no political agenda and no desire to prove the superiority of French, Condillac is free to adopt a relativistic view of what constitutes good, rational language. However, Rivarol's partisan perspective allows no such luxury, and like the majority of his era, he supports the one-natural-order position.

For Rivarol, agents are necessary antecedents to the actions they perform and therefore supercede them in importance. Processes and actions are required antecedents to the people or things that they affect and so occupy a place of greater importance than their objects. The sequencing of events in reality is for thinkers such as Rivarol the ideal model that languages should strive to emulate in their structures. The artifice of discourse must follow the nature of things. Since in this particular language-mind-world model the nature of things is common to all humankind, the perception of that nature is in itself a global or universal quality. Indeed the concept of common sense, that is, the idea of a central faculty of the mind bringing together and coordinating the data taken in by all of the senses, is a notion that fuses together both Condillacian sensualism and Cartesian rationalism, redefining "the most shared quality" among all human beings in Rivarol's text.

However, even with this being the case, not all languages are equally rational, as seen in Rivarol's previous discussions of Italian, Spanish, German, and English. Rivarol explains the root of this discrepancy:

> cet ordre si favorable, si nécessaire au raisonnement, est presque toujours contraire aux sensations, qui nomment le premier l'objet qui frappe le premier:

c'est pourquoi tous les peuples, abandonnant l'ordre direct, ont eu recours aux tournures plus ou moins hardies, selon que leurs sensations ou l'harmonie l'exigeait; et l'inversion a prévalu sur la terre, parce que l'homme est plus impérieusement gouverné par les passions que par la raison. (44)

(this order so favorable, so necessary to reasoning, is almost always contrary to sensations, which first name the object that first strikes us: this is why all peoples, abandoning the direct order, have had recourse to more or less risky turns of phrase, depending on what their sensations or what harmony demanded; and inversion prevailed around the world, because men are more imperiously governed by their passions than by reason.)

Just as social order precedes culture, linguistic order precedes reason. Rivarol applies Vaugelas' language-as-sovereign idea to Condillac's language-as-reason principle. However, there exists for Rivarol a clear opposition between the disposition of things in the natural world (including the intelligible relationships between them) and the physical stimulations they provoke in us through perception. If language and the order it provides are removed from the mix, then our perceptions distort the natural order.[20] Condillac too had addressed this problem in his *Essai* in explaining the relationship between the refinement of language and how it brings about the refinement of thought. He, like Rivarol, had argued that we perceive before engaging in any other mental operation. So in early primitive languages, Condillac claims in his *Essai,* a man says "fruit want Pierre" rather than "Pierre want fruit" (137). The primitive thinking subject perceives first, and with the greatest intensity, the object desired, then second, the relationship between that object and self, and last and least, the need to distinguish the speaking self from other selves. However, for Rivarol, this point is more than a simple argument for the necessity of linguistic order for analytical thinking. It is one more argument for the superiority of French over other languages, again going one step further than Condillac was willing to go.

For Rivarol, even in modern languages one sees a paradoxical relationship between sensation, language, and reason. Language provides for reason *because* it deviates from sensation. The cause for this lies in the opposition of reason and passions—that is to say between rational thought and, in Cartesian terms, all aspects of human activity not related to rational thought, including all physical sensations and emotions. Where the modern rational mind identifies the speaking self first, paralleling Condillac's civilized example of "Pierre want fruit," the passionate mind identifies first the object of desire, as in Condillac's primitive example of "fruit want Pierre." So strong are the passions, in Rivarol's view, that all nations prefer to follow this latter order, which deviates from the norms of reason. The rational order is natural because it is a direct exposition of the order of things. It is thus objective because it presents above all objects and the relations between them, with little reference to the speaking subject except as a necessity recognized by a disembodied observer, to indicate to whom the perception belongs. The inverted order is subjective since it is rooted in the passions, which place all objects in the context of how the speaking subject feels about them.

Rivarol's text suggests that in modern languages, unlike in Condillac's primitive languages, this phenomenon occurs on the level of the nation rather than on the level of the individual. It is the result of collective physical perceptions of the surrounding environment (colored by existing language, in a continual cycle of perception feeds language feeds perception) and also of the emotional effects of language dictated by collective aesthetic taste (again colored by language in a similar cyclical relationship between language and emotion). These two sources of communal, national subjectivity prevent all languages other than French from having a universal character that appeals to the common sense belonging to all of humanity. Such is the force of the passions and their expression that their power to govern the mind cannot be broken *from the inside.* The speakers of a language cannot opt to change their language of their own accord to make it more rational. To do so would require the very rational thought that their own language currently cannot provide them. This leaves them devoid of the universal character necessary to spread themselves throughout the world.

For French, however, this is not the case. The moderate environment of France previously cited by Rivarol calms French passions to a level where common sense and reason are able to stay in charge:

> Le Français . . . est seul resté fidèle à l'ordre direct, comme s'il était tout raison . . . et c'est en vain que les passions nous bouleversent et nous sollicitent de suivre l'ordre des sensations; la syntaxe française est incorruptible. C'est de là que résulte cette admirable clarté, base éternelle de notre langue. *Ce qui n'est pas clair n'est pas français;* ce qui n'est pas clair est encore anglais, italien, grec ou latin. (44)

> (The Frenchman . . . alone has remained faithful to the direct order, as if he were all reason . . . and it is in vain that passions overwhelm us and beg us to follow . . . the order of sensations; French syntax is incorruptible. *That which is not clear is not French;* that which is not clear is instead English, Italian, Greek or Latin.)

The French have kept to the natural order as if they were beings of pure logic. The passions have no corrupting influence on the structures of the French language. French, seen from this perspective, possesses a purity unknown by other languages and defined through its fidelity to the structure of reality. Its purity makes it a language of all times and of all places and provides it with an ability to express ideas without ambiguity. Rivarol's celebrated formula—that "*ce qui n'est pas clair n'est pas français; ce qui n'est pas clair est encore anglais, italien, grec ou latin*"—is reflective of the equation of clarity with purity and therefore, by extension, is reflective of a barbarity associated with all other languages including those of the ancients. All other languages are not eternal but finite. They are not pure, and lacking purity (of expression, race, and nationality) they are barbaric in both the general sense of not belonging to the community and in the moral sense of being uncivilized and uncouth. Such are the clarity and purity of the French language and such is its rational character, Rivarol claims, that even when foreigners learn French (as opposed to learning the classical languages), "on dirait que c'est d'une géométrie toute élémentaire, de la simple ligne droite, que s'est formée la langue française; et que ce sont les courbes et leurs variétés infinies qui ont présidé aux langues grecque et latine" (one would say that it is from a completely elementary geometry, from a simple straight line, that the French language was formed; and it is curves and their infinite variety which have presided over the Greek and Latin languages, 44). Rivarol privileges a Cartesian classicism over a Montaignian baroque.

The only danger that the rational character of the French language could potentially pose to its own universality is in those areas where emotion is at a premium. This was a concern for a number of French writers of the eighteenth century. As seen earlier, Condillac's *Essai* underlines the weakness of French poetry relative to other genres, stressing instead the language's qualities of analysis and exactitude (166). Likewise, Diderot's *Lettre sur les sourds et muets* also raises the question, claiming that while French is indeed the language of philosophy, other languages such as Latin, Italian, and English are far more suited to poetry (114–15). In a similar vein Rivarol too admits that the logical character of French makes it less suitable than other languages for music and poetry, whose express purpose is to represent the passions (45). Indeed this is a crucial point, since after all, part of the universality of the language as previously underlined by Rivarol lies in the language as literary "product" and also in the literary "marketing" of the language abroad. In the realm of verse Rivarol states that it is necessary for French poetry to please the reader or listener by the thoughts it expresses, by its organization, and by its connections of ideas (46).

French has succeeded to an extent in doing this, adding further to its appeal to the common human characteristic of reason. However, where French literature really shines is in its prose, where its clarity and the elegance of its purity and directness dominate and render French's qualities accessible to all the world (47). After all, Rivarol begins his discourse by underlining the link between the French language and philosophy and by insisting on philosophy as the most significant portion of the domain of letters over which French rules. Rivarol's own century was referred to as the era of Enlightenment, its greatest writers called themselves philosophes, and prose was fast becoming the dominant genre, gaining more and more in prestige and eventually equaling or even surpassing the prestige of the sixteenth century's poetry and the seventeenth century's theater. For Rivarol, "rien n'est en effet comparable à la prose française" (nothing in fact is comparable to French prose, 47). This ultimately justifies his belief regarding the French language that "ce n'est plus la langue française, c'est la langue humaine" (it is no longer the language of France, it is the language of humanity, 51).

It has been claimed by Comfort, and rightfully so, that Rivarol's discourse is "faulty in composition, somewhat desultory in its emphasis, and a little rhetorical in places" (v).[21] In particular the desultory nature of the text can make getting to the heart of Rivarol's thought difficult. In essence, though, Rivarolian thought can be said to rest clearly on certain recognizable principles once the ironic convolutions of his style are cleared away.

Feeling is the most fundamental human cognitive faculty. It precedes language and thought, both on an individual level and on a societal level. Reason, however, or common sense, is the highest and most universal quality that man possesses. Any language aspiring to universality must appeal to this human quality—it must have a rational character. The character of a language is determined by the character of the nation that speaks it. This national character is derived from natural factors of a nation's climate and environment. In this way feeling leads to language, which leads to thought, and further, the thought processes created by language lead to a cultural worldview.

The problem is that feeling, as the first cognitive function, is so primal that human beings are dominated by their passions. Almost all nations suffer from this, and the character of their people is such that passions are the driving force behind their languages. Hence their languages provide a thinking framework or worldview that is passion-oriented rather than reason-oriented. Unlike reason, the passions vary from nation to nation, and such variability prevents these languages from having a universal quality. In all cases the languages and cultures of the "others," because their character deviates from one's own norms, are inevitably judged to be barbaric.

France, however, represents a special and unique case. France's moderate conditions allow Frenchmen to dominate their passions with reason. No other nation, for Rivarol, has conditions that permit this. Additionally stability and constancy are provided for by the strong central government of France, which helps fix the moderate, rational French character.[22] Linguistically the manifestation of the rational character of the French people lies in the direct order of French syntax, which gives clarity to French sentence structure. Clarity of structure makes French more appropriate to the expression of reason than to the expression of the passions. As the only language of reason, French appeals to the only universal human quality and therefore is not judged by anyone else as barbaric.

While moderate conditions and a strong monarchy were the prerequisites for the stable, rational universal language that French was to become, there is nevertheless a two-part process to a language actually becoming a universal tongue: producing a quality linguistic-cultural product and then marketing it. Writers above anyone else are responsible for the perfection of the product. Given the language/culture association assumed by Rivarol, this makes sense since writers produce cultural artifacts that are essentially "made out of language." So in the first stage of universalization writers create and perfect the product, imbuing it with a universal quality. The linguistic-cultural product is then exported beyond the borders of the nation and marketed abroad, satisfying the needs of a global "demand" for reason in the Republic of Letters, which by universal consent has elected the French linguistic-cultural complex as sovereign.

In addition to the desultory nature of Rivarol's writing style, the content also forces the reader to recoil somewhat. The fundamental premise used to justify French's status as a universal language, its special genius, frankly borders on the ridiculous for the modern reader. Some of the ideas, in particular the masculinity/femininity of a language, the positive and negative connotations given to masculinity and femininity, and the idea that some languages and therefore cultures are inherently irrational, can be thoroughly offensive. However, the very fact that these ideas would not stand up today is what makes them of interest historically, because they made perfect sense to Rivarol and other thinkers of his era. The fact that they made sense tells us something about the mind-set of the intelligentsia of the time and their desperate need to find an ideological justification for the political, economic, and social reality of the French language's international prominence. The political, economic, and social factors are not sufficient for the late eighteenth-century mind. There has to be more, some inherent quality that makes French language and culture, and the French nation, *fundamentally better* than everyone else's.

This idea of French as a universal language has implications in terms of identity. First, within the national community of France, it is clear that the inferiority complex that defined French intellectual identity in the early sixteenth century is long gone. It has been replaced with a firm, even exaggerated national pride and an overglorified sense of place in history. French no longer needs to be defended or illustrated. It is dominant and illustrious, and it shines to such a degree and in such a manner that it surpasses even the languages of the ancients. The ancients are glorious only in the memory of their past. French is seen to be eternally glorious as a living, breathing medium of thought and culture in a never-ending present.

Additionally the universality factor suggests that French intellectual identity transcends national borders. The author, the philosopher, the man of reason and letters is a citizen of the world in the era of the Enlightenment. French has become the language of this world, rhetorically expanding the Republic of Letters into an empire. The French language is no longer a vehicle merely for French letters, French ideology, and French culture. It is a vehicle for world letters, world ideology, and world culture. The elite segments of European society who speak, read, and write in French constitute an intellectual and cultural upper class—taking the place of Vaugelas' social upper class—who perfect not French culture but human culture. If man is a rational animal and French is the language of reason, then French language and, by extension, French cultural identity become, in the context of this newly developed sense of excessive national pride, the language and cultural identity of all humanity.

Conclusion
Binary Relationships and the Making of Myth

The thinkers of early modern France who addressed the question of the language triangle continually reshaped the relationships between its constituent elements of thought-expression-reality and, consequently, the manner in which that three-part complex defines identity. They did so by weaving a complex web of binary concepts including France and antiquity, France and its contemporaries, the individual and the group, idiolect and language of the community, the self and the other, civilization and barbarity, doubt and certainty, conception and perception, being and doing, thinking and speaking, manner and matter, existence and thinking, flux and stability, imitation and creation, nature and acquisition, state and process, will and instinct, determinism and freedom, evolution and stagnation. The connections linking the parts of these binary pairs range from parallel and interplay to tension and opposition. While the oppositions of France and antiquity and of France and its contemporaries bookend my discussion, manifesting themselves explicitly in du Bellay and Rivarol respectively, the other binary relationships are equally if not more important in the overall evolution of a collective thought scheme that allows French intellectuals to move from one bookend paradigm to the other. Indeed the binary pairs that my analysis has drawn from the early modern texts examined can be categorized into three groups—environment, process, and agency—that provide for that movement of self-perception from barbarism to universality.

Of primary importance are the binary pairs related to the establishment of an environment that permits language and identity evolution to occur. The tensions between flux and stability, instinct and will, determinism and freedom, nature and acquisition represent the essential environmental view required for the amelioration of a language, a culture, and their status. The assumption of a universe in flux makes anything possible. That we who exist in that universe have both the will and the freedom to act and the capacity not simply to be what nature has made us but to become instead what we choose to make of ourselves means that we are not condemned to a condition of barbarity. Even though this may be where we began, we can choose to build our own civilization. Our essence consists not in our present state or condition but rather in the processes we choose to create a condition.

It is in the context of an environment favorable to evolution that the ideology of process, manifesting itself in the outer triangle of expression-thought-reality, takes on its greatest importance. This outer triangle floats on the binary relationships of doubt and certainty, conception and perception, existence and thinking, thinking and speaking, being and doing. There is an uneasy tension in the flux of the universe and our desire to know it. Navigating the straits between doubt and certainty requires a fragile alliance between perception and conception, how we view the world, what we consider to be reality, and the conclusions we draw about that reality. Our sense of self and sense of community depend not on what we perceive in the world, but on what we choose to do with our perceptions, how we use ideas to create expression, and how we use expression to create ideas. Doing defines being, such that how we think and speak the world establishes and affirms who we are in relation to our surroundings and in relation to each other. The willful construction of an identity, the rise from barbarism to civilization, requires a combined intellectual and linguistic agency.

Agency, in the intellectual and linguistic terms suggested by early modern French texts, is fundamentally semiotic in nature—it consists of the act of creating meaning. The binary pairs of the self and the other, the individual and the group, idiolect and the language of the community, manner and matter, imitation and creation establish the framework of how meaning is formed. All meaning is rooted in a relationship between self and other, speaker and listener, writer and reader, for language is a group activity. If the individual has his own way of expressing himself, it is simultaneously different and familiar for those to whom the individual speaks. Since neither random gibberish nor parrotlike mimicry can be considered to have meaning, all expression must be, at one and the same time, both an imitation and a creation. It is in the way we walk the line between imitation and creation that meaning is made. We build a sense of self and community in *how* we make the connections between expression, thought, and reality rather than in *what* we say.

The ideology ultimately traced out by the collective work of early modern French authors is one in which an evolution in language and identity can occur only in a universe that provides conditions making change possible, through the existence of mechanisms for making change, and through the will of an agent to utilize those tools. In the end du Bellay's exhortation is a call to his compatriots to take advantage of those conditions, to employ those mechanisms and to act as agents of change, while Rivarol's hymn to the glory of France is an acknowledgment that what du Bellay had called for had been done. In the transition from du Bellay's text to that of Rivarol, a narrative emerges from diverse philosophical considerations on thought, reality, and expression, suggesting that if French would rise, was rising, or had risen to become the new universal language of Europe, this was possible only through those three principles of environment, process, and agency. In removing the rise of French from the actual social, political, and economic factors that had pushed the language into a position of higher and higher status throughout the era, early modern thinkers managed to construct a myth, rather than a history, of their own inherent value as universal models.

The mythical nature of this ideology becomes evident when placed for perspective back alongside the history of the French language at the end of the early modern period. Certainly French was spoken widely outside of France, in court and intellectual circles, and indeed more widely than any other language. However, as Baggioni writes, "le caractère d' 'universalité' qu'on attribuait à la langue française ne concernait en fait qu'une mince couche privilégiée qu'on estimait porteuse des 'progrès de l'esprit humain'" (the "universal" character attributed to the French language concerned only a thin, privileged layer of society that held itself to be the bearers of the "human mind's progress," 192). So there was a limit to French's influence. Outside of these circles French was spoken practically nowhere. Furthermore just after Rivarol wrote his prizewinning essay and as the revolution took on steam, the importance of French in Europe actually began to diminish (Baggioni, 192).

Additionally it is not clear that French had as much impact as the mythology would suggest even within the confines of the country's borders. Kay, Cave, and Bowie have noted:

> In 1794 the abbé Grégoire had calculated that 6 million inhabitants of France, from a total population of 28 million, were ignorant of the French language, and that as many again had only a rudimentary knowledge of it. The continuing strength of Breton, Occitan, Basque and a variety of local patois was thought by successive governments to be inimical to the very idea of a national democracy, and the presence of German and Flemish speakers in the border territories of the hexagon, and of Italian speakers offshore, gave the project of linguistic unification outlined by Grégoire still greater urgency. . . . Francien, which had until now been the language of the court, of centralized government, and of the professional bourgeoisie, was being aggressively repromoted as the language of national identity. (198)

While we should, of course, be somewhat suspicious of the abbé's statistics, they are no doubt adequate to make us wonder just how many people in France actually spoke French during his era. In a time and place where, according to the abbé, about 42 percent of the population had nothing more than a rudimentary knowledge of the French language and where it was necessary to outline a project to make French the language of national identity, it is difficult to speak of French as already being the language of that national identity. I think this means not so much that language does not equate with identity but rather that French, either at home or abroad, was in reality far from being the truly universal language its emerging mythology claimed, and that the so-called national identity was the identity of an extended Vaugelasian elite, a nation within nations abroad, and a nation within a nation at home.

At the same time, however, I would argue that the myth of the universal quality of French is just as significant as the more sober historical reality. First, in a pragmatic sense, the myth is a historical fact that should take its place alongside the other social, political, and economic facts that actually caused the rise of France and the French language over the course of the early modern era. Second, the myth has relevance in a more theoretical sense. Myths are stories that symbolically represent philosophical, social, and metaphysical forces in the world we inhabit. Myths do not simply break with history; they transform it, and they do so for a reason. They are idealizations of selected aspects of reality, idealizations that represent ways of thinking and acting, idealizations that represent fundamental collective aspirations and communal metaphysical needs.

Consequently the placing of the French language on a pedestal is more than a simple jingoistic reflex. It is a manifestation of the collective desire of an intelligentsia eager to match the illustrious civilizations of antiquity, as well as an exhortation and inspiration to engage in the creative and intellectual effort needed to achieve that equality. Early modern France's discourse of the journey from barbarism to universality is a philosophical and ideological construct conceived to concretize sense of self in an all-too-ephemeral reality.

APPENDIX

Historical Overview of French's Rise in Status

The following summary gives an overview of significant events and trends in the historical rise of French over the course of the early modern era. All of the information in the summary is taken from the works of Rickard, Lodge, Padley, Burke, Oakes, Waquet, Henry, and Baggioni. I strongly encourage anyone interested in a detailed accounting of the history of French's growth in status to consult these excellent works.

Prelude: The Middle Ages

Latin dominates the Middle Ages. Latin is the language of all international diplomacy and is the most widespread language of internal law and administration. It is spoken by the educated elite and is a language of power. Latin is the language of the church and all theology and is the sole language of instruction in education. Latin is the language of the sciences and philosophy. All scholarly work is published in Latin. Along with Latin, French is used in literature, though French is considered less serious by some.

The Sixteenth Century

During this period French struggles for legitimacy and Latin begins to decline. Latin still dominates international diplomacy. In 1539 the Ordinance of Villers-Cotterêts makes French the official language of internal law and administration. In the realm of religion, Lefèvre d'Étaples produces the first French translation of the New Testament in 1523. During the Reformation, Protestants tend toward the use of French in many religious contexts. The Catholic Church offers some sermons in French; however, the remainder of the Mass and all theological works are in Latin. In education most instruction is in Latin, although in 1530 the Collège de France is founded, and there French is employed as a language of instruction. That same year Palsgrave's *Eclaircissement de la langue Française*, the first French grammar, appears and is intended for instruction of foreigners. Despite this, French is generally considered to lack an established grammar. In scholarship and publication the era sees increasing translation of Latin and other classical works into French. Latin is still a common literary medium, and "defenses" of both French and Latin are written, but French slowly takes the lead. Latin dominates scholarship. Some original works in mathematics and natural sciences appear in French. There is an expanding publishing market for French. At the start of the century less than 10 percent of books published in Paris are in French; by the end of the century over 75 percent are in French.

The Seventeenth Century

The period sees the French quest for linguistic perfection, codification, and prestige. In 1635 the Académie française is founded. French is used increasingly in international diplomacy (for example, the 1679 Treaty of Nijmegen and the 1682 Treaty of Frankfurt). The upper and educated classes abroad begin to speak more French. In religion Latin maintains its position in church and theological matters. In education most instruction is still in Latin, but the French role increases. The Oratoire uses French as its language of instruction. Some lectures in politics, law, medicine, and agriculture are given in French at various venues. In 1680 a government edict requires lectures on French law to be given in French. In scholarship and publishing the century sees continued translation of philosophical and scientific works from Latin. Latin virtually disappears as a literary medium, and foreigners (for example, Leibniz) begin to use French as a scholarly and literary language. At the start of the century about 80 percent of books published in France are in French, and by the end of the century this figure grows to over 90 percent. There is also an explosion in periodical publishing: 80 percent of scholarly periodicals published in France are in French. In 1685 Louis XIV repeals the Edict of Nantes.

The Eighteenth Century

French expands in international presence and prestige. French Protestants leave the country, spreading French abroad. In 1744 Frederick the Great declares French the official language of the Berlin Academy. French sees continue use in international diplomacy (for example, the 1714 Treaty of Rastatt, the 1735 Treaty of Vienna, the 1748 Treaty of Aix-la-Chapelle, and the 1774 Russo-Turkish Treaty). French remains the international diplomatic standard until World War I. By the end of the century French is spoken by the regent class of the Dutch Republic, in the German and Russian courts, and as a second language for *mondaine* conversation with foreigners in England and Spain. Still, Latin maintains its position in church and theological matters. In education universities continue to use Latin as the primary language of lectures and examinations, but by midcentury French spelling and grammar are taught in all *collèges*, as the use of Latin there declines. In scholarship and publishing by midcentury over 95 percent of all books published in France are in French. Expatriate French Huguenots create a ready market for

French texts abroad, and French thinkers dominate the European Enlightenment. French is the language of the Republic of Letters, and individuals such as Frederick the Great, Catherine the Great, Gibbon, Grimm, d'Holbach, Walpole, Hamilton, Casanova, and Galiani correspond or compose in French. Many English novels, popular across Europe, are read in French translation, while French dominates periodical publication in most European capitals.

NOTES

Introduction

1. This book does not explore the history of France's rise from poverty to prestige. However, the appendix contains a brief historical overview. For a thorough treatment of that history, see Baggioni, Burke (*Languages* and "Heu Domine"), Henry, Lodge, Oakes, Padley, Rickard, and Waquet.

2. Joseph states, "Already we have seen three apparent pairs of subtypes of personal identity: one for real people and one for fictional characters; one for oneself and one for others; one for individuals and one for groups. Although in each case there are clear differences involved, it is not obvious that all these differences are so fundamental as to demand that we establish six separate analytical categories" (*Language,* 3–4).

3. See for example, Abalain, Barlow and Nadeau, and Henry.

Chapter One: Du Bellay's *Deffence et Illustration*

1. Sébillet, for example, compares the greatness of the works of the Marotic poets with that of the *Iliad* and the *Aeneid* (Chamard, 92).

2. Actually there were three, though the third is not particularly relevant to this study. Du Bellay and company suffered not only from the critique of French poetic traditions and the argument against the superiority of neo-Latin poetry but also from the shocking ego blow of seeing their own idea of imitating the ancients published by Sébillet before they themselves could get it into print (Chamard, 92; Saulnier, 35–36).

3. This tendency of writing laws in Latin is, of course, inherited from the Middle Ages. As Lusignan points out, "Si les médiévaux apprennent le latin, c'est que certains registres d'expressions sont fermés au français. Le latin s'identifie entre autres au savoir et par conséquent à l'écrit. Jean le Danois le désigne comme l'idiome des philosophes. On a vu Bacon soutenir qu'on ne pourrait exprimer la logique en français" (If medieval men learned Latin, it was because certain expressive registers were closed to French. Latin was equated with knowledge and, consequently, with the written text. Jean le Danois designated it as the idiom of philosophers. Bacon was seen to uphold the idea that one could not express logic in French. *Parler vulgairement,* 83). Law was problematic in that laws were written in regional (not national) vernaculars or in Latin, with the latter being privileged. Lusignan states that "à la fin du Moyen Âge, certains actes de chancellerie française et tous les arrêts et jugés du Parlement de Paris étaient en latin" (at the end of the Middle Ages, certain acts of the French chancellery

and all the decrees and judgments of the Paris parliament were in Latin. *Langue des rois,* 17). French, according to Lusignan, encounters two difficulties in asserting itself as the language of the legal system. First, it is viewed as less capable of expressing with precision the technical aspects of the law (*Langue des rois,* 18). Second, as human laws were seen largely to derive from divine law, Latin, the language of the church, was considered the ideal language of interaction between man and God (*Langue des rois,* 19). It was finally the Ordinance of Villers-Cotterêts in 1539 that officially made French the language of law in France.

4. Du Bellay's *Poematum Libri Quatuor* (1558) was offered to Marguerite, sister of Henri II. The anthology editors Céan and Tin write: "que l'auteur de la *Défense et illustration de langue française* ait composé des poèmes latins, voilà qui peut surprendre, mais du Bellay cultive le paradoxe et la palinodie, comme le montre l'épître au lecteur" (that the author of the *Defense and Illustration of the French Language* wrote poems in Latin might be surprising, but du Bellay cultivates paradox and disavowal, as the epistle to the reader shows, 573).

5. Étienne Dolet states, for example, in his *Manière de bien traduire d'une langue en aultre* (1540), that "par le passé j'ay faict, & fais encores mainteāt profeßion totalle de langue Latine. Mais . . . mon affection est telle envers l'honneur de mon pais, que je veulx trouver tout moyen de l'illustrer. Et ne le puis myeulx faire, que de celebrer sa langue, comme ont faict Grecs, & Rommains la leur" (in the past I made, and make even now, a profession of the Latin language. But . . . my affection toward the honor of my country is such that I seek any means to render it illustrious. And I cannot do this better than in celebrating its language, as the Greeks and Romans did their own, 3).

6. The character of Peretto made the very same argument. I cite the passage here in the original Italian as well as in the French translation of Genot and Larivaille to demonstrate just how closely du Bellay stuck to Speroni's text when it came to this metaphor: "Dunque, non nascono le lingue per sé medesme, a guisa di alberi o d'erbe, quale debole e inferma nella sua specie, quale sana e robusta e atta meglio a portar la soma di nostri umani concetti; ma ogni loro vertù nasce al mondo dal voler de' mortali" (35). And in French: "les langues ne naissent point d'elles-mêmes, à la façon d'arbres ou d'herbes, les unes infirmes et débiles en leurs espèces, les autres saines et robustes et plus aptes à porter le faix de nos conceptions humaines; mais toute leur vertu est né au monde du vouloir des mortels" (in Speroni, 35). Du Bellay's borrowings have been well documented—for example, Meerhoff cites not only Speroni's text but also the works of Cicero, Horace, Quintilian, Polititien, Valla, Vida, Erasmus, Bruni, Ricci, Bembo, Longueil, Dolet, Landin, Lemaire des Belges, Fabri, and the Rhétoriqueurs (111). On the other hand, some argument can be made that du Bellay is nevertheless original in his redirection and reapplication of others' ideas (Melehy, "Du Bellay," 509; Navarrete, 149).

7. As Gillot points out, the Italians in particular were "toujours prêts à mépriser les 'barbares' d'Outre-Monts et à se targuer de leur descendance des illustres Romains,

fanfarons d'orgueil qu'une estime démesurée d'eux-mêmes porte aux pires calomnies à l'égard de la France" (always ready to scorn the "barbarians" from across the mountains, and to vaunt their descendance from the illustrious Romans, swaggering blowhards that an excessive self-esteem led to the worst slander with respect to France, 23). Gillot adds that the Italians were particularly fond of denigrating the lack of knowledge of Greek or Roman letters in France: "Qua in re Galli, ut homines sunt ingenio simplici atque barbaro" (As for the Gauls, they are men of simple, and indeed barbarous, wit, 24).

8. Chapter 2 of Pasquier's *Les recherches de la France* is entitled "Que Jules Cesar n'eut les Gaulois en opinion de Barbares, et que l'occasion de ce vint de leur ancienne police, ensemble de ce que *quelques Autheurs Italiens nous veulent blasonner de ce tiltre*" (That Julius Caesar Did Not Hold the Gauls to Be Barbarians, and That the Origins of This Name Came from Their Ancient Social Administration, along with the Fact That *Certain Italian Authors Seek to Hang Us with This Epithet*, 1:258, emphasis added). As for Estienne's inversion of Franco-Italian attributions of the term "barbaric," we see reference to courtesans who speak an Italianized French as being "lourdement barbarisans" (heavily barbarizing, *Deux dialogues,* vi) and as speaking a "iergon sauvage" (savage jargon, *Deux dialogues,* viii).

9. It should also be noted that despite the debt owed to Speroni by du Bellay, there is one significant difference between them, and that is that the dialogic nature of Speroni's text admits for some debate and for some degree of validity to many of Lazaro's pro-Latin ideas. Du Bellay's text, by its monologic structure, utterly excludes all possible support for any part of a pro-Latin position.

10. Aneau's critique of du Bellay's *Deffence* is probably the most virulent of all the ripostes the work received, and some of what he has to say, as here, is tainted by the fact that he is responding not out of an intellectually honest appreciation of things but rather out of an impassioned defense of Marot. According to Chamard, Aneau was a great friend of Marot and a fervent admirer of "old poetry" (152–53). As a result, Chamard states, the *Quintil* quickly stoops to insults (152–53).

11. This fact was pointed out by others as well, such as Chamard (104) and Painter (67).

12. Though du Bellay's text here deals with "manly" virtues or behavior, rather than language, it is interesting to note that his reference to such comportments parallels the general trend associated with language in sixteenth-century France, studied by Bullock and Eilderts's article "Prononcer mâle ou prononcer mal," in which "male" or "manly" speech was considered virtuous while "effeminate" speech—such as that of the "*mignons* of the court of Henri III . . . and . . . the Italianate court before Henry's reign" (283)—was viewed as morally corrupt.

13. Beaune, for example, mentions it in his *Discours comme une langue vulgaire se peult perpétuer* (1548): "ceulx mesmes de qui nous sommes descenduz, ont heu par plusieurs siecles fantasie que l'escripre, & manier livres, en quel que congnoissance

que peult estre, estoit chose pernicieuse & dommageable au peuple qui se vouloit renommer par armes, & faictz victorieux, pensant . . . que trop plus estoit aisé d'escripre chose memorable, que d'icelle n'estoit l'executer" (even those from whom we are descended had for several centuries the fantasy that to write and make books, whatever the subject matter, was a thing pernicious and harmful to a people who sought military renown and victorious deeds, thinking . . . that it was too much easier a thing to write something memorable than it was to execute it, n.p.). Pasquier mentions this as well in his *Recherches de la France*. The very first chapter of *Les Recherches* is entitled "Du tort que les anciens Gaulois, et ceux qui leur succederent se firent, pour estre peu soucieux de recommander par escrits leur Vertu à la posterité" (Of the Error of the Ancient Gauls, and Those Who Succeeded Them, of Being Too Little Concerned with Writing Down Their Virtuous Deeds for Posterity, 1:253).

14. This passage shows clearly du Bellay's debt to Speroni's *Dialogo*. Again, I include here the original in Italian, along with Genot and Larivaille's translation of it: "io vi dico questa lingua moderna, tutto che sia attempatetta che no, esser però ancora assai picciola e sottile verga, la quale non ha appieno fiorito, non che frutti produtti che elle può fare: certo non per defetto della natura di lei, essendo così atta a generar come le altre, ma per colpa di loro che l'ebbero in guardia, che non la coltivorno a bastanza, ma a guisa di pianta selvaggia, in quel medesimo deserto ove per sé a nascere cominciò, senza mai né adacquarla né potarla né difenderla dai pruni che le fanno ombra, l'hanno lasciata invecchiare et quasi morire" (Speroni, 21); in translation: "je vous dis que cette langue moderne, bien qu'elle soit déjà quelque peu ancienne, reste encore une tige fort courte et menue, qui n'a ni pleinement fleuri ni produit les fruits qu'elle peut porter: et ce n'est certes pas en raison d'un défaut de sa nature, car elle est tout autant que les autres apte à engendrer, et au contraire, bien par la faute de ceux qui l'ont eue en garde, et qui ne l'ont pas cultivée à suffisance, mais, à la façon d'une plante sauvage, dans le désert même où par elle-même elle avait pris naissance, l'ont laissé, sans jamais ni l'arroser, ni la tailler, ni la défendre des ronces qui lui font ombre, vieillir et presque mourir" (Speroni, 21).

15. The etymological root of "humanism" is *humanitas* in Latin, meaning "culture."

16. The character of Bembo in Speroni's *Dialogo* maintains that even if, admittedly, Tuscan has produced no authors yet of the status of the best writers from the ancient world, it is certainly not impossible that with time, vulgar literature will have authors to rival Virgil and Homer (8). Further on Bembo states that instead of saying that Latin "is" better than Tuscan, we should say that it "was" better than the vulgar and that the time will come perhaps when the vulgar will equal the ancients in excellence (22).

17. Meigret writes: "Or et il qe notre lang' et aojourdhuy si enriçhíe par la professíon e experiençe de' langes Latin' e Grecqe, q'il n'et poīt d'ar, ne siençe si diffiçil' e subtile, ne méme çete tant haote theolojíe . . . dōt elle ne puysse tretter amplement, e elegamment" (Yet our language is today so enriched by the profession and experience of the

Latin and Greek languages, that there is neither art nor science so difficult and subtle, not even high theology . . . which it cannot amply and elegantly treat, 2–3). Beaune states: "Mais quand à moy me plaira la langue qui ha grace à exprimer ce qu'elle veult dire encores quelle soit plus prolixe, pensant toute chose qui plaist au jugemēt naturel estre le plus beau et meilleur, Et en ce la nostre vulgaire me semble bien avoir autant de grace en beaucoup de choses que la Latine ou Grecque" (But as for me, I like a language which has the grace to express what it wishes however prolix, thinking that all things which please natural judgment are the best and most beautiful; And in this our vernacular seems to me to have as much grace in many respects as Latin or Greek, n.p.). For Pasquier: "nostre langue n'est moins capable que la Latine des traits Poëtiques hardis" (our language is no less capable than Latin when it comes to bold Poetic strokes, 2:1440).

18. The weakness of translation suggested by du Bellay's text would not be universally accepted, especially by French translators of the seventeenth and eighteenth centuries. As Hayes points out in her excellent study *Translation, Subjectivity and Culture*, many early modern translators took a free approach to translation, emphasizing the literary values of the contemporary audience and reshaping an eloquence handed down from antiquity, making classical authors speak the vernacular in a manner reflecting the principles of taste of the translator's own era (3). In so doing, these translators effectively turned translation into a far more creative and original endeavor than du Bellay would give them credit for.

19. Peletier does, however, add that "une bonne traduction vaut trop mieus qu'une mauvaise invancion" (a good translation is far more worthy than a poor invention, 31).

20. According to Chamard, this point is a major feature of Sebillet's own response to the *Deffence*, as he contrarily defends the practice of translation (146).

21. Fauchet's *Recueil de l'origine de la langue et poésie française* (1581) echoes this idea: "j'estime que si les hommes doctes continuent à escrirre leurs conceptions en nostre langue vulgaire, que cela pourra nous rendre l'honneur perdu: l'enrichissant tous les jours, par tant de fideles translations de livres Grecs & Latins: mais plus (à mon advis) par tant de sçavans personnages, qui employent les forces de leur vif esprit, à l'augmentation de la poesie Françoise" (I believe that if learned men continue to write their conceptions in our vernacular, it will bring back to us our lost honor: enriching it every day, through so many faithful translations of Greek and Latin books: but more (in my opinion) through so many learned persons who employ the forces of their vivid minds to the augmentation of French poetry, 48).

22. Dolet, for example, underlines it as well in his *Manière de bien traduire* (4).

23. The criticism of translation was not universally accepted in the sixteenth century. For example, Dolet claimed in his rules for translation that effective translation was possible provided the scholar obeyed certain principles scrupulously: fully understanding the sense and the "manner" of the author translated; acquiring perfect knowledge of the original author's language as well as of the language into which the

work was to be rendered prior to attempting translation; and grasping the inherent spirit of both the original and the target languages (11–13). In contrast, Speroni presents us with a dialogue between Peretto and Lascari in which Lascari points out that when reading the Greek writer Alessandro Afrodiseo translated into Latin, he finds the author to be a different man than when read in the original, suggesting that much of the essence of a work is effectively lost in translation (31).

24. Book 7, chapter 10 of Pasquier's *Recherches* is entitled "Que nos Poëtes François, imitans les Latins, les ont souvent esgalez, et quelquefois surmontez" (That Our French Poets, Imitating the Latins, Have Often Equaled, and Sometimes Surpassed Them, 2:1444).

25. For Peletier du Mans, in all human arts and activities we learn from the masters who preceded us; we want to produce things that resemble what was good and avoid that which was bad in their works. So the first thing we need to do is learn to discern virtue from vice. However, at the same time the poet who wishes to excel must not limit himself to being an "imitateur juré ni perpetuel" (a sworn and perpetual imitator). He must add in his own original qualities; otherwise "cét le fèt d'un homme pareceus e de peu de keur, de marcher tousjours apres un autre: Celui sera tousjours dernier, qui tousjours suivra" (it is the act of a lazy man, and of little courage, to always march behind another: He who follows will always be last, 23–24).

26. Indeed, Rivarol in his *Universalité de la langue française* (1784) would ultimately criticize the poets of the Pléiade for having done precisely this, accusing them of "having spoken Greek in French" (28–29).

27. According to Chamard, this point was at the root of the response of another of du Bellay's critics, Guillaume des Autelz, who argues against the doctrine of imitation of the ancients and upholds the value of French predecessors (148–49).

28. In Speroni's text Bembo does, on the other hand, advise the Courtesan to speak in Tuscan, as courtly practice and inclination from birth drive him to do. After all, by expressing himself elegantly in the vernacular, the Courtesan will be admired and appreciated far more in society than if he expressed himself poorly in Latin (13–14). Peletier writes: "Le Poëte pourra il james étre parfet, auquel é deniee la perfeccion du langage auquel il doèt ecrire, qui n'ét que l'un des moindres instrumans de son metier? Car il ét certein, qu'une Langue aquisitive n'antre james si avant an l'antandemät comme la native . . . nous nous montrons de petit courage, qui emons mieux suivre tousjours les derniers, que nous metre au rang auquel nous puißions étre premiers. . . . Ne voudrons nous james exceler?" (Can the Poet ever be perfect, to whom is denied the perfection of the language in which he must write, which is only one of the most basic instruments of his craft? For it is certain that an acquired Language never enters so deeply into the mind as one's native tongue. . . . We show ourselves of little courage, who prefer to follow always last, rather than putting ourselves in a rank where we can be first. . . . Will we never wish to excel?, 35). The image of words in language being analogous to stones in masonry also appears in Peletier du Mans (36).

29. Fragments/*pièces*/*poudre*.

30. This is in spite of the fact, as mentioned previously, that du Bellay wrote in Latin on occasion.

31. According to Paré: "Joachim Du Bellay avait saisi, lors de son voyage à Rome, l'ampleur décisive de ce paradoxe. Les *Regrets* et surtout les *Antiquitez de Rome* soulignaient la nécessité de transformer les 'ruines' linguistiques et morales des cultures méditerranéennes en un terreau de renouvellement pour les nations du nord" (Joachim du Bellay had grasped, during his trip to Rome, the decisive amplitude of this paradox. The *Regrets* and above all the *Antiquities of Rome* underline the necessity of transforming the linguistic and moral "ruins" of the Mediterranean cultures into a loam for renewing the northern nations, 55). The same, I think, could already be said for the *Deffence*.

32. This foreshadows the quarrel of the ancients and the moderns.

33. Dolet too closed his *Manière de bien traduire* with an exhortation to his readers to write in French, saying, "Si vers ta langue as quelque affection: / Dolet t'y donne une introduction / Si bonne en tout, qu'il n'y a que redire, / Car il t'enseigne (ò noble invention) / D'escrire bien, bien tourner, & bien dire" (If toward your language you have some affection: / Dolet gives you an introduction to it / So good in all respects, there is nothing to dispute, / For he teaches you (oh noble invention) / to write well, to express well and to say well, 39).

Chapter 2: Montaigne's *Essais*

1. As Melehy has pointed out in *Writing Cogito,* "Montaigne is . . . the 'first' to write an entire book made up of statements originating in a contingent subjectivity rather than in the higher authority of God, to use the first-person singular pronoun to represent an autonomous writing subject, . . . to examine the problem of how such a subjectivity emerges and locates itself, of the impossibility of its being metaphysically grounded—to examine the metaphysical basis of authorship" (5).

2. This story comes to us from Montaigne himself and is accepted by Jeanson, for example, as fact (13–14). Even if it were not true, however, it would still have validity and relevance as an ideological backdrop against which the ideas on language in the *Essais* can be examined.

3. He also clearly seems to suggest that French has left barbarism behind. In "De la Praesumption" (bk. 2, chap. 17, 712–48) Montaigne states: "mon langage françois est alteré, et en la prononciation et ailleurs, par la barbarie de mon creu: je ne vis jamais homme des contrées de deça, qui ne sentit bien evidemment son ramage et qui ne blessast les oreilles pures françoises" (my French is deformed, both in my pronunciation and elsewhere, by the barbarity of my stock: I never saw a man from the outlying countries who didn't obviously hear his own squawking and who didn't offend pure French ears, 721). Thibaudet indicates that the "contrées de deça" are the *pays de langue d'oc* (in Montaigne, 721n2). Montaigne does not refer to French as a

"barbaric" vernacular, implying it to have some claim to status (if still less than Latin). He reinforces the idea that French is not barbarous by using it as the yardstick of civilized language, by which other languages such as the various regional patois can be judged as meriting that denigrating qualification.

4. *Simple/naturel/ordinaire.*

5. *Parer/présenter/étudier/contention/artifice.*

6. *Je/suis/moi/même/mon.*

7. Sánchez writes in *That Nothing Is Known* (1581), "Being is the object, subject, and the first principle of all understanding" (238).

8. In Speroni's *Dialogo* the character of Lascari argues, for example, against translation because when reading the Greek Alessandro Afrodiseo translated into Latin, Lascari finds him to be a completely different man than when read in the original Greek (31).

9. Rider, for example, has highlighted in Montaigne the role of the author as "social go-between" (102). I believe it is in the sense I have underlined here that the authorial function identified by Rider is most fully and deeply executed.

10. *Humeurs/opinions/[être] autre/changer.*

11. Sánchez states: "You will say that what you define by the terms 'animal,' 'rational,' 'mortal' is a thing (namely Man), not a verbal concept. This I deny; for I have further doubts about the word 'animal,' the word 'rational,' etc. You will further define these concepts by higher genera and differentiae, as you call them, until you arrive at the thing's 'Being.' I will ask the same question about each of these names in turn. Finally I will ask it concerning the last of them, namely Being; for you do not know what this term signifies. You will say that you will not define this Being, for it has no higher genus to which it belongs. This I do not understand; nor do you. *You do not know what Being is; much less do I*" (175).

12. Galen, alongside Hippocrates, was one of the most celebrated physicians of antiquity. Living in the second century, Galen elaborated on Aristotle's theory of humors, holding that the elements of earth, fire, water, and air acted within the body in the form of yellow bile, black bile, blood, and phlegm. For Galen, the equilibrium of these four humors affected a person's temperament. His work was highly valued by Renaissance humanists and had a long-standing impact on western medical thought.

13. The French *cours* and the English "course" are both derived from the Latin *cursus*, "to run"; the French *discours* and the English "discourse" are derived from the Latin for "to run to and fro, to run about."

14. This play between the creation and re-creation of reality through language foreshadows the coming debate between proponents of rationalist (Cartesian) and empiricist (Condillacian) theories of language that was to dominate the philosophy of language in the seventeenth and eighteenth centuries.

15. Though it is certainly a possibility, as indicated in "De l'Art de conférer" where Montaigne notes: "Publiant et accusant mes imperfections, quelqu'un apprendra de

les craindre" (Publishing and condemning my imperfections, someone will learn to fear them, 1031).

16. This is an idea reiterated further on in the essay when Montaigne writes: "Je tors bien plus volontiers une bonne sentence pour la coudre sur moy, que je ne tors mon fil pour l'aller querir . . . c'est aux paroles à servir et à suivre" (I'd rather twist a good phrase to make it fit me, than to twist the thread of my thought to go after it . . . it is words who must serve and follow, 206–7).

17. Shadow/ambiguity/[un]raveling.

18. *Simple/naïf/succulent/nerveux/court/serré/véhément/brusque/difficile/déréglé/ décousu/hardi/soldatesque.*

19. *Délicat/ennuyeux/affecté/pédantesque/plaideresque.*

20. Sánchez writes, for example: "you are not to look in me for an elegant, polished style. Indeed, I should provide it, did I wish to do so; but Truth slips away while we substitute one word for another and employ circumlocutions—for this is verbal trickery. . . . I shall speak prettily enough if I speak truly enough. Elegant language is seemly for rhetoricians, poets, courtiers, lovers, harlots, pimps, flatterers, parasites, and people of that sort, for whom elegant speech is an end in itself; but for science, accurate language suffices—indeed, is indispensable; and on the other hand this cannot coexist with the former kind" (171). Similarly Agrippa states that "the speache of Trueth . . . is simple, not seekinge for painted and coloured woords" (12).

21. Agrippa states that "the preceptes of pleading doo more hurte, then profite the life of men: and to speake the truthe, it is cleare that al the whole doctrine of Rhetorike is nothing els, but the arte of fauninge flatterie, and as some more boldely speake of lyinge, to the ende that that whiche he cannot bring to effect, with the veritie of the matter, he may persuade with the painted glosse of talke" (43). He adds that "if by the meanes of nature there is nothinge, whiche maye not be expressed with true woordes, what can be more pestilent, then to studie for coloured words? The speache of truthe is simple, liuely, percinge, and a searcher of the inwarde intentions of the harte, and like a hatchet and twoo handed sworde dothe separate and cut a sunder al the Artificial argumentes of Oratours" (46).

22. Sánchez states: "A man is a single thing, yet you describe him by several names: Being, Substance, Body, Living, Animal, Man, and finally Socrates. Are these then not words? Of course they are. If they refer to the same things, then there are too many of them; but if they mean different things, then a man is not a single thing possessing identity" (175).

23. Critical works have shown how the question of religion was the central, driving force behind the composition of the "Apologie" (Baraz, 209–10; Brahami, 7–8; Hallie, 7–8). I focus on the (possibly secondary) element of epistemology, only because of its direct relationship to the concepts of language, mind, reality, and identity that are the center of the present study.

24. Similarly, in treating the truth of distinctions, Sextus Empiricus uses man and animal as models for undermining the distinction of the two based on the principle

of reason. In treating animal reason, Empiricus uses the dog as example: "If, then, it has appeared that the animal on which we have rested our argument for the sake of example chooses what is appropriate and avoids what is disturbing, has an expertise which provides what is appropriate, can grasp and relieve his own feelings, and is not outside the scope of virtue, then since in these things lies the perfection of internal reasoning, the dog will be, in this respect, perfect" (21).

25. Translation is based on that of Thibaudet (in Montaigne, 557n3). Thibaudet identifies the quotation from Cicero's *On Divination,* book 2, chapter 3 (in Montaigne, 557n3).

26. This distinction between judgment and knowledge is not unique to Montaigne. For example, Sánchez in *That Nothing Is Known* presents the idea that "I do not *know* even this one thing, namely that I know nothing. I infer, however, that this is true both of myself and of others" (172). The discord between language and reality crops up in Sánchez as well: "Let us deduce the thing from the name; for as far as I am concerned every definition, and almost every enquiry, is about names . . . [but if] we cannot comprehend the *natures* of things; . . . how are we to assign names to something we do not understand?" (174). Similar thoughts had appeared in Sextus Empiricus: "Thus even as far as the more general remarks of those who belong to other schools go, signs are inconceivable. For they say that they are both relative to something and revelatory of what is signified (to which they are relative). Hence, if they are relative to something and relative to what is signified, they must necessarily be apprehended together with what is signified—just like what is to the left and what is to the right, what is up and what is down, and the other relatives. But if they are revelatory of what is signified, they must necessarily be apprehended before them, in order that, having been recognized beforehand, they may lead us to a conception of the object known on the basis of them. But it is impossible to conceive of an object which cannot be recognized before something before which it must necessarily be apprehended. Therefore it is impossible to conceive of something which is both relative to something and revelatory of that relative to which it is thought of. But they say that signs are both relative to something and revelatory of what is signified: therefore it is impossible to conceive of signs" (98).

27. Montaigne reinforces the idea of the doubtful character of knowing, and of expressing, what is supposedly true in other passages from the "Apologie" as well. For example: "Tout ainsi que les femmes employent des dents d'yvoire où les leurs naturelles leur manquent, et, au lieu de leur vray teint, en forgent un de quelque matiere estrangere; comme elles font des cuisses de drapt et de feutre, et de l'embonpoint de coton, et, au veu et sçeu d'un chacun, s'embellissent d'une beauté fauce et empruntée: ainsi faict la science . . . elle nous donne en payement et en presupposition les choses qu'elle mesmes nous aprend estre inventées" (Just as women employ ivory teeth when their own are missing, and, in place of their true complexion create one of some foreign substance; as they pad their hips with cloth and felt, and their

busts with cotton, and to the view and knowledge of everyone, improve their looks with a false and borrowed beauty: thus does knowledge do . . . it gives us in payment and in presupposition things that it tells us itself are made up, 601). A similar view appears further on in the "Apologie": "Toutes choses produites par nostre propre discours et suffisance, autant vrayes que fauces, sont subjectes à incertitude et debat. C'est pour le chastiement de nostre fierté, et instruction de nostre misere et incapacité que Dieu produisit le trouble et la confusion de l'ancienne tour de Babel. . . . La diversité d'ydiomes et de langues, dequoy il troubla cet ouvrage, qu'est-ce autre chose que cette infinie et perpetuelle altercation d'opinions et de raisons qui accompaigne et embrouille le vain bastiment de l'humaine science" (All things produced by our own discourse and pretension, both true and false, are subject to uncertainty and debate. It is for the punishment of our pride, and the awareness of our misery and incapacity that God produced the disturbance and confusion of the ancient tower of Babel. . . . The diversity of idioms and languages, with which he troubled that construction, is nothing more than the infinite and perpetual altercation of opinions and reasoning that accompanies and confuses the vain edifice of human science, 621), and "l'essence même de la verité, qui est uniforme et constante, quand la fortune nous en donne la possession, nous la corrompons et abastardissons par nostre foiblesse" (the very essence of truth, which is uniform and constant, when fate give us possession of it, is corrupted and bastardized by our weakness, 621).

28. In his chapter on grammar, for example, Agrippa of Nettesheim points out, "We may speake more things and greater, of the corrupte interpretation of woords, with which they doo so muche deceiue the whole worlde" (24).

29. Thibaudet indicates that the reference is to the debate between Catholics, Lutherans, and Calvinists over the meaning of *Hoc est corpus meum* (in Montaigne 589n1).

30. This, of course, assumes that it is possible to know even that something is true in the first place, an idea already questioned by Montaigne.

31. Some skeptics go even further, questioning the very existence or usefulness of logic itself: Agrippa writes, for example: "Logike is . . . nothinge els, but a skilfulnes of contention and darkenesse, by whiche al other sciences are made more obscure, and harder to learne, and shee more ouer termeth her selfe *Logike*, that is the science of speakinge and reasoninge . . . the Logitioners promisse . . . that they are able to finde out the *essential* definition of euery thinge: not withstanding they can neuer make it plaine with any woordes, but that the minde is as ignoraunt as it was before" (48).

32. A similar analysis could be done of the legendary claim of Socrates that he knew only that he knew nothing—a prime allusion in Montaigne's concept of the unknowability of the world. Interestingly enough, Sánchez provided a rather clever answer to such contentious enemies of skepticism: "Let this proposition be my battle colour—it commands my allegiance—'Nothing is known.' If I come to *know* how to establish this, I shall be justified in drawing the conclusion that nothing is known;

whereas if I *do not know* how to establish it, then all the more so—for that was what I claimed. But you will say, 'If you *know* how to establish it, this will result in a contradiction, for you already know *something*. I have, however, anticipated your objection by coming to the opposite conclusion. Now I begin to upset the argument: it already follows, *from this very consideration,* that nothing is known. Perhaps you have failed to grasp my meaning and are calling me ignorant, or a quibbler. You have told the truth; but I have a better right to say this of you, since you have failed to understand. So we are both ignorant. This being so, you have unwittingly arrived at the conclusion I was looking for" (172–73).

33. The slogan "Que sçay-je?" was in fact adopted by Montaigne while he was writing the "Apologie." Popkin tells us that "a large part of the 'Apologie' was written in 1575–76, when Montaigne, through studying the writings of Sextus Empiricus, was experiencing the extreme trauma of seeing his entire intellectual world dissolve into complete doubt. Slogans and phrases from Sextus were carved into the rafter beams of his study so that he could brood on them as he composed his 'Apologie.' It was in this period that his motto, 'Que sais-je?' was adopted" (47). The interrogative tactic was employed as well by Sánchez, who closes both his preface to the reader and his text proper with the capitalized interrogative "WHAT?" (172, 290).

34. The first layer is *ecrits/dire/sens/corriger*. The second is *imagination/jugement/opinion/esprit/raison/avis*. The third is *Ne pas retrouver/ne pas savoir/aller et venir/pas toujours en avant/flotter/vaguer/contraire/tourner/ne plus trouver/s'en départir*.

35. As Joukovsky has pointed out, his intellectual life is a "continual metamorphosis" (239).

36. As Hallie writes, "these essays are a portrait, or rather a jumpy, moving picture, of a jumpy, moving mind" (2).

37. The transformation of language over time is a commonplace in Renaissance thought. We see, for example, in Fauchet's *Recueil* the claim that all languages change so quickly that "à peine nous pouvons entendre le langage de nos bisayeulx" (we can barely understand the language of our forefathers, 2). Pasquier's *Recherches* suggest the same through a rhetorical question: "Dirons nous que les langages resemblent aux rivieres, lesquelles demeurans tousjours en essence, toutefois il y a un continuel changement des ondes: aussi nos langues vulgaires demeurans en leur general, il y ayt changement continu de paroles particulieres, qui ne reviennent plus en usage?" (Will we say that languages resemble rivers which, remaining the same in their essence, nevertheless undergo a changing of their waves: thus our vernaculars remaining the same overall, there is a continual changing of particular words that never come back into usage?, 3:1526).

38. Sánchez's skepticism connects language change to unknowing: "What of the fact that words are continually corrupted, and that there exist French and Spanish books in which you may find a great many words of which the meanings are quite unknown? Moreover, in the realm of Latin are there not a great many words that are

obsolete, while others are invented afresh every day? In the spoken language the same phenomenon occurs as in other departments: there is a change through continual use, and finally so much change occurs that the language degenerates completely and becomes a different language" (219). He adds that this same change occurs in the realm of things: "one more reason for our ignorance remains, in the realm of things, namely the everlasting permanence of some of them and *per contra* the endless coming-to-be and passing-away, or endless change, of some others; so that you could give an account neither of the former class, since you do not live forever, nor of the latter class, since they are never wholly the same, and moreover sometimes exist and sometimes do not" (225–26).

39. Translation of the Latin citation is based on that of Thibaudet (in Montaigne, 654n3). Thibaudet identifies the quotation from Cicero's *On Ends,* book 5, chapter 21 (in Montaigne, 654n3).

40. Knowing the man through his text is yet another idea that has a general hold on the Renaissance mind. For example: Pasquier's *Recherches* underline that "nos langages tant en particulier comme en général, accompagnent la disposition de nos esprits: car si vous vous arrestez au particulier, mal-aisément trouverez-vous un homme brusque en ses mœurs, qui n'ait la parole de mesme, et peu de personnes tardives et Saturniennes, qui n'ayent aussi un langage morne et lent" (our languages both in particular and in general, accompany the disposition of our minds: for if you look at particular cases, you will be hard-pressed to find a man brusque in his behavior, whose speech is not also so, and few slow and melancholic people who do not have a slow and mournful speech, 3:1503–4). Pasquier, like Montaigne, equates means of expression with the man. Additionally Sánchez affirms the inability of one to know anything through the text, while at the same time the text is the basis for judging the judgments (or in terms Montaigne would use, judging the opinions) of the writing self. Sánchez states: "As for the thoughts I am now thinking, the words I am writing on this page, assuredly neither do I understand them, nor will you have understood them once you have read them. Yet you will, perhaps, judge them to be fine and true utterances. And I, for my part believe them to be such. Yet neither of us knows anything" (239–40).

41. While it is true, as Jeanson claims, that Montaigne seeks knowledge of men in general (33), I believe it can be argued that the quest to know man in general manifests itself through knowing individual men in particular, hence the value of the written text.

Chapter 3: Descartes' *Discours*

1. Grayling has argued that Descartes may have served as a spy during the Thirty Years' War (8).

2. Other works in the four-part *Essais philosophiques* treated geometry, optics, and meteors.

3. The *Méditations* were first published in Latin as *Meditationes de Prima Philosophia*.

4. One notable exception that comes to mind is Scipion Dupleix's *Cours de Philosophie* (1607).

5. Derrida states: "son acte n'est pas simplement révolutionnaire, même s'il paraît relativement singulier dans l'ordre philosophique et s'il a quelque apparence de rupture. En vérité, s'il s'écarte d'une certaine pratique et renonce à un usage dominant, s'il complique ses relations avec la Sorbonne, il suit néanmoins la tendance étatico-monarchique" (his act is not simply revolutionary, even if it seems relatively singular in the realm of philosophy and if it presents some appearance of a rupture. In truth, if he strays from certain practices and renounces the prevailing usage, if he complicates his relations with the Sorbonne, he is nevertheless following the tendency of the monarchical state, *S'il y a lieu de traduire,* 306). In the context of the present study, I think the philosophical revolution, rather than the political motivation, is the more important factor.

6. Dassonville indicates that Ramée, in opting to write in French, conceived "l'émancipation de la langue comme le moyen d'échapper à une tradition avilie" (the emancipation of language as a means to escape a degraded tradition, 9).

7. As Limbrick has indicated, "In rebelling against Latin, the language of his Jesuit teachers at the *Collège de la Flèche* and of his professors in the universities of France and Holland where the Aristotelian system of knowledge and Scholastic dialectic still dominated the university curriculum, Descartes was boldly asserting the claims of his 'completely new science'" (75).

8. Although Chomsky has noted a scarcity and variability in Descartes' comments on language (2), he nonetheless argues that "there is, in the period under review here, a coherent and fruitful development of a body of ideas and conclusions regarding the nature of language in association with a certain theory of mind and that this development can be regarded as an outgrowth of the Cartesian revolution" (2–3). I would extend this view of a coherent and fruitful body of ideas beyond the generalization on the period and apply it to Descartes' work itself.

9. *Méthode* is from the Latin *methodus,* adopted from the Greek *methodos* from *hodos,* meaning "path."

10. *Méthode/raison/vérité/sciences*.

11. The verb *conduire* by simple definition implies going somewhere, while the verb *chercher* is derived from the Latin *circare,* meaning to "go around."

12. This is distinctly different for those who will follow Descartes. Locke, for example, in his *Essay Concerning Human Understanding* (1690), divides the mind into two fundamental faculties—perception and reason. Condillac, in his *Essai sur l'origine des connaissances humaines* (1746), as we shall see in more detail in chapter 5 of this present study, breaks the mind down into some sixteen individual faculties that constitute the global capacity of human understanding.

13. Descartes indicates further on in the *Discours* that "la raison, ou le sens, . . . est la seule chose qui nous rend hommes, et nous distingue des bêtes" (reason, or sense, . . . is the only thing that makes us men, and distinguishes us from animals, 30).

14. Arnauld and Nicole write: "On a considéré . . . en ce qui regarde la Rhetorique, que le secours qu'on en pouvoit tirer pour trouver des pensées, des expressions, & des embellissemens, n'etoit pas si considerable. L'esprit fournit assez de pensées, l'usage donne les expressions; & pour les figures & pour les ornemens, on n'en a toujours que trop. Ainsi tout consiste presque à s'éloigner de certaines mauvaises manieres d'écrire & de parler, & sur-tout d'un stile artificiel & rhetoricien composé de pensées fausses & hyperboliques & de figures forcés, qui est le plus grand de tous les vices" (It has been considered . . . regarding Rhetoric, that the aid received from it for finding thoughts, expressions, and ornamentation was not so considerable. The mind furnishes plenty of thoughts, usage provides expressions: and as for figures and ornaments, we have only too many of those. Thus it all comes down practically to distancing oneself from certain poor manners of writing and speaking, and above all from an artificial and rhetorical style, composed of false and hyperbolic thoughts and forced figures, which is the greatest of all vices, 29).

15. See, for example, Pascal (594), Lamy (343–44), and Hobbes (39).

16. Pascal is probably the best known and the most compelling in this group. For him, those orations, "qui ont cette liaison tout ensemble, et avec les vérités avouées, et avec les désirs du cœur, sont si sûres de leur effet, qu'il n'y a rien qui le soit davantage dans la nature. Comme au contraire ce qui n'a de rapport ni à nos créances, ni à nos plaisirs, nous est importun, faux et absolument étrangère" (which establish this connection fully, between avowed truths and the desires of the heart, are so sure of their effect, that there is nothing more so in all of nature. Just as, contrarily, that which has no relation to our beliefs, or our pleasures, is annoying to us, false and completely foreign, 594).

17. Lee, for example, has indicated that thought for Descartes is fundamentally propositional (224).

18. It has been argued by Clarke, for example, that for Descartes, "Language is essential for metaphysical or abstract thinking, although all languages are not equally suitable for the task" (159)—an assessment indicating that speakers of different languages would have different capacities for abstract thinking due to the languages they speak. However, the present analysis would suggest that the more traditional interpretation of the Cartesian mind-language link is more accurate: thought is what it is, and language is overlaid upon it. If a language follows the order of thought, regardless of which language is in question, it will convey thought accurately. Language expresses thought and does not create it, though it may, as Clarke suggests, assist it: "The Cartesian theory of language thus straddles any dichotomy, in the relationship between thought and language, which implies that we either can or cannot think without words. It suggests instead that human beings have a limited capacity of thinking

without words, and that this is considerably enhanced by the acquisition of linguistic skills" (179). I think what can be added to this claim is that language enhances thought only to the extent that language follows the order that thought itself has already laid out.

19. Davies too recognizes these two elements as the "component parts" of the Cartesian mind (91).

20. As Davies has correctly asserted, "Considered as the causes constituting the faculty for judging, the intellect and the will must both be operative for the operation of that faculty; and if either is non-operative, then the composite ceases to exist" (91).

21. The baroque is suggested by imperfection; ugliness; disorder; patchwork composition; contradiction; disproportion; age; deterioration; lack of coordination toward a particular end; chance; poor conception, structure, and layout; curvature; irregularity; and imbalance. The classical is suggested by that which is perfect, beautiful, unified, ordered, even, balanced, elementary, simple, straight, regular, crafted by art, logically laid out, and conceived by will and by reason.

22. This problem has been previously identified within the context of the integrity of the sign by Melehy in *Writing Cogito*: "Descartes's confrontation is with the integrity of the sign; it is also with the excesses that present themselves when the sign is considered in relation to written language (Descartes no longer accepts the authority of the books through which he was educated, and then must write his own book to publicize his ideas)" (6).

23. In fact this point is made explicitly further along in the *Discours* when Descartes writes: "je déracinais cependant de mon esprit toutes les erreurs qui s'y étaient pu glisser auparavant. Non que j'imitasse pour cela les sceptiques, qui ne doutent que pour douter, et affectent d'être toujours irrésolus: car, au contraire, tout mon dessein ne tendait qu'à m'assurer, et à rejeter la terre mouvante et le sable, pour trouver le roc ou l'argile" (I uprooted from my mind all the errors that had slipped into it previously. Not that in this I imitated the skeptics, who only doubt for doubt's sake, and affect perpetual irresolution: but, on the contrary, all my purpose was directed toward finding certainty, and toward abandoning bogs and sand in favor of clay and rock, 57).

24. Descartes was not alone in assigning a place of prime importance to Logos. The idea of the natural order of the universe serving as the basis of thought and language appears also in the *Rhetoric* of Bernard Lamy (182, 198).

25. The question of essences would become a contentious one. For example, Locke in particular would argue against them, distinguishing between "real" essences and merely "nominal" ones. For Locke, even if real essences exist, we cannot know them or anything about them, so it is useless even to think about them. The only essences within our grasp are nominal essences—for example, the abstract terms applied to collections of simple ideas, by which we essentially give the collection of simple ideas substance (239).

26. This idea recurs as well in the *Méditations* where Descartes writes: "Je ne suis donc, précisément parlant, qu'une chose qui pense, c'est-à-dire, un esprit, un entendement ou une raison" (Strictly speaking, therefore, I am only a thing which thinks, which is to say, a mind, an understanding, or a reason, 419), and further that "je ne remarque point qu'il appartienne nécessairement aucune autre chose à ma nature ou à mon essence, sinon que je suis une chose qui pense, je conclus fort bien que mon essence consiste en cela seul, que je suis une chose qui pense, ou une substance dont toute l'essence ou la nature n'est que de penser (I do not remark that anything else belongs necessarily to my nature or to my essence, except that I am a thing that thinks, I conclude then that my essence consists in this alone, that I am a thing that thinks, or a substance whose whole essence and nature is only to think, 488). A similar idea would later be echoed by Malebranche: "La pensée seule est essentielle à l'esprit. Sentir & imaginer n'en sont que des modifications" (Thought alone is essential to the mind. Feeling and imagination are only modifications of it, 1:381).

27. Chomsky has identified this concept as one of the key derivatives of Cartesian thinking in period discussions on language (31–51).

28. The *Grammaire* goes on to add that "la connoissance de ce qui se passe dans notre esprit, est necessaire pour comprendre les fondemens de la Grammaire" (the understanding of what goes on in our mind is necessary to understand the foundations of Grammar, Lancelot and Arnauld, 26) and that man's language "est une des plus grandes preuves de sa raison" (one of the greatest proofs of his reason, 27).

29. The influence of Descartes' thought on this matter has been identified by a number of sources, such as Clarke, who stresses its influence on Port-Royal: "the distinction between natural and conventional signs, and the distinction between rational and non-rational animals that depends on it, is a central feature of the *Port Royal Logic*" (171), and Chomsky, who highlights this point in terms of the principle of "creative language use" in works across the era (3–31). Gontier has suggested that Montaigne is Descartes' "privileged interlocutor" here (233).

30. Séris has noted, "What interests him [Descartes] . . . is the performance of the act of thinking by the mind. What is spoken interests him only as an expression of that performance" (189). Rodis-Lewis has indicated that despite the diversity of languages, connected to the institutional character of signs, every man makes himself understood by others such that language manifests the universality of reason (*Anthropologie* 239).

31. Descartes makes a similar statement relative to the automatons he imagines: "Car on peut bien concevoir qu'une machine soit tellement faite qu'elle profère des paroles, et même qu'elle en profère quelque-unes à propos des actions corporelles qui causeront quelque changement en ses organes: comme, si on la touche en quelque endroit, qu'elle demande ce qu'on lui veut dire; si en un autre, qu'elle crie qu'on lui fait mal, et choses semblables; mais non pas qu'elle les arrange diversement, pour

répondre au sens de tout ce qui se dira en sa présence, ainsi que les hommes les plus hébétés peuvent faire" (For one can easily conceive of a machine built such that it says words, and even such that it says some appropriate to certain bodily actions that would cause a change to its organs: such as if one touches it in some spot, and it asks what one wishes to say to it; or if in another, it cries out that one is hurting it, and other similar things; but not because it arranges them differently in order to respond to the meaning of all that might be said in its presence, such as even the most unintelligent men can do, 85–86).

32. Although this term is not used in the deaf community today (and is, in fact, an erroneous term in and of itself), I have employed it here because Descartes uses it.

33. This is in Descartes' view. The deaf are, however, capable of producing speech and cannot be considered mute.

Chapter 4: Vaugelas' *Remarques*

1. See, for example, Rickard (102–3) or Lodge (174–78).

2. Ibid.

3. This is the excessive tendency ridiculed by Molière in his *Précieuses ridicules*.

4. Additionally Aronson indicates that there was much intellectual substance to language discussions at Rambouillet and that Madame de Rambouillet encouraged discussions of interest to writers such as Malherbe, Voiture, Vaugelas, or Chapelain on etymology, correct forms, or even the pronunciation of words (236).

5. This was largely, Combaz tells us, for his reputation as a fine speaker well versed in grammar and for his reputation as an ardent defender of the French language (*Mousquetaire*, 258).

6. Combaz claims that this text and the academy's dictionary with which he was charged were so connected that some of his correspondents referred to the *Remarques* as "the dictionary of Monsieur de Vaugelas" (*Mousquetaire*, 261).

7. As Ayres-Bennett writes in "Evolving Genre," "From the outset the *remarqueurs* orientate themselves and their observations in relation to those of others working in the genre and notably in relation to Vaugelas" (365).

8. Ayres-Bennett defines this divergence in terms of the principle of reason and authorial intent. Regarding reason she writes: "When we think of la raison in the context of seventeenth-century French grammar, we generally associate it with the meaning 'rational' in the sense of 'analogical to the structure of the human mind' as typified in the *Grammaire générale et raisonnée*. While there is some indication that Vaugelas subscribes to the view that language mirrors thought and ultimately the world, you will remember that his exemplification of usage acting *sans raison* demonstrated a fundamental belief in the arbitrary nature of the relationship between symbol and meaning" ("Usage and Reason," 239). With respect to authorial intent, she states: "an understanding of the purpose, intended audience and social context of the *Remarques* is crucial in determining how this work differs from the *Grammarie*

générale et raisonnée. While the latter, as a companion to the equally famous *Logique* (1662), promotes a theory of general and universal grammar, Vaugelas's work is intended rather as a kind of courtesy book, as a way of improving one's speech and consequently one's position in the court society, a vital concern in a period of rapid social mobility" ("Usage and Reason," 240).

9. This is an idea that shows the influence of the Hôtel de Rambouillet. Vincent states: "Hôtel de Rambouillet stood for the art of conversation. It was a place where men and women met for the interchange of ideas, and the only place where excellence in talk conferred with social distinction" (8).

10. Ayres-Bennett writes in *Vaugelas and the Development of the French Language:* "Vaugelas . . . apparently had good linguistic reasons for favouring the Court. If Henri Estienne, for instance, rejected the authority of the Court, it was because he believed that the language spoken there was corrupted by Italian influence. Vaugelas, on the other hand, considers the Court to be the most neutral source of good usage, the least affected by regionalisms and extremes of variation, and hence probably the most easily comprehensible to all" (13).

11. This partnership existed in the Hôtel de Rambouillet. As Vincent writes: "The Marquise de Rambouillet did more perhaps than any other one woman to secure for authors the privilege of being received into the 'best society' on equal terms with the aristocracy" (20). Vincent notes this as a novelty at the time, when an author was frequently attached to a patron who considered the author his "property" (20).

12. Aristotle saw spoken words as the signs of "impressions of the soul" and written words as signs of spoken ones (Harris and Taylor, 21).

13. In modern terms one might think of spoken language being an original document, while written language is a photocopy of it. The copy is never quite as good, as clear or sharp, as the original. A degradation process comes into play.

14. This comes back to the fact that Vaugelas refers to usage from the very start as the "sovereign" that makes the "laws" of language.

15. This notion is underlined by the subtitle of Vaugelas' book. Combaz has pointed out that those who wanted to write and speak well were numerous, and that many people of the time aspired to a better life and thus were led to imitate the fine manners and language of courtly folk (*Mousequetaire,* 264).

16. *Résoudre/éclaircir/doutes/difficultés.*

17. Vaugelas in fact later refers explicitly to the court, the authors, and the savants of the language as the "trois tribunaux" (three tribunals, n.p.).

18. "If the *Remarques* are essentially concerned with topics where usage is doubtful, how then can Vaugelas justify appealing to usage in any of his examples? There are two possible interpretations, both of which apparently apply to the *Remarques:* firstly, that the work does not cover only doubtful usage, and secondly, that usage is not the only criterion on which the decisions are based" (Ayres-Bennett, *Vaugelas,* 19). Alternatively there is a third possibility that could be added as a corollary to

Ayres-Bennett's second proposed interpretation: that the criterion beyond usage is what I have called "general" (as opposed to "specific") usage.

19. In this it could be argued that Vaugelas distinguishes himself from the Malherbian view that reason and clarity are aesthetic ideals.

20. The preceding passage supports the traditional view mentioned in Ayres-Bennett's *Vaugelas* that "the competing roles of usage and reason in Vaugelas' work have been the subject of much discussion. The traditional view, which sees Vaugelas purely as a recorder of usage, the pragmatist as opposed to the Rationalists of Port-Royal, is found in many standard textbooks on the history of the language and is repeated in Noam Chomsky's *Cartesian Linguistics*" (13).

21. One might argue that the surrealists of the twentieth century did just this, but it is impossible that such writing would have appealed to the aesthetic sensibilities of early modern society. While it may appeal to us, this appeal is the result of an evolution in aesthetic perceptions and appreciations.

Chapter 5: Condillac's *Essai*

1. Knight writes, for example: "In the spring of 1756 the Abbé de Condillac received—and declined—an invitation to visit Voltaire's Swiss retreat, Les Délices. Voltaire had hoped that he could give Condillac the leisure and facilities to write a work containing 'all that man is permitted to know about metaphysics.' The invitation reflects the esteem in which Condillac was held by the philosophes; his refusal suggests the caution, amounting to almost fearfulness, with which he regarded them. J-J Rousseau called him one of 'the best thinkers and profoundest metaphysicians' of the century. Diderot and d'Alembert praised his attack on *l'esprit de système* and borrowed from his writings for the *Encyclopédie*" (1).

2. Even the reception of the *Traité* at the time seems to suggest this. Grimm writes in *Correspondance littéraire* that "vous ne trouverez pas dans ce Traité ces traits de génie, cette imagination sublime et brillante . . . qui caractérise la métaphysique de nos Buffon et de nos Diderot" (you will not find in this Treatise the strokes of genius, the sublime and brilliant imagination . . . that characterize the metaphysics of our Buffons and of our Diderots, 2:440) and that Condillac "est naturellement froid, diffus, disant peu de choses en beaucoup de paroles, et substituant partout une triste exactitude de raisonnement au feu d'une imagination philosophique. . . . On disait . . . que M. l'abbé de Condillac avait noyé la statue de M. de Buffon dans un tonneau d'eau froide. N'en déplaise à M. l'abbé de Condillac, quand on veut être lu il faut savoir écrire" (is naturally cold, vague, saying few things with many words, and substituting everywhere a sad precision of reasoning for the fire of philosophical imagination. . . . It is said . . . that M. l'abbé de Condillac has drowned M. de Buffon's statue in a barrel of cold water. Let it not displease M. l'abbé de Condillac, when one wants to be read, one must know how to write, 3:111–13).

3. See, for example, Harris and Taylor (121).

4. The importance of language is evident in the *Essai*, the *Traité des animaux* (1755), and several books of the *Cours d'Etudes* for the Prince of Parma (1776)—notably the *Grammaire*, the *Art d'Écrire*, and the *Art de Penser*. Only in the *Traité des sensations* and the *Traité des systêmes* (1749), though, is human cognition treated without an overconcern with language.

5. This is a point commonly recognized in studies on Condillac, whose *Essai*, according to Aarsleff, aims to be a radical critique of Locke, who failed to distance himself from Descartes and take into account the possibility of discursive thought as a precondition of knowledge (in Bertrand, 87); centers, according to Parret, on the question of whether language was an "expression" or an "articulation" epistemologically speaking (7); and, as Charrak claims, goes so far as to interpret metaphysics as the science of human understanding in semiotic terms (71–72). As N. Rousseau points out, language operates as the driving force behind all human understanding (32). While some may question this assessment on the basis of Condillac's letter to Maupertuis, in which the former states: "j'ai trop donné aux signes" (I gave too much to signs), I believe that Aarsleff has convincingly argued that this does not represent a deviation on Condillac's part from this basic doctrine but rather shows the simple indication that he had not adequately taken into account the social component in the formation of language and thus of human reason (in Bertrand, 101–2).

6. As Bertrand indicates, Condillac shows that the operations of the mind are rooted in "animal organization" (15).

7. Man is considered, for example, "un Animal de son espèce" (his own type of an animal") in La Mettrie's *Homme machine* (162); and as a preface to the development of society and inequality among men, J-J Rousseau states in his second *Discours*: "Toutes les connaissances qui demandent de la réflexion, toutes celles qui ne s'acquièrent que par l'enchaînement des idées et ne se perfectionnent que successivement, semblent être tout à fait hors de la portée de l'homme sauvage. . . . Son savoir et son industrie se bornent à sauter, courir, se battre, lancer une pierre, escalader un arbre" (All knowledge that demands reflection, all that which requires the connecting of ideas and which only perfects itself progressively, seems to be completely beyond the reach of savage man. . . . His knowledge and industry are limited to jumping, running, fighting, throwing stones, climbing trees, 175n1).

8. Similarly Pariente points out that the verb becomes the sign not of an idea but of an operation of the mind (in Sgard, 260). It should also be noted that to a certain extent the definition of judgment in Condillac's *Essai* is similar to a "standard" view of judgment found in the *Logique* and the *Grammaire* of Port-Royal, which were, according to Tsiapera and Wheeler, from the time of their publication until at least a century later considered "classics" in the field of logic and language (21). The Port-Royal *Grammaire* defines judging as affirming that some object is or is not such—for example, we conceive the idea of the earth and the idea of roundness, and we affirm that "the earth is round" (Lancelot and Arnauld, 28). The sole difference between this

definition and Condillac's is a subtle but important one. While the thinkers of Port-Royal believe that one first conceives of this relationship and then expresses it, Condillac holds that only the linguistic expression of it allows the mind to think the relationship in that manner.

    9. See, for example, Beattie (239–40), Horne Tooke (27), Monboddo (1:5), and Court de Gébelin (1).

    10. For example, La Mettrie states in *L'Homme machine:* "Rien de plus simple . . . que la Mécanique de notre Education! Tout se réduit à des sons, ou à des mots" (Nothing is simpler . . . than the mechanism of our education! It can all be reduced to sounds, or to words, 162). He adds that once we receive sensations, "le cerveau ne peut pas ne pas voir leurs images & leurs différences; de même, lorsque les Signes de ces différences ont été marqués ou gravés dans le cerveau, l'Ame en a nécessairement examiné les rapports; examen qui lui étoit impossible, sans la découverte des Signes, ou l'invention des langues" (the brain cannot not see their images and their differences; similarly, when the Signs of these differences have been marked or engraved in the brain, the mind has necessarily examined the relationships; an examination which was impossible without the discovery of Signs, or the invention of languages, 163–64). For Maupertuis, languages form a "map of ideas" that directs our thinking (31–32). J-J Rousseau exhorts in his second *Discours:* "Qu'on songe de combien d'idées nous sommes redevables à l'usage de la parole; combien la grammaire exerce et facilite les opérations de l'esprit" (Let us think of how many ideas we owe to the use of speech; how much grammar exercises and facilitates the operations of the mind, 198); acknowledging a debt to Condillac, he adds that "les idées générales ne peuvent s'introduire dans l'esprit qu'à l'aide des mots, et l'entendement ne les saisit que par des propositions" (general ideas can enter the mind only with the aid of words, and the understanding does not grasp them except through propositions, 206). Turgot writes further, "Avant les langages établis, il n'y avait aucune proposition; toutes nos idées devaient être des sensations ou des peintures de l'imagination" (Before established languages, there were no propositions; all our ideas must have been sensations or the painting of the imagination, 68). It is true that not all necessarily saw this dependence of thought on language as a good thing. For example, Diderot argues: "la sensation n'a point dans l'âme ce développement successif du discours; et si elle pouvait commander à vingt bouches, chaque bouche disant son mot, toutes les idées . . . seraient rendues à la fois" (sensation does not have in the mind the successive development of discourse; and if it could command twenty mouths, each mouth having its say, all the ideas . . . would be rendered at once, 109). This view leads to the idea that language limits reason to some extent because the simultaneity, rather than linearity, of ideas is necessary for such operations as comparison, judgment, and reason. Diderot continues: "si nous n'avons pas plusieurs perceptions à la fois, il est impossible de raisonner et de discourir. Car discourir ou raisonner, c'est comparer deux ou plusieurs idées. Or comment comparer des idées qui ne sont pas présentes à l'esprit dans le même temps?"

(if we do not have several perceptions at once, then it is impossible to reason and to speak. For to speak or to reason is to compare two or several ideas. But how can one compare ideas that are not present in the mind at the same time?, 112). Nevertheless, one typically finds at the very least the idea presented by Condorcet that, whatever its weaknesses, language on the whole "facilitates" new combinations of ideas (6:11).

11. See, for example, Court de Gébelin (16) and Beattie (301–6).

12. See, for example, Monboddo (1:12) and Herder (87–99).

13. See, for example, J-J Rousseau's second *Discours* (209) and Maupertuis (33).

14. Herder would later explicitly reject Condillac's hypothetical model for two reasons, both based on misreading. First, Herder mistakes its author's intention. Herder interprets the two-children model as an actual historical narrative and then proceeds to argue that the two children would never have survived in the wilderness (100). Of course, Condillac only meant the model in the same spirit as Rousseau's state of nature—as a theoretical construct intended simply to provide a contrast for the present-day's observable reality. Second, Herder misreads Condillac's evolution of signs, arguing that it makes no sense that the children should learn "the natural signs of language through a mutual exchange" (100), when, of course, Condillac as shown in this chapter never presents any such idea.

15. The social element is a key factor in the philosophy of Condillac. As O'Neal has pointed out, one of the differences in Condillacian thought between man's progress and animal's lack thereof is the solitary nature of animal experience versus the collective nature of human experience (174).

16. There was a fair amount of discussion regarding the relationship of natural or "animal" language to human language. Most thinkers, such as Condillac, while they did not see animal language and human language as the same, nevertheless saw animal communication as the *source* of human speech—La Mettrie (160–63) and J-J Rousseau (*Discours,* 205), for example, both felt this way. Herder, however, was a notable standout, claiming, "While still an animal, man already has language. . . . In all aboriginal languages, vestiges of these sounds of nature are still to be heard, though, to be sure, they are not the principal fiber of human speech. . . . I cannot conceal my amazement that philosophers . . . ever conceived of the idea that the origin of human language might be explained from these outcries of the emotions: for is not this obviously something quite different? . . . Children, like animals, utter sounds of sensation. But is not the language they learn from other humans a totally different language?" (88–99). Herder later specifically criticizes Condillac and Rousseau by name on this point (102).

17. Again, this is what in Cartesian terminology would have constituted "animal spirits"—everything that is part of the autonomous machine of the body, exclusive of everything that is part of the rational essence.

18. As Aarsleff has indicated, emotions, passions, and gestures cannot be separated from communication (in Bertrand, 95).

19. Others also underline this idea in the development of language. For example, J-J Rousseau, in his *Essai sur l'origine des langues,* says, "On ne commença pas par raisonner mais par sentir" (We did not begin by reasoning but by feeling, 66)—such that in the gentle climates of the south the first words were "aimez-moi" (love me, 110), while in the harsh climes of the north the first words were "aidez-moi" (help me, 110). Thus for many thinkers any natural origin of speech comes down to a combination of needs and emotions, as for Turgot: "Dans une émotion vive, un cri, avec un geste qui indique l'objet, voilà la première langue" (In a powerful emotion, a cry, with a gesture that indicates the object, that was the first language, 75).

20. This point is emphasized clearly in Condillac's *Traité des animaux* (357–59, 375–82). The role of habit in the development of language is also stressed by Monboddo (1:490).

21. As Condillac states in the *Essai,* "Les signes d'institution, ou ceux que nous avons nous-mêmes choisis, et qui n'ont qu'un rapport arbitraire avec nos idées" (Institutional signs, or those which we have ourselves chosen, and which have only an arbitrary relationship to our ideas, 34).

22. Knight writes: "Taking off from Locke's psychology of uneasiness, Condillac found in desire the moving force behind the development of the entire human mind. Where Locke had found desire at the root of the will, Condillac saw it as the spring of both the will and the understanding" (96).

23. Taylor states that "Condillac's argument . . . although question-begging, is that man's growing familiarity with the connection between natural sign and its sensation-stimulus gave him the power to produce it at will" (294). Roos has indicated that the "spectacle" mentioned above is a key moment in the transition between the natural and institutional sign and has correctly underlined the importance of the "mediation of vision" (684–85). I believe my reading of the text, in conjunction with Roos's reading, helps substantially to resolve at least some of the question begging indicated by Taylor. In the moment of the spectacle, vision, as underlined by Roos, works in conjunction with hearing. Just as in the *Traité des Sensations* Condillac argues that sight in conjunction with touch enables man to understand ideas such as distances and three-dimensional shapes, here it is vision working with hearing that makes the transition of language possible through a naturally shared sense of identity. Further, it is not mere familiarization but rather *naturalization* of the accidental sign that leads man to institutional signification—in other words, the first institutional signs are paradoxically imposed on man by nature, through the transitional mechanism of the accidental sign, which expresses *common,* natural emotions through a fusion of visual and auditory stimuli. It can be argued that my reading represents a prime manifestation of Andreson's notion that Condillac "introduit l'idée qu'il existe un continu entre le naturel et l'artificiel, et qu'ils diffèrent l'un de l'autre quantitativement et non qualitativement" (introduces the idea that continuity exists between the natural and the artificial, and that they differ from one another quantitatively rather than qualitatively, in Sgard, 280).

24. While the first languages were simple and limited to the most basic human needs, Maupertuis posits that "*bientôt* les idées se combinèrent les unes avec les autres, et se multiplièrent; on multiplia les mots, et souvent même au-delà du nombre des idées" (*soon* ideas combined themselves with one another and multiplied; we multiplied words, and often even beyond the number of ideas, 32, emphasis added).

25. J-J Rousseau states in his second *Discours:* "qu'on pense aux peines inconcevables, et au temps infini qu'a dû coûter la première invention des langues ... et l'on jugera combien il eût fallu de milliers de siècles, pour développer successivement dans l'esprit humain les opérations dont il était capable" (think of the inconceivable difficulties, and of the infinite time that the first invention of languages must have required ... and you will realize how many thousands of centuries were needed to develop successively in the human mind the operations of which it was capable, 198–99). This idea is reinforced by the inherent difficulty of the mutual interdependence of language and thought also stressed in the *Discours:* "car si les hommes ont eu besoin de la parole pour apprendre à penser, ils ont eu bien plus besoin encore de savoir penser pour trouver l'art de la parole" (for if men needed speech to learn how to think, they had even more need to know how to think in order to find the art of speech, 204). Equally interesting is the representation of language provided by Monboddo: "in its *infancy*,—first mute; then lisping and stammering; next by slow degrees learning to speak, very lamely and imperfectly at first; but at last, from such rude essays, forming an art the most curious, as well as the most useful among men" (1:2).

26. Not all thinkers agree on this, of course. For Herder, to take an example, only reasoning raises us above the vague, uncontrollable feelings of mere sensation and enables us to know something outside ourselves (117)—which in effect means that identity is rational for Herder, while its origins are emotional for Condillac, only later evolving into a more reasoned sense of identity—and even then the emotional and sensory factors still play their role. See, for example, Coski, "Emotion and Poetry in Condillac's Theory of Language and Mind."

27. This idea was becoming commonplace. The notion of climate also appeared two years later in *De l'Esprit des lois* (1748), and Montesquieu would become famous for it.

28. Per Charrak, analogy is "at the heart" of Condillacian language theory (76).

29. This form of genius must not be underestimated, as Derrida has correctly pointed out: "la méthode générale proposée par Condillac ... ne peut s'établir qu'après une découverte—un coup de génie" (the general method proposed by Condillac ... can be established only after a discovery—a stroke of genius, *Archéologie,* 23). According to Derrida, one must recognize that "*la combinatoire soit une énergétique, et l'élément taxinomique une puissance germinale*" (combinatorial analysis is a high energy source, and the taxonomical element a germinating force, *Archéologie,* 28), and "il existe des 'combinaisons neuves.' L'invention d'une science en est à la fois l'exemple et la découverte, la production de l'un de ces événements et le concept de cette loi. *L'Essai* l'attribue au génie plutôt qu'au talent" (there exist "new combinations." The invention of a science is at one and the same time an example and a discovery,

the production of one of these events and the concept of this law. The *Essai* attributes it to genius rather than to talent, *Archéologie,* 49–50). Derrida also states: "L'avènement d'une science nouvelle tient au coup de génie, et d'un génie individuel. Dont la qualité essentielle paraît être l'imagination" (the advent of a new science derives from the stroke of genius, and of an individual genius. Whose essential quality seems to be imagination, *Archéologie,* 53).

30. See Herder (104) and see Coski, "Rousseau: le langage et la problématique de la perfectibilité." Condorcet, for example, speaks of the "moyens d'assurer et d'accélérer les nouveaux progrès que sa nature [celle de l'homme] lui permet d'espérer encore . . . la nature n'a marqué aucun terme au perfectionnement des facultés humaines; . . . la perfectabilité de l'homme est réellement indéfinie" (means to assure and accelerate new progress that his [man's] nature permits him to hope for in time to come . . . nature placed no limit upon the perfecting of human faculties; . . . the perfectibility of man is in fact infinite, 6:13).

31. The discussion contained in the preceding five paragraphs appeared in my article "Emotion and Poetry in Condillac's Theory of Language and Mind" (164–65). Used with permission of the *French Review* © 2006. Permission conveyed through Copyright Clearance Center, Inc.

32. As Auroux has underlined, a well-made language is one in which analogy allows us to see the identity between ideas (in Sgard, 180). I would argue that Auroux's thought is correct not only in terms of the identity of ideas expressed by words but also in the mind-sets of individuals who use the language—which is what makes progress possible.

33. Eighteenth-century French poetry, although extremely popular, was considered even by writers of the time to be weak when compared to that of other nations. Condillac suggests the idea here, and other writers, such as Diderot in his *Lettre sur les sourds et muets,* also make this point, arguing that French was the language of philosophy, while Latin, Italian, English, etc. were more suited to poetry (Diderot, 114–15).

Chapter 6: Rivarol's *De l'Universalité*

1. He was sometimes called the comte de Rivarol. It has been suggested by some, such as Jünger (12), Loiseau (29–30), and Callot (156), that there is evidence to support this. Dutourd questions it (5).

2. According to Jünger, "La réputation de ses mots parvint jusqu'au roi qui le fit venir et l'engagea à lui en fournir un exemple:—*Donnez-moi, Sire, un sujet.*—*Eh bien, faites-en un sur moi.*—*Sire, le Roi n'est pas un sujet*" (The reputation of his words made its way all the way to the king, who summoned him and requested of him an example of one of his witticisms:—*Sire, give me a subject.*—*Very well, say something witty about me.*—*Sire, the King is not a subject,* 17).

3. Rivarol also began but never completed a "Nouveau Dictionnaire de la langue française." Rivarol's first writings, such as the *Lettre sur le Globe aérostatique* and his *Universalité de la langue française,* have been referred to by Le Breton as "hymnes en l'honneur des arts, des sciences et des lettres" (hymns in the honor of the arts, sciences and letters, 92–105). Certainly in the case of the latter it would be appropriate to specify a hymn in honor of *French* art, science, and letters.

4. According to Dutourd, although modern philologists scorn Rivarol's text for its numerous contestable and false ideas, a French writer will inevitably read it with emotion as it is "a prodigious act of literary patriotism" (7).

5. Thanks to Jünger (37), Callot (163), and Ricken (130), we know that Rivarol had, in fact, read and been influenced by Condillac in particular.

6. To these factors Schwab adds the fact that printing had not been invented at the time of the Italian Renaissance, which hampered the diffusion of Italian literature, and furthermore the fragmentary nature of the Italian states prevented the establishment of a truly unified language (97–100).

7. The question of inversions was widely discussed in the seventeenth and eighteenth centuries. It was generally accepted by most French thinkers that there was a natural order to language and/or thought and that this was based on the natural order of the world. For them, the natural order of things in the world involved the sequence subject-verb-object. French was considered by many of them to follow this order more closely than any other language did. Examples where languages did not follow this order as scrupulously were considered inversions. Inversions were acknowledged to have aesthetic and poetic value but were generally considered to distort the logic of expression.

8. Estienne, speaking of the Italian tongue in the "Condoléance aux courtisans," which closes his *Deux dialogues,* describes it as "ce son feminin" (that feminine sound) and further qualifies it as "ce son vilain & infame" (that villainous and infamous sound, n.p.).

9. This was not an uncommon idea during the Enlightenment. A typical hierarchy of rational beings from most rational to least rational, or from the infinitely rational to the absolutely nonrational, went something like this: God—man—women and children—animals—plants.

10. The man-as-machine premise was also common in the Enlightenment. Descartes had posited that animals along with every nonrational aspect of human beings were material and mechanical. La Mettrie in 1748 took Descartes' theory and eliminated the spiritual essence in man—man was only material; there was no ghost in the machine.

11. This idea is similar to the use of distinguishing marks in the theories of Maupertuis and Herder.

12. Schwab, on a similar note, claims that the Frenchman is the most communicative of all Europeans (122).

13. A similar idea appears in Schwab's *Dissertation* (121).

14. Interestingly enough Schwab presents a similar argument to explain why Italian never came to dominance during the Renaissance, stating that apart from Dante and Petrarch, Italy hardly produced any poets of note (97).

15. This is a somewhat ironic point, as many have since argued that Malherbe effectively killed French poetry for a period of nearly two hundred years. Of course this condemnation relates only to lyric poetry and not the classical theater of the seventeenth century, whose writers were still referred to as poets.

16. Schwab too, in his *Dissertation,* asserts the importance (and superiority) of French literature in the propagation of the French language across Europe.

17. This is a point to which Rivarol's treatment of Italian alluded earlier.

18. According to Diderot, "la communication de la pensée étant l'objet principal du langage, notre langue est de toutes les langues la plus châtiée, la plus exacte et la plus estimable; celle en un mot qui a retenu le moins de ces négligences que j'appellerais volontiers des restes de la *balbutie* des premiers âges. Ou pour continuer le parallèle sans partialité, je dirais que nous avons gagné à n'avoir point d'inversions, de la netteté, de la clarté, de la précision, qualités essentielles du discours" (the communication of thought being the principal object of language, our language is of all tongues the most disciplined, the most exact and estimable; that language, in a word, which has retained fewer of those negligences that I will readily call the leftovers of the *babble* of a primitive age. Or, to continue the parallel impartially, I would say that thanks to having no inversions, we have gained exactitude, clarity, and precision, all qualities essential to discourse, 113).

19. The article "Construction" in the *Encyclopédie* indicates that a construction is natural "parce qu'elle suit la nature, je veux dire parce qu'elle énonce les mots selon l'état où l'esprit conçoit les choses" (because it follows nature, by which I mean because it enunciates words according to the state in which the mind conceives of things, 4:75). A similar idea is at the root of the article "Inversion." Ironically this latter article actually accuses Abbé Batteux of having inverted the notion of inversion: "il déclare directement ordonnées des phrases où tout le monde croyoit voir l'inversion; & il la voit, lui dans les tours que l'on avoit jugés les plus conformes à l'ordre primitif" (he declares directly ordered those sentences in which everyone else sees inversion; and he sees it in expressions which have been judged to conform to the primitive order, 8:852)—which for our purposes here is interesting in that this "contrary" idea nevertheless still supposes, just as the mainstream idea espoused by the article itself does, the existence of a natural order and the necessity of following it with our linguistic constructions. Schwab claims, on the subject of the genius of the French language, "C'est l'ordre naturel, la marche régulière de la construction françoise, qui forment particulièrement ce caractère" (It is the natural order, the regular march of French sentence structure, which specifically forms this character, 106).

20. One main principle of the Cartesians was that sensations without reason cannot be trusted, as they will often trick us. Only reason (for the Cartesians a faculty independent from sensation) can guide the mind safely through the minefield of perceptions.

21. Le Breton gives a similar assessment, indicating that Rivarol's best works are short, fragmentary pieces and pointing out that in his longer works he has difficulties in following an organized plan (266–85). This is particularly true, I think, of *De l'Universalité*.

22. Even in this early piece of work we see Rivarol's attachment to the monarchy. As would eventually be seen in his political writings to come later with the revolution, Rivarol was ardently antidemocratic and antirepublic. He held a low opinion of the masses. Jünger writes: "Pour lui le peuple est toujours mineur, toujours à l'état infantile, souvent cruel et extrêmement crédule. Il suit ses impulsions sentimentales" (For him the people are always at an age of minority, always in an infantile state, often cruel, and extremely credulous. They follow their sentimental impulses, 56). Instead his universality applied only to the upper elements of society.

BIBLIOGRAPHY

Aarsleff, Hans. *From Locke to Saussure: Essays on the Study of Language and Intellectual History.* Minneapolis: University of Minnesota Press, 1982.
Aarsleff, Hans, et al. *La Grammaire générale des modistes aux idéologues.* Villeneuve-d'Ascq: Presses Universitaires de Lille III, 1977.
Abalain, Hervé. *Le Français et les langues historiques de la France.* Paris: Gisserot, 2007.
Académie Française. *Observations de l'Académie françoise sur les Remarques de M. de Vaugelas.* 1705. Reprint, Geneva: Slatkine, 1972.
Agrippa of Nettesheim. *Of the Vanitie and Uncertaintie of Artes and Sciences.* 1530. Rev. ed., Northridge: California State University Foundation, 1974.
Aisy, Jean d'. *Le Génie de la langue française.* 1685. Reprint, Geneva: Slatkine, 1972.
Alanen, Lilli. *Descartes' Concept of Mind.* Cambridge, Mass.: Harvard University Press, 2003.
Almog, Joseph. *What Am I?: Descartes and the Mind-Body Problem.* Oxford: Oxford University Press, 2002.
Aneau, Barthélémy. *Quintil Horatian.* 1550. *Deffence et illustration de la langue françoyse.* Edited by Henri Chamard, ix–xiv. Rev. ed., Paris: Didier, 1961.
Arnauld, Antoine, and Pierre Nicole. *La Logique.* 1662. Rev. ed., Paris: Presses Universitaires de France, 1965.
Aronson, Nicole. *Madame de Rambouillet, ou La magicienne de la Chambre bleue.* Paris: Fayard, 1988.
Auroux, Sylvain. "Condillac, inventeur d'un nouveau matérialisme." *Dix-Huitième Siècle* 24 (1992): 153–63.
———. "L'Intentionnalité, le langage et la cognition." *Modèles Linguistiques* 15, no. 1 (1994): 7–23.
Ayres-Bennett, Wendy. "An Evolving Genre: Seventeenth-Century *Remarques* and *Observations* on the French Language." In *Interpreting the History of French,* edited by Rodney Sampson and Wendy Ayres-Bennett, 353–68. Amsterdam: Rodopi, 2002.
———. "Observations et remarques sur la langue française: Histoire d'un genre." *Licorne* 19 (1991): 1–24.
———. "Usage and Reason in Seventeenth-Century French Grammar: A Fresh Look at Vaugelas." In *Papers in the History of Linguistics: Proceedings of the Third International Conference on the History of the Language Sciences,* edited by Hans Aarsleff, Louis G. Kelly, and Hans-Josef Niederehe, 233–46. Amsterdam: Benjamins, 1987.

———. *Vaugelas and the Development of the French Language.* London: Modern Humanities Research Association, 1987.

Baggioni, Daniel. *Langues et nations en Europe.* Paris: Payot & Rivages, 1997.

Baraz, Michaël. *L'Être et la connaissance selon Montaigne.* Paris: Corti, 1968.

Barbour, Stephen, and Cathy Carmichael, eds. *Language and Nationalism in Europe.* Oxford: Oxford University Press, 2000.

Barlow, Julie, and Jean-Benoît Nadeau. *La Grande Aventure de la langue française.* Montreal: Québec-Amérique, 2007.

Beattie, James. *Dissertations Moral and Critical.* 1783. Edited by Bernhard Fabion. Rev. ed., Hildesheim: Verlag, 1974.

Beaune, Jacques de. *Discours comme une langue vulgaire se peult perpetuer.* 1548. Reprint, Geneva: Slatkine, 1972.

Bellay, Joachim du. *Deffence et illustration de la langue françoyse.* 1549. Rev. ed., Edited by Henri Chamard. Paris: Didier, 1961.

Bertrand, Aliénor, ed. *Condillac: L'Origine du langage.* Paris: Presses Universitaires de France, 2002.

Bizer, Marc. "'Qui a païs n'a que faire de patrie': Joachim Du Bellay's Resistance to a French Identity." *Romanic Review* 91, no. 4 (2000): 375–95.

Blancpain, Marc. Avant propos. In *Discours sur l'universalité de la langue française,* by Antoine Rivarol. Edited by Hubert Juin. Paris: Belfond, 1966.

Bots, Wilhelmus J. A. *Joachim du Bellay: Entre l'histoire littéraire et la stylistique.* Groningen: Drukkerij van Denderen, 1970.

Bouhours, Dominique. *Doutes sur la langue françoise.* 1674. Rev. ed., Paris: Didier, 1998.

———. *Remarques nouvelles sur la langue françoise.* 1675. Reprint, Geneva: Slatkine, 1973.

Bowen, Barbara C. *Words and the Man in French Renaissance Literature.* Lexington, Ky.: French Forum Publishers, 1983.

Bracken, Harry M. *Mind and Language: Essays on Descartes and Chomsky.* Cinnaminson, N.J.: Foris, 1984.

Brahami, Frédéric. *Le Scepticisme de Montaigne.* Paris: Presses Universitaires de France, 1997.

Bras, Hervé Le, and Emmanuel Todd. *L'invention de la France: Atlas anthropologique et politique.* Paris: Livre de poche, 1981.

Breton, André le. *Rivarol: Sa vie, ses idées, son talent.* 1895. Reprint, Geneva: Slatkine Reprints, 1970.

Buffum, Imbrie. *Studies in the Baroque from Montaigne to Rotrou.* New Haven, Conn.: Yale University Press, 1957.

Bullock, Barbara E., and Luke L. Eilderts. "*Prononcer mâle ou prononcer mal:* Linguistic Markers of Effeminacy in Early Modern French." *French Review* 83, no. 2 (2009): 282–93.

Burckhardt, Jacob. *The Civilization of the Renaissance in Italy.* Translated by S. G. C. Middlemore. New York: Modern Library, 2002.

Burke, Peter. "Heu domine, adsunt Turcae: A Sketch for a Social History of Postmedieval Latin." In *Language, Self, and Society: A Social History of Language,* edited by Peter Burke and Roy Porter, 23–50. Cambridge: Polity, 1991.

———. *Languages and Communities in Early Modern Europe.* Cambridge: Cambridge University Press, 2004.

Burkhardt, Hans. "Modalities in Language, Thought and Reality in Leibniz, Descartes and Crusius." *Synthèse: An International Journal for Epistemology, Methodology and Philosophy of Science* 75, no. 2 (1988): 183–215.

Callot, Émile. *Six Philosophes français du XVIIIe siècle: La vie, l'œuvre et la doctrine de Diderot, Fontenelle, Maupertuis, La Mettrie, D'Holbach, Rivarol.* Annecy: Gardet, 1963.

Caron, Philippe, ed. *Les Remarqueurs sur la langue française du XVIe siècle à nos jours.* Rennes: Presses Universitaires de Rennes, 2004.

Céard, Jean, and Louis-Georges Tin, eds. *Anthologie de la poésie française du XVIe siècle.* Paris: Gallimard, 2005.

Chamard, Henri. *Joachim Du Bellay.* Geneva: Slatkine, 1969.

Charrak, André. *Empirisme et métaphysique: L'Essai sur l'origine des connaissances humaines de Condillac.* Paris: Vrin, 2003.

Cherel, A. Notice. In *Discours sur l'universalité de la langue française* by Antoine Rivarol. Paris: Hatier, 1929.

Chiflet, Laurent. *Essay d'une parfaite grammaire de la langue françoise.* 1659. Reprint, Geneva: Slatkine, 1973.

Chomsky, Noam. *Cartesian Linguistics: A Chapter in the History of Rationalist Thought.* New York: Harper & Row, 1966.

Clarke, Desmond M. *Descartes's Theory of Mind.* Oxford: Oxford University Press, 2003.

Combaz, André. *Claude Favre de Vaugelas: Mousquetaire de la langue française.* Paris: Klincksieck, 2000.

———. "Vaugelas, ce fameux Savoyard qui a réformé la langue française." *Studi Francesi* 47, no. 1 (2003): 39–51.

Comfort, W. W. Preface. In *De l'Universalité de la langue française,* by Antoine Rivarol. Boston: Ginn, 1919.

Compagnon, Antoine. *Nous, Michel de Montaigne.* Paris: Seuil, 1980.

Condillac, Etienne Bonnot, Abbé de. *Essai sur l'origine de connaissances humaines.* 1746. Rev. ed., Paris: Vrin, 2002.

———. *Traité des sensations; Traité des animaux.* 1754; 1755. Paris: Fayard, 1984.

Condorcet, Marie Jean Antoine Nicolas de Caritat, Marquis de. *Œuvres.* 12 vols. Stuttgart-Bad Cannstatt: Fromann, 1968.

Coski, Christopher. "Condillac: Language, Thought, and Morality in the Man and Animal Debate." *French Forum* 28, no. 1 (2003): 57–75.

---. "Condillac's Metaphysical Paradox: The Nature of the Soul versus the Natural Origin of Language and Reason." *Dalhousie French Studies* 67 (2004): 3–15.

---. "Condillac's Modernization of Rationalist Language Theory: Evidence, Propositions, and a Newtonian Linguistics." *1650–1850: Ideas, Aesthetics, and Inquiries in the Early Modern Era* 10 (2004): 153–71.

---. "Emotion and Poetry in Condillac's Theory of Language and Mind." *French Review* 80, no. 1 (2006): 157–70.

---. "Rousseau: Le langage et la problématique de la perfectibilité." *Working Papers in Romance Literatures and Philology* 2 (1997): 1–12.

Court de Gébelin, Antoine. *Histoire naturelle de la parole.* 1776. Rev. ed., Paris: Plancher, Eymery, Delaunay, 1816.

Cramer-Vos, Marianne. "Rivarol: Ou la seconde 'Illustration' de la langue française." *Language Quarterly* 25, nos. 3–4 (1987): 40–43.

Dassonville, Michel. "L'Originalité de la 'Dialectique' de Pierre de la Ramée." In *La Dialectique,* by Pierre de la Ramée, 7–19. 1555. Rev. ed., Geneva: Droz, 1964.

Davies, Richard. *Descartes: Belief, Scepticism, and Virtue.* London: Routledge, 2001.

Derrida, Jacques. *L'Archéologie du frivole.* Paris: Galilée, 1990.

---. "S'il y a lieu de traduire." In Derrida, ed., *Du Droit à la philosophie.* Paris: Galilée, 1990.

Descartes, René. *Discours de la méthode, suivi des Méditations.* 1637, 1641. Rev. ed., Paris: Editions 10/18, 1951.

Dickson, William J. "Descartes: Language and Method." *Seventeenth-Century French Studies* 19 (1997): 61–72.

Diderot, Denis. *Lettre sur les sourds et muets.* 1751. *Lettre sur les aveugles; Lettre sur les sourds et muets,* 87–197. Rev. ed., Paris: Flammarion, 2000.

Dolet, Étienne. *La manière de bien traduire d'une langue en aultre.* 1540. Reprint, Geneva: Slatkine, 1972.

Dubu, Jean. "De l'Ordonnance de Villers-Cotterêts à la *Deffence et illustration de la langue françoise:* Affirmation politique et revendication littéraire." In *Langues et nations au temps de la Renaissance,* edited by M. T. Jones-Davies, 137–51. Paris: Klincksieck, 1991.

Duchesneau, François. "Condillac et le principe de liaison des idées." *Revue de Métaphysique et de Morale* 1 (1999): 53–79.

Duddy, Thomas. *Mind, Self, and Interiority.* Aldershot: Avebury, 1995.

Dutourd, Jean. *Rivarol.* Paris: Mercure de France, 1963.

Ehrlich, Hélène H. *Montaigne: La Critique et le langage.* Paris: Klincksieck, 1972.

Encyclopédie (1751–72). 35 vols. Stuttgart-Bad Cannstatt: Frommann, 1966.

Estienne, Henri. *Deux dialogues du nouveau langage françois italianizé.* 1578. Reprint, Geneva: Slatkine, 1972.

---. *La précellence du langage françois.* 1579. Paris: Colin, 1896.

Fauchet, Claude. *Recueil de l'origine de la langue et poesie française*. 1581. Geneva: Slatkine, 1972.

Favergeat, Maurice. Notice in *Discours sur l'universalité de la langue française* by Antoine Rivarol. Paris: Larousse, 1958.

Febvre, Lucien. "Langue et nationalité en France au 18ᵉ siècle." *Revue de synthèse historique* 42 (1926): 19–40.

Formigari, Lia. *A History of Language Philosophies*. Translated by Gabriel Poole. Amsterdam: Benjamins, 2004.

———. *Signs, Science and Politics: Philosophies of Language in Europe, 1700–1830*. Translated by William Dodd. Amsterdam: Benjamins, 1993.

Frame, Donald M. *Montaigne's Discovery of Man: The Humanization of a Humanist*. New York: Columbia University Press, 1967.

François, Alexis. *La grammaire du purisme et l'Académie française au XVIIIe siècle*. Geneva: Slatkine, 1973.

Gadet, Françoise. "Identités françaises différentielles et linguistique du contact." In *The French Language and Questions of Identity*, edited by Wendy Ayres-Bennett and Mari C. Jones, 206–16. Leeds: Maney, 2007.

Gillot, Hubert. *La Querelle des anciens et des modernes en France*. Geneva: Slatkine, 1968.

Girardet, Raoul. *Le nationalisme français, 1871–1914*. Paris: Colin, 1970.

Glucksmann, André. *Descartes, c'est la France*. Paris: Flammarion, 1987.

Goldsmith, Elizabeth. *Exclusive Conversations: The Art of Interaction in Seventeenth-Century France*. Philadelphia: University of Pennsylvania Press, 1988.

Gontier, Thierry. *De l'Homme à l'animal: Montaigne et Descartes ou les paradoxes de la philosophie moderne sur la nature des animaux*. Paris: Vrin, 1998.

Grayling, A. C. *Descartes: The Life and Times of a Genius*. New York: Waller, 2005.

Grayson, Cecil. *A Renaissance Controversy, Latin or Italian?* Oxford: Clarendon Press, 1960.

Grimm, Friedrich Melchior, and Denis Diderot. *Correspondance littéraire, philosophique et critique*. 16 vols. Paris: Garnier, 1877.

Hall, Stuart. "Who Needs 'Identity'?" In *Questions of Cultural Identity*, edited by Stuart Hall and Paul du Gay, 1–17. London: Sage, 1996.

Hallie, Philip P. *Montaigne, and Philosophy as Self-Portraiture*. Middletown, Conn.: Center for Advanced Studies, Wesleyan University, 1966.

Hampton, Timothy. *Literature and the Nation in the Sixteenth Century: Inventing Renaissance France*. Ithaca, N.Y.: Cornell University Press, 2001.

Harris, Roy, and Talbot J. Taylor. *Landmarks in Linguistic Thought: The Western Tradition from Socrates to Saussure*. New York: Routledge, 1989.

Hartley, David. *Patriotism in the Work of Joachim Du Bellay: A Study of the Relationship between the Poet and France*. Lewiston, N.Y.: Mellen, 1993.

Hausman, David, and Alan Hausman. *Descartes's Legacy: Minds and Meaning in Early Modern Philosophy.* Toronto: University of Toronto Press, 1997.

Hayes, Julie Candler. *Translation, Subjectivity, and Culture in France and England: 1600–1800.* Stanford, Calif.: Stanford University Press, 2009.

Henry, Freeman G. *Language, Culture and Hegemony in Modern France.* Birmingham, Ala.: Summa, 2008.

Herder, Johann Gottfried. *Essay on the Origin of Language.* 1772. Translated by Alexander Gode. *On the Origin of Language.* Rev. ed., New York: Ungar, 1966.

Hobbes, Thomas. *Briefe of the Art of Rhetorique.* 1637. In *The Rhetorics of Thomas Hobbes and Bernard Lamy,* edited by John T. Harwood, 39–132. Rev. ed., Carbondale: Southern Illinois University Press, 1986.

Hoffmann, Charlotte, ed. *Language, Culture and Communication in Contemporary Europe.* Philadelphia: Multilingual Matters, 1996.

Horne Tooke, John. *The Diversions of Purley.* 1798. Reprint, Menston: Scolar, 1968.

Jeanson, Francis. *Montaigne.* Paris: Seuil, 1994.

Johnstone, Barbara. "Communication in Multicultural Settings: Resources and Strategies for Affiliation and Identity." In *Language, Culture and Identity,* edited by Torben Vestergaard, 25–46. Aalborg: Aalborg University Press, 1999.

Joseph, John E. *Eloquence and Power: The Rise of Language Standards and Standard Languages.* New York: Blackwell, 1987.

———. *Language and Identity: National, Ethnic, Religious.* New York: Palgrave-Macmillan, 2004.

Joseph, John E., and Talbot J. Taylor, eds. *Ideologies of Language.* London: Routledge, 1990.

Jouanna, Arlette. *L'idée de race en France au XVIème siècle et au début du XVIIème siècle: 1498–1614.* Paris: Champion, 1976.

Joukovsky, Françoise. *Montaigne et le problème du temps.* Paris: Nizet, 1972.

Juliard, Pierre. *Philosophies of Language in Eighteenth-Century France.* The Hague: Mouton, 1970.

Jünger, Ernst. *Rivarol et autres essais.* Paris: Grasset, 1974.

Kale, Steven. *French Salons: High Society and Political Sociability from the Old Régime to the Revolution of 1848.* Baltimore, Md.: Johns Hopkins University Press, 2004.

Katz, Jerrold J. *Cogitations: A Study of the Cogito in Relation to the Philosophy of Logic and Language and a Study of Them in Relation to the Cogito.* New York: Oxford University Press, 1986.

Kay, Sarah, Terence Cave, and Malcolm Bowie. *A Short History of French Literature.* Oxford: Oxford University Press, 2003.

Keating, L. Clark. *Joachim du Bellay.* New York: Twayne, 1971.

Knee, Philip. *La Parole incertaine: Montaigne en dialogue.* Saint-Nicholas: Presses Universitaires Laval, 2003.

Knight, Isabel F. *The Geometric Spirit: The Abbé de Condillac and the French Enlightenment.* New Haven, Conn.: Yale University Press, 1968.

Lamy, Bernard. *The Art of Speaking.* 1675. In *The Rhetorics of Thomas Hobbes and Bernard Lamy,* edited by John T. Harwood, 133–44. Rev. ed., Carbondale: Southern Illinois University Press, 1986.

Lancelot, Claude, and Antoine Arnauld. *Grammaire générale et raisonnée.* 1660. Reprint, Menston: Scolar, 1969.

Lathuillère, Roger. *La Préciosité: Étude historique et linguistique.* Geneva: Droz, 1966.

Lee, Benjamin. "Semiotic Origins of Mind-Body Dualism." In *Semiotics, Self, and Society,* edited by Benjamin Lee, Greg Urban, and Thomas Sebeok, 193–228. Berlin: Mouton de Gruyter, 1989.

Leibniz, Gottfried. *New Essays on Human Understanding.* Translated and edited by Peter Remnant and Jonathan Bennet. Rev. ed., Cambridge: Cambridge University Press, 1996.

Levine, Alan. *Sensual Philosophy: Toleration, Skepticism, and Montaigne's Politics of the Self.* Lanham, Md.: Lexington, 2001.

Limbrick, Elaine. "To Write in Latin or in the Vernacular: The Intellectual Dilemma in an Age of Transition: The Case of Descartes." *History of European Ideas* 16, nos. 1–3 (1993): 75–80.

Lipiansky, Edmond M. *L'Identité française: Représentations, mythes, idéologies.* La Garenne-Colombes: L'Espace Européen, 1991.

Locke, John. *An Essay Concerning Human Understanding.* 1690. London: Everyman, 1993.

Lodge, R. Anthony. *French: From Dialect to Standard.* London: Routledge, 1993.

Loiseau, Ivan. *Rivarol.* Paris: Palatine, 1961.

Lusignan, Serge. *La Langue des rois au moyen âge.* Paris: Presses Universitaires de France, 2004.

———. *Parler vulgairement: Les Intellectuels et la langue française aux XIIIe et XIVe siècles.* Montreal: Presses Universitaires de Montréal, 1986.

Malebranche, Nicolas. *De la Recherche de la vérité.* 1674. In Malebranche, *Œuvres,* 1:39–437. Rev. ed., Paris: Vrin, 1962.

Martin, Marie-Madeleine. *La Formation morale de la France: Histoire de l'unité française.* Paris: Gallimard, 1949.

Matyaszewski, Pawel. "Langue et politique: Essai de relecture du Discours sur l'universalité de la langue française d'Antoine de Rivarol." *Roczniki Humanistyczne: Annales de Lettres et Sciences Humaines/Annals of Arts* 45, no. 5 (1997): 5–20.

Maupertuis, Pierre-Louis Moreau de. *Réflexions philosophiques sur l'origine des langues et la signification des mots.* 1740. In *Sur l'Origine du langage,* edited by Ronald Grimsley, 29–46. Rev. ed., Geneva: Droz, 1971.

Meerhoff, Kees. *Rhétorique et poétique au XVIe siècle en France: Du Bellay, Ramus et les autres.* Leiden: Brill, 1986.

Meigret, Louis. *Le tretté de la grammère françoèze*. 1550. Reprint, Geneva: Slatkine, 1972.

Melehy, Hassan. "Du Bellay and the Space of Early Modern Culture." *Neophilologus* 84, no. 4 (2000): 501–15.

———. *Writing Cogito: Montaigne, Descartes, and the Institution of the Modern Subject*. Albany: State University of New York Press, 1997.

Ménage, Gilles. *Le Parnasse alarmé*. 1649. Reprint, Geneva: Slatkine, 1972.

Meschonnic, Henri, ed. *Et le génie des langues?* Saint-Denis: Presses Universitaires de Vincennes, 2000.

Mettrie, Julien Offray de la. *L'Homme machine*. 1747. Edited and with an introduction by Aram Vartanian. Rev. ed., Princeton, N.J.: Princeton University Press, 1960.

Monboddo, James Burnett, Lord. *Of the Origin and Progress of Language*. 1773–92. Reprint, 6 vols., Menston: Scolar, 1967.

Monnin, Luc. "Condillac: Le Rêve d'un réductionniste." *Modern Language Notes* 119, no. 4 (2004): 819–44.

Montaigne, Michel de. *Essais*. 1580–95. Edited and with annotations by Albert Thibaudet. Rev. ed., Paris: Gallimard, 1950.

Moreau, Pierre-François, and Jean Robelin, eds. *Langage et pouvoir à l'âge classique*. Paris: Belles Lettres, 2000.

Montesquieu, Charles de Secondat, Baron de la Brède et de. *De l'Esprit des lois*. 1748. Rev. ed., Paris: Société des Belles Lettres, 1950.

Navarrete, Ignacio. "Strategies of Appropriation in Speroni and Du Bellay." *Comparative Literature* 41, no. 2 (1989): 141–54.

Nuri, Doatéa. *L'Incertain: Lecture de Descartes*. Saint-Denis: Presses Universitaires de Vincennes, 2005.

Oakes, Leigh. *Language and National Identity: Comparing France and Sweden*. Amsterdam: Benjamins, 2001.

Ojala, Jeanne A., and William T. Ojala. *Madame de Sévigné: A Seventeenth-Century Life*. New York: St. Martin's, 1990.

O'Neal, John. "L'Evolution de la notion d'expérience chez Boullier et Condillac sur la question de l'âme des bêtes." *Recherches sur Diderot et sur l'Encyclopédie* 29 (2000): 149–75.

Padley, G. A. *Grammatical Theory in Western Europe, 1500–1700: The Latin Tradition*. Cambridge: Cambridge University Press, 1976.

Painter, Douglas. "Humanist Insights and the Vernacular in Sixteenth-Century France." *History of European Ideas* 16, nos. 1–3 (1993): 67–73.

Palsgrave, John. *L'éclaircissement de la langue française*. 1530. Rev. ed., Paris: Champion, 2003.

Paré, François. "L'Impact sur l'Italie des débats français sur la langue au milieu du XVIe siècle." *Renaissance and Reformation/Renaissance et Réforme* 27, no. 2 (2003): 53–63.

Parret, Herman. *Idéologie et semiologie chez Locke et Condillac: La question de l'autonomie du langage devant la pensée.* Lisse: de Ridder, 1975.

Pascal, Blaise. *De l'esprit géométrique et de l'art de persuader.* 1658. In Pascal, *Œuvres complètes,* 575–604. Rev. ed., Paris: Gallimard, 1954.

Pasquier, Etienne. *Les recherches de la France.* 1560. Rev. ed., 3 vols., Paris: Champion, 1996.

Pécharman, Martine. "Signification et langage dans l'Essai de Condillac." *Revue de Métaphysique et de Morale* 1 (1999): 81–103.

Peletier du Mans, Jacques. *L'art poétique.* 1555. Reprint, Geneva: Slatkine, 1971.

Phillips, James E., and Don C. Allen. *Neo-Latin Poetry of the Sixteenth and Seventeenth Centuries.* Los Angeles: University of California at Los Angeles, 1965.

Popkin, Richard Henry. *The History of Scepticism from Erasmus to Descartes.* Assen: Van Gorcum, 1960.

Price, Glanville. "Vaugelas: A Reassessment Long Overdue." *Seventeenth-Century French Studies* 11 (1989): 72–79.

Regosin, Richard. "Language and Nation in 16th-Century France: The Arts Poétiques." In *Beginnings in French Literature,* edited by Freeman G. Henry, 29–40. New York: Rodopi, 2002.

———. *The Matter of My Book: Montaigne's* Essais *as the Book of the Self.* Berkeley: University of California Press, 1977.

Rickard, Peter. *A History of the French Language.* London: Unwin Hyman, 1989.

Ricken, Ulrich. *Linguistics, Anthropology and Philosophy in the French Enlightenment.* Translated by Robert E. Norton. London: Routledge, 1994.

Rider, Frederick. *The Dialectic of Selfhood in Montaigne.* Stanford, Calif.: Stanford University Press, 1973.

Riley, Philip. *Language, Culture and Identity.* London: Continuum, 2007.

Rivarol, Antoine. *De l'Universalité de la langue française.* 1784. Rev. ed., Boston: Ginn, 1919.

Robinet, André. *Le Langage à l'âge classique.* Paris: Klincksieck, 1978.

Rodis-Lewis, Geneviève. *L'Anthropologie cartésienne.* Paris: Presses Universitaires de France, 1990.

———. *L'Individualité selon Descartes.* Paris: Vrin, 1950.

Roos, Suzanne. "Consciousness and the Linguistic in Condillac." *Modern Language Notes* 114, no. 4 (1999): 667–90.

Ross, George M. "Hobbes and Descartes on the Relation between Language and Consciousness." *Synthèse: An International Journal for Epistemology, Methodology and Philosophy of Science* 75, no. 2 (1988): 217–29.

Rousseau, Jean-Jacques. *Discours sur l'origine de l'inégalité.* 1755. Rev. ed., Paris: Flammarion, 1971.

———. *Essai sur l'origine des langues.* 1781. Rev. ed., Paris: Gallimard, 1990.

Rousseau, Nicolas. *Connaissance et langage chez Condillac.* Geneva: Droz, 1986.

Sainte-Beuve, Charles-Augustin. "De la Tradition en littérature." In Sainte-Beuve, *Causeries du lundi,* 15:356–82. Paris: Garnier, 1862.

Sampson, Rodney, and Wendy Ayres-Bennett, eds. *Interpreting the History of French.* Amsterdam: Rodopi, 2002.

Sánchez, Francisco. *That Nothing Is Known.* 1581. Translated by Douglas F. S. Thomson. Cambridge: Cambridge University Press, 1988.

Saulnier, Verdun L. *Du Bellay.* Paris: Hatier, 1968.

Scaglione, Aldo, ed. *The Emergence of National Languages.* Ravenna: Longo, 1984.

Schwab, Johann Christoph. *Le Grand Concours: "Dissertation sur les causes de l'universalité de la langue françoise et la durée vraisemblable de son empire."* 1784. Translated by Denis Robelot. Rev. ed., New York: Rodopi, 2005.

Sébillet, Thomas. *Art poétique français.* 1548. Rev. ed., Paris: Droz, 1932.

Séris, Jean-Pierre. "Language and Machine in the Philosophy of Descartes." In *Essays on the Philosophy and Science of René Descartes,* edited by Stephen Voss, 177–92. New York: Oxford University Press, 1993.

Sextus Empiricus. *Outlines of Scepticism.* Translated by Julia Annas and Johnathan Barnes. Cambridge: Cambridge University Press, 1994.

Sgard, Jean, ed. *Condillac et les problèmes du langage.* Geneva: Slatkine, 1982.

Skenazi, Cynthia. *Le Poète architecte en France: Constructions d'un imaginaire monarchique.* Paris: Champion, 2003.

Skirry, Justin. *Descartes and the Metaphysics of Human Nature.* London: Continuum, 2005.

Speroni, Sperone. *Dialogo delle lingue.* 1542. Translated by Gérard Genot and Paul Larivaille. Rev. ed., Paris: Belles Lettres, 2001.

Streichler, Jeanne, ed. *Commentaires sur les* Remarques *de Vaugelas par La Mothe le Vayer, Scipion Dupleix, Ménage, Bouhours, Conrart, Chapelain, Patru, Thomas Corneille, Cassagne, Andry de Boisregard, et l'Académie française.* Paris: Droz, 1936.

Strömholm, Stig. "Défense et illustration et Rivarol: Ébauche d'une réflexion historique sur la francophonie." *Moderna Språk* 88, no. 1 (1994): 67–72.

Suran, T. Preface. In *De l'universalite de la langue francaise* by Antoine Rivarol. Paris: Didier, 1930.

Taylor, Talbot J. "Condillac: Language as an Analytic Method." *Language & Communication: An Interdisciplinary Journal* 9, no. 4 (1989): 289–97.

Thiesse, Anne-Marie. *La Création des identités nationales: Europe XVIIIe–XXe siècle.* Paris: Seuil, 1999.

Tory, Geoffroy. *Champfleury.* 1529. Rev. ed., New York: Johnson Reprint, 1970.

Trudeau, Danielle. *Les Inventeurs du bon usage (1529–1647).* Paris: Minuit, 1992.

Tsiapera, Maria, and Gordon Wheeler. *The Port-Royal Grammar: Sources and Influences.* Münster: Nodus, 1993.

Turgot, Anne-Robert-Jacques, Baron de l'Aune. *Remarques critiques sur les réflexions philosophiques de Maupertuis sur l'origine des langues et la signification des mots.* 1805.

Maupertuis, Turgot et Maine de Biran: Sur l'origine du langage. Edited by Ronald Grimsley. Rev. ed., Geneva: Droz, 1971.

Vaugelas, Claude Favre de. *Remarques sur la langue françoise.* 1647. Reprint, Paris: Droz, 1934.

Vestergaard, Torben. Introduction. In *Language, Culture and Identity,* edited by Vestergaard. Aalborg: Aalborg University Press, 1999.

Vincent, Leon H. *Hôtel de Rambouillet and the Précieuses.* Boston: Houghton Mifflin, 1900.

Waquet, Françoise. *Le Latin ou l'empire d'un signe XVIe–XXe siècle.* Paris: Michel, 1998.

Watson, R. A. *Language and Human Action: Conceptions of Language in the Essais of Montaigne.* New York: Lang, 1996.

Winock, Michel. *Les Nationalismes français.* Barcelona: Institut de Ciències Polítiques i Sociales, 1994.

Zalloua, Zahi. "Reading the *Essais:* Where Does the Critic Begin?" In *Beginnings in French Literature,* edited by Freeman G. Henry, 41–55. Amsterdam: Rodopi, 2002.

INDEX

Académie française, 78–79, 81, 89, 95, 138, 154
accidental signs, 116–18, 119, 126
accidental traits, 12, 75, 118, 119, 126
Agrippa of Nettesheim, 41, 42
Aisy, Jean d', 93
analogy, 90–91, 100, 101, 102, 120–21, 122–24, 127
Aneau, Barthélémy, 9, 14
Arnauld, Antoine, 64, 67, 71
arbitrary signs. *See* institutional signs
artificial signs. *See* institutional signs
artificial traits, 12, 19, 30, 33, 58–59, 67
authority, 15, 54–55, 64, 75, 79, 80, 81, 83, 89, 90–91, 92, 138–39

barbarism, 13–16, 19, 30, 97–99, 100, 137–140, 145, 146–47
baroque, 49–50, 52, 63, 66, 138, 145
Beattie, James, 113, 114
Beaune, Jacques de, 20
Bellay, Joachim Du, 9–31, 32, 33, 36, 47, 51, 53, 54, 55, 56, 64, 76, 80, 88, 94, 96, 99, 121, 122, 127, 129, 138, 139
Berlin Academy, 128, 154
Bouhours, Dominique, 77, 79, 88, 93

Chiflet, Laurent, 79–80, 81, 88
classicism, 63, 66, 75–76, 101, 138, 145
Condillac, Etienne Bonnot abbé de, 56, 103–27, 130, 131, 135–36, 137, 142, 143–44, 145
Condorcet, Marie Jean Antoine Nicolas de Caritat Marquis de, 114, 122
Court de Gébelin, Antoine, 113, 114

Descartes, René, 54–76, 83, 84, 87, 91, 92, 104, 105–6, 106–7, 107–8, 113, 122, 123, 127, 134, 135
Diderot, Denis, 103, 114, 142, 145
Dolet, Etienne, 10, 13
doubt, 33, 44, 45–46, 48, 56, 58, 65–69, 75, 79, 81, 85–86, 87–88, 89, 90–91, 100, 101, 107–8

emotion, 34, 38, 60–61, 94, 110, 116–17, 121, 123, 143–44, 145. *See also* feeling
empiricism, 107. *See also* sensualism
Encyclopédie, 142
Estienne, Henri, 13, 77, 133
evolution. *See* progress

feeling, 75, 110, 111, 115, 116–17, 118, 123–24, 126, 134, 135–36, 144, 146. *See also* emotion

genius, 21, 22, 23, 24, 33, 46, 47, 48, 51, 94, 98, 100, 120–24, 127, 130, 132–33, 134–35, 136, 138, 141–42, 147
grammar, 36, 45–46, 48, 62, 71, 77, 78, 79–81, 92–93, 94–96, 138, 141–42

Herder, Johann Gottfried, 114, 122
hierarchy, 57–58, 67, 68, 73, 74, 75, 76, 83, 91, 104–5, 112, 124, 141–42
Hobbes, Thomas, 61
Horne Tooke, John, 113

innate ideas, 67, 104
institutional signs, 117–20, 123, 126

Lamy, Bernard, 61, 71
Lancelot, Claude, 67, 71
Leibniz, Gottfried, 71
Locke, John, 67, 71, 72, 103–8, 109, 113, 114
logos, 68, 75, 92

Malebranche, Nicolas, 65
Maupertuis, Pierre-Louis Moreau de, 106, 114, 115, 119
Meigret, Louis, 20
Ménage, Gilles, 77, 93, 95–96
Mettrie, Julien Offray de la, 106, 114
Monboddo, James Burnett, Lord, 113, 114, 119, 130
Montaigne, Michel de, 32–53, 54–55, 56–57, 58, 59, 61, 62, 63, 64, 66, 69, 71, 75, 76, 84, 87, 95, 114, 123, 127, 133, 135

natural order, 92–94, 126, 141–44, 146
natural signs, 71, 115–19
nature, 12, 18–19, 23, 29–30, 42, 57–58, 60, 70, 76, 105–6, 112, 142
Nicole, Pierre, 64, 67

order, 27, 46, 52, 56, 60, 62–64, 65–69, 72, 73–74, 75, 87, 97, 98, 135, 138–39. *See also* natural order
origin of language, 11–12, 16, 28, 104, 108–9, 114–19, 126, 130–31

Pascal, Blaise, 61, 62, 64
Pasquier, Etienne, 13, 20, 22, 77
Peletier du Mans, Jacques, 10, 21, 23, 26
perfection, 11, 12, 19, 29, 62–63, 73, 75, 81, 88–89, 97–98, 99, 100, 101, 102, 117–18, 120, 122, 124–26, 127, 138–40, 147, 148
Pléiade, 9, 32
Port-Royal, 59, 61, 64, 67, 71, 72, 80, 92, 113, 142
progress, 12–13, 16–17, 19, 25, 28, 30, 33, 57, 64, 88, 95, 97–101, 106, 108, 112, 114, 118–27, 130–31

Rambouillet, Mme de, 78
rationalism, 142
Rivarol, Antoine, 17, 31, 105, 127, 128–48
Rousseau, Jean-Jacques, 103, 106, 114, 115, 119, 122, 130

Sainte-Beuve, Charles-Augustin, 101
salons, 78, 80, 85
Sánchez, Francisco, 36, 38, 41, 42, 64
scholasticisim, 54, 64
Schwab, Johann Christoph, 128, 142
Sébillet, Thomas, 9, 10, 12, 25
sensationism. *See* sensualism
sensualism, 109. *See also* empiricism
Sextus Empiricus, 43–44
skepticism, 43, 45–46, 50, 68–69
Speroni, Sperone, 11, 14, 20, 26, 28, 36, 158

translation, 20–22, 23, 24, 28–29, 33, 97–99
Turgot, Anne-Robert-Jacques, baron de l'Aune, 106, 114

Vaugelas, Claude Favre de, 77–102, 104–5, 119, 122–23, 124, 125, 127, 130, 135, 136, 137, 138, 143, 148